Best Hikes Detroit and Ann Arbor

The Greatest Views, Wildlife, and Forest Strolls

Second Edition

Matt Forster

FALCON GUIDES

GUILFORD, CONNECTICUT

No wealth can buy the requisite leisure, freedom, and independence, which are the capital in this profession. It comes only by the grace of God. It requires a direct dispensation from Heaven to become a walker.

—Henry David Thoreau, *Excursions*

FALCONGUIDES®

An imprint of The Rowman & Littlefield Publishing Group, Inc.
4501 Forbes Blvd., Ste. 200
Lanham, MD 20706
www.rowman.com
Falcon and FalconGuides are registered trademarks and Make Adventure Your Story is a trademark of The Rowman & Littlefield Publishing Group, Inc.

Distributed by NATIONAL BOOK NETWORK

Copyright © 2019 The Rowman & Littlefield Publishing Group, Inc.
Maps: Hartdale Maps
Photos by the author unless otherwise noted

A previous paperback edition was published by FalconGuides in 2013.

British Library Cataloguing in Publication Information available

A previous paperback edition was catalogued by the Library of Congress as follows:

Library of Congress Cataloging-in-Publication Data

Forster, Matt, 1971-
  Best hikes near Detroit and Ann Arbor / Matt Forster.
     pages cm
  Includes index.
  ISBN 978-0-7627-8182-9
  1. Hiking—Michigan—Detroit—Guidebooks. 2. Hiking—Michigan—Ann Arbor—Guidebooks. 3. Trails—Michigan—Detroit—Guidebooks. 4. Trails-Michigan—Ann Arbor—Guidebooks. 5. Michigan—Guidebooks. I. Title.
  GV199.42.M5F67 2013
  796.5109774—dc23
                              2013019925

ISBN 978-1-4930-3840-4 (paperback)
ISBN 978-1-4930-3841-1 (e-book)

∞™ The paper used in this publication meets the minimum requirements of American National Standard for Information Sciences—Permanence of Paper for Printed Library Materials, ANSI/NISO Z39.48-1992.

Printed in the United States of America

The author and The Rowman & Littlefield Publishing Group, Inc. assume no liability for accidents happening to, or injuries sustained by, readers who engage in the activities described in this book.

Contents

The Hikes

Overview

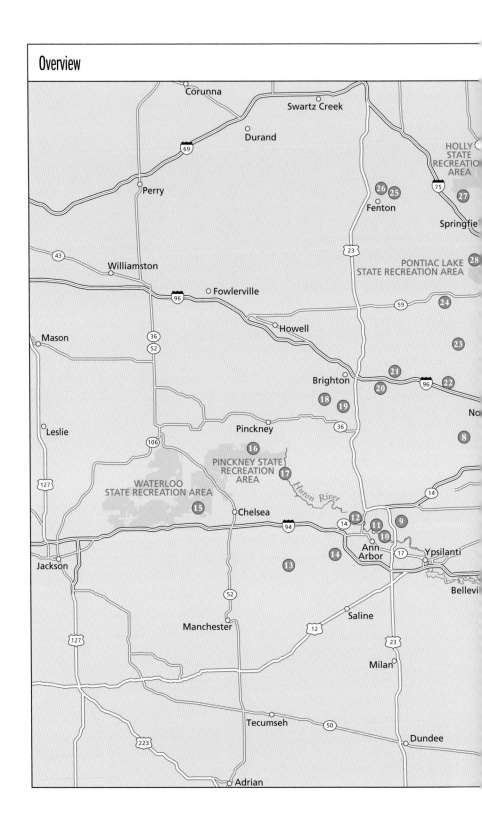

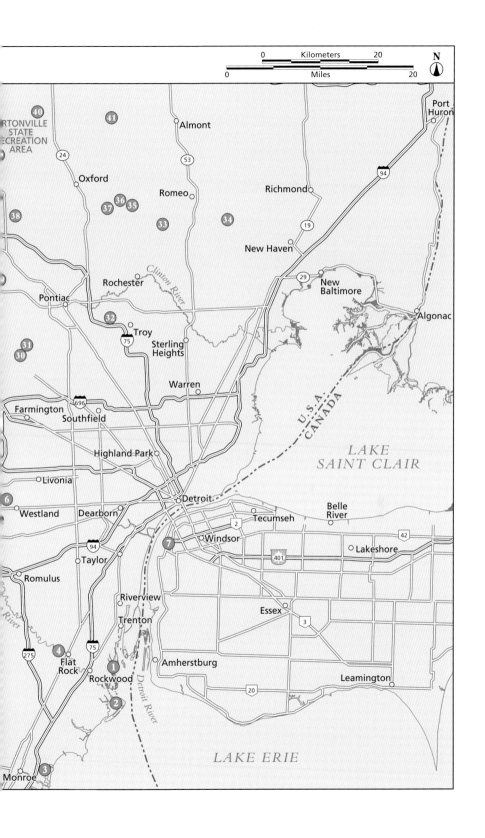

Acknowledgments

Writing a book, even a guide to hiking trails, is a lot like taking a long hike. There are hills to climb, places to rest, moments that need some reflection. Most important, when both writing and walking, you have to keep moving forward. Sometimes walking becomes plodding. That's when it helps to have a companion on the trail, someone to share the motivational load. Someone to remind you to keep putting one foot in front of the other—or one word after the last. To those precious individuals who walk with me every day, in good weather and bad: Thank you.

I also want to share my appreciation for the thousands of people who not only hike in southeast Michigan but also volunteer to build and maintain trails, remove invasive species, advocate for expanding our natural spaces, and generally make this state a better place in which to live.

Legend

94	Interstate	‖‖‖‖‖	Boardwalk/Stairs
12	US Highway	⬥	Boat Ramp/Launch
53	State Highway	⌣	Bridge
401	Trans-Canada Highway	■	Building/Point of Interest
3	Canada Provincial Highway	▲	Campground
= = = =	Unpaved Road	○	City/Town
⊢—⊢—⊢	Railroad	⬤	Gate
════	Featured Trail on Road	?	Information Center
▬ ▬ ▬	Featured Trail	P	Parking
- - - - -	Trail	▲	Peak/Hill
———	Paved Trail	⛙	Picnic Area
∿	River or Stream	🚻	Restroom
⋯⋰	Intermittent Stream	⬥	Scenic View/Viewpoint
▭	State/City Park	1 ■	Trail Marker
⨯	Wetland	40	Trailhead
⬭	Lake/Pond	?	Visitor/Information Center
▭	Bench		

Introduction

It wasn't too long ago, less than 200 years, that southeast Michigan was a wilderness. When Alexis de Tocqueville and his companion traveled from Detroit to Saginaw Bay in 1831, an innkeeper in Pontiac reacted in surprise: "Do you know that Saginaw is the last inhabited spot toward the Pacific, that between this place and Saginaw lies an uncleared wilderness?" The next day, as the two made their way north along the old Saginaw Trail (now Woodward and Dixie Highway), they found solitude as deep as the "solitary passes of the Alps, where Nature refuses to obey the hand of man." They found a land of lakes, streams, and marshes, of hills and valleys.

Tocqueville lamented the inevitable ruin of that wilderness, predicting settlers would soon clear the land and civilize the place. He was right of course, but some of the natural beauty he saw on the trail can still be found in and around Metro Detroit

White-tailed deer are common enough, and many have grown accustomed to living around people.

and Ann Arbor. There are state parks, county parks, metroparks, nature centers, wild-life preserves, and recreational areas; and you will find trails running through them all.

It's not like us to let a good wilderness—be it an ancient forest, a restored marsh-land, or a managed nature preserve—go unexplored, so we have trails. Hundreds of miles of trails. A few are for horseback riding, and mountain bikers all have their favorites, but the best are the ones you can walk.

Hiking near the headwaters of the Clinton River or through hills forested with maple, oak, beech, and hickory around the shore of a quiet lake, you know for a time what Tocqueville saw here. You experience the primeval beauty of the place.

Where to Hike

The state of Michigan manages numerous parks in southeast Michigan. There are state parks, state recreation areas, and state game areas. There are, however, no state forests (or national forests, for that matter). Those are all found north of Saginaw Bay. This means state land here is managed for access and recreation. Funding has been a problem for state parks for many years. A recent change in how fees are collected has resulted in a $10 Recreation Pass. Residents pay for the pass when they renew their car plates. A small "P" on the sticker means you have access to all of Michigan's parks.

Another group of parks you will find here are the Huron-Clinton Metroparks. This park system has parks in five counties. As the name suggests, these are all on the Huron and Clinton Rivers, two important regional waterways. These proper-ties are usually pretty big. Though no two parks are the same, many feature splash parks, nature centers, and golf courses, as well as unique educational opportunities, such as historic farms.

Oakland County in the north end of Metro Detroit has an excel-lent park system. Closer to urban areas, these parks feature wave pools and water parks. In more rural areas the focus is on conservation, environ-mental education, and offering space for people to get outside.

The aptly named shagbark hickory is an easy tree to identify.

Weather

The weather in and around Metro Detroit follows the usual Midwest patterns. Spring is cool and rainy. In April and May rain and snowmelt swell streams and ponds. Wetlands become very wet, and trails near water become muddy. Later in May and into June, mosquitoes and flies make their first appearance of the year. Deerflies are a particular nuisance, and when it's deerfly season, they will hound you through a hike.

In June things start to warm up, and by the height of summer, the weather is typically very hot and very humid. It's then that we start hoping for a summer thunderstorm to break the heat. The lake effect means western Michigan gets more than its fair share of storms, but plenty of fronts hold onto their water long enough to dump it on our side of the state. Thunderstorms blow in from the west, and if you have a good view of the sky, dark clouds will give you fair warning of rain.

One of the best parts of summer in Michigan is the long days. Back during World War II the decision was made to include Detroit in the eastern time zone. This made some sense and kept Detroit on the same time as the banks in New York, but the rest of Michigan had to follow suit. So in the summer the sun doesn't set here until after 9 p.m. (Further north, the effect is even more dramatic.)

Come September you can feel the days getting shorter. The temperature drops, and even warm days cool quickly in late afternoon. Fall showers are not uncommon—fewer thunderstorms, more gray, drizzly days. As the colors begin to change in autumn, some people believe this is the best time for hiking: cooler temps, fewer bugs, and great fall colors.

Aside from the usual Internet sources, the best way to get your weather information is good old-fashioned radio. WWJ, AM 950, does "weather on the 8s." That means every 10 minutes (at 8 minutes, 18 minutes, 28 minutes, etc., after the hour) you can get a quick idea of whether it's going to rain. They're also a good source for weather alerts. A big concern for hikers should be tornado season. Officially the season begins in April and goes through October, after which it's typically too cold for tornadoes, but the peak is in June, when the longer, warmer days are wrestling with winter's leftover cold.

In the end, don't let the chance of foul weather keep you from a good hike, but do keep a weather eye open.

Flora and Fauna

The forests in the southern half of Michigan's Lower Peninsula are part of the eastern broadleaf forest that covers portions of Ohio, all of Indiana, and stretching down to Missouri and up into Minnesota. The trees are primarily hardwoods—oak and hickory in particular—and lose their leaves in the fall.

Wetlands create a mix of habitats. Grassy marshes form on the borders of rivers and lakes, creating important feeding and nesting grounds for hundreds of birds. The

Poison ivy may grow along the ground, like this, or climb up forest trees.

water and wading birds of the Great Lakes rely on the marshes along the western shore of Lake Erie but are just as common in marshes farther inland. Where wetlands overlap with forest, we have swamps. Cedar swamps are common in southeast Michigan, as are wetlands filled with oaks and other hardwoods. You will also find bogs and fens in the area. When you have the opportunity, be sure to visit a bog or fen. This is the only habitat that can support Michigan's carnivorous pitcher plant.

In May and June the woods are full of spring ephemerals. These flowers (often very small) shoot up early, hoping to snag enough sunlight, before the trees fill with leaves, to bloom and be pollinated. The rest of the year the green leaves produce energy, which is stored for a long winter. The most curious of these flowers is the skunk cabbage. This decidedly pungent plant begins its seasonal growth cycle before the snow has even melted, creating enough heat in the process to melt the snow around it and protect it from freezing temperatures.

Summer flowers (like spotted touch-me-not) can be found in the woods as well, but some species thrive in the open. Prairies and meadows are full of goldenrod, Queen Anne's lace, milkweed, buttonbush, and thistle.

Some woodland plants that have been doing very well are the vines. If you see a vine climbing a tree, it's probably Virginia creeper (five leaflets), wild grape (with the broad, toothed leaf), poison ivy (leaves of three), or oriental bittersweet (roundish leaves alternating along the vine). You might see the more-delicate American bittersweet as well, but if the blanket of vines is taking down a section of forest, it's the hardier oriental invasive.

Poison ivy—the dangers of which are discussed below—is often seen as a nuisance plant, but it is a great food source for wildlife. Deer eat its leaves and stems, and birds devour its fruit.

The animals you are most likely to see in the woods are squirrels and chipmunks. Black squirrels, which were once more common closer to Detroit, have been spreading out and can be found all over the area. The larg-

I am always thankful when trail markers are this clear.

est mammals you're likely to run into are white-tailed deer. In more urban areas the deer gather wherever they can find food to eat and space to make a bed. This often means nature centers are teeming with deer.

If you look at some bird guides, you will see that the bluebird's range does not include Michigan. It once did, but the loss of nesting places and food sources has pushed the bird south. For many years now area parks have been erecting nesting boxes in prime habitat, and a number of birds, including the bluebird, are making a comeback. Other birds that were believed lost to us have been making appearances as well. In particular, it's not uncommon to spot a bald eagle or two every summer now. Other large birds are found closer to the water—great blue herons, sandhill cranes, and egrets, to name a few.

Trail Hazards

Unlike other parts of the country that are crawling with bears and mountain lions, scorpions and rattlesnakes, and large birds of prey bent on scooping up small children for a quick meal, Michigan is relatively tame country.

The biggest mammalian threat would be deer. They're not likely to attack, but they do cause more than 60,000 car accidents a year. So on your drive to the trailhead, be sure to watch the road. And remember: If you see a deer, don't veer. Many people have been hurt because a driver swerved out of the way and either hit a tree or another car. It's much better to hit the deer . . . for you at least.

Many people don't know that Michigan has a rattler. The Michigan rattler, otherwise known as the Massasauga or Eastern Massasauga rattlesnake, prefers grassy prairies and fields near wetlands. Many of the trails highlighted in this book pass through grassy prairies and fields near wetlands. The most likely time you will see a

Virginia creeper is a common vine in southeast Michigan.

Massasauga is on a hot day, perhaps sunning itself on the trail.

The snake has a triangular-shaped head, wide and flat, with a narrow neck. It has a short tail with a rattle, saddle-shaped markings, and a thick midsection. It looks nothing like the garter snakes or blue racers you are more likely to see. The Massasauga is Michigan's only venomous snake. Though not aggressive, it will strike when cornered. Keep kids and pets far away, and give the snake a wide berth.

The final hazards to mention are the plant hazards: poison ivy and poison sumac. The latter is relatively scarce. It looks like sumac but has white fruit. You find this near wetlands, close to the water. Poison ivy, on the other hand, seems to be spreading. Vines do a great job of processing carbon dioxide. Our atmosphere has had really high levels of carbon dioxide lately, and vines in general have been thriving. Poison ivy is no exception.

The basic rule with poison ivy is "Leaves of three, let it be." Technically it should be "Leaflets of three . . .," but that's not as catchy. Poison ivy has a compound leaf, meaning that each leaf is composed of multiple leaflets. Since there are other plants with three leaves, you can identify poison ivy by its two lower leaflets, which attach directly to the stem. The middle leaflet is farther up the stem. Also, since you will see a lot of poison ivy climbing up trees next to the trail, I will share another rhyme I learned recently: "If it's got a hairy rope, don't be a dope." The poison ivy vine has small hairlike roots that cling to the tree.

The allergic reaction is caused by the sap, which contains an oil called urushiol. Every part of the plant carries this oil, and any damage to the plant will release it. Burning poison ivy actually sends the oil into the air where it can be breathed, causing all sorts of problems. The rule of thumb bears repeating: Leaves of three, let it be.

Getting Around

Michigan in general, and Metro Detroit in particular, is car country. Aside from the trails in the city of Ann Arbor, none of the parks and preserves mentioned here are readily accessible by public transportation.

How to Use This Guide

This guide contains just about everything you'll ever need to choose, plan for, enjoy, and survive a hike near Metro Detroit. Stuffed with useful area information, *Best Hikes Detroit and Ann Arbor* features forty-one mapped and cued hikes. Here's an outline of the guide's major components:

Each section begins with an **introduction to the region** in which you're given a sweeping look at the lay of the land. Each hike then starts with a short **summary** of the hike's highlights. These quick overviews give you a taste of the hiking adventures to follow. You'll learn about the trail terrain and what surprises each route has to offer.

Following the overview you'll find the **hike specs:** quick, nitty-gritty details of the hike. Most are self-explanatory, but here are some details:

Start: This is where the hike begins; the trailhead.

Distance: The total distance of the recommended route—one-way for loop hikes, the round-trip on an out-and-back or lollipop hike, point-to-point for a shuttle. Options are additional.

Hiking time: The average time it will take to cover the route. It is based on the total distance, elevation gain, and condition and difficulty of the trail. Your fitness level will also affect your time.

Difficulty: Each hike has been assigned a level of difficulty. The rating system was developed from several sources and personal experience. These levels are meant to be a guideline only, and specific hikes may prove easier or harder for different people depending on ability and physical fitness. The difficulty is specific to southeast Michigan.

> **Easy:** Three miles or less total trip distance, minimal elevation gain, and paved or smooth-surfaced dirt trail.
>
> **Moderate:** Up to 4 miles total trip distance, moderate elevation gain, and potentially rough terrain.
>
> **Difficult:** More than 4 miles total trip, strenuous elevation gains, and rough and/or rocky terrain.

Trail surface: General information about what to expect underfoot.

Best season: General information on the best time of year to hike.

Other trail users: Horseback riders, mountain bikers, in-line skaters, etc.

Canine compatibility: Know the trail regulations before you take your dog hiking with you. Dogs are not allowed on several trails described in this book.

Fees and permits: Whether you need to carry any money with you for park entrance fees and permits.

Schedule: Hours the trail and visitor centers, offices, etc. are open to the public.

Maps: This is a list of other maps to supplement the maps in this book. Local park maps are usually the best source for accurate information. Check out the agency's website or the park office. However, they rarely show topographical details. If that's something you're looking for I would suggest the TOPO! maps produced by National Geographic.

Trail contacts: This is the location, phone number, and website URL for the local land manager(s) in charge of all the trails within the selected hike. Before you head out, get trail access information. Or contact the land manager after your visit if you see problems with trail erosion, damage, or misuse.

Other: Other information that will enhance your hike.

Special considerations: This section calls your attention to specific trail hazards, such as a lack of water or hunting seasons.

The **Finding the trailhead** section gives you dependable driving directions to where you'll want to park. **The Hike** is the meat of the chapter. Detailed and honest, it's a carefully researched impression of the trail. It also often includes lots of area history, both natural and human. Under **Miles and Directions,** mileage cues identify all turns and trail name changes, as well as points of interest. **Options** are also given for many hikes to make your journey shorter or longer, depending on the amount of time you have. The **Hike Information** section provides information on local events and attractions, restaurants, hiking tours, and hiking organizations. **Green Tips** throughout the book provide suggestions for how to keep the spectacular scenery of the Detroit/Ann Arbor area clean, beautiful, and healthy.

Don't feel restricted to the routes and trails that are mapped here. Be adventurous, and use this guide as a platform to discover new routes for yourself. One of the simplest ways to do this is to just turn the map upside down and hike any route in reverse. The change in perspective is often fantastic, and the hike should feel quite different. With this in mind, it'll be like getting two distinctly different hikes on each map.

For your own purposes, you may wish to copy the route directions onto a small sheet of paper to help you while hiking, or photocopy the map and cue sheet to take with you. Otherwise, just slip the whole book in your backpack and take it all with you. Enjoy your time in the outdoors—and remember to pack out what you pack in.

How to Use the Maps

Overview map: This map shows the location of each hike in the area by hike number.

Route map: This is your primary guide to each hike. It shows all the accessible roads and trails, points of interest, water, landmarks, and geographical features. It also distinguishes trails from roads, and paved roads from unpaved roads. The selected route is highlighted, and directional arrows point the way.

Trail Finder

Hike No.	Hike Name	Best Hikes with Children	Best Hikes with Dogs	Best Hikes for Birders	Best Hikes for Nature Lovers	Best Hikes for Water Lovers	Best Hikes for Wetland Lovers	Best Hikes for History Lovers	Best Hikes for Forest Lovers
1	Lake Erie Metropark			●	●		●		
2	Pointe Mouillee State Game Area			●			●		
3	Sterling State Park			●			●		
4	Oakwoods Metropark					●			
5	Crosswinds Marsh Wetlands Interpretive Preserve	●		●	●		●		
6	William P Holliday Forest & Wildlife Preserve				●				
7	Ojibway Prairie Provincial Nature Reserve				●				
8	Maybury State Park		●						●
9	Matthaei Botanical Gardens	●		●	●				
10	Furstenberg Nature Area and Gallup Park			●		●			
11	Nichols Arboretum			●					●
12	Bird Hills Nature Area								●
13	Brauer Preserve			●					
14	Scio Woods Preserve	●			●		●		●
15	Waterloo State Recreation Area								●

Hike No.	Hike Name	Best Hikes with Children	Best Hikes with Dogs	Best Hikes for Birders	Best Hikes for Nature Lovers	Best Hikes for Water Lovers	Best Hikes for Wetland Lovers	Best Hikes for History Lovers	Best Hikes for Forest Lovers
16	Pinckney State Recreation Area					●			●
17	Hudson Mills Metropark	●							
18	Brighton State Recreation Area								●
19	Huron Meadows Metropark						●		
20	Island Lake State Recreation Area					●			
21	Kensington Metropark			●					
22	Lyon Oaks County Park			●					
23	Proud Lake State Recreation Area					●			
24	Highland State Recreation Area						●	●	
25	Seven Lakes State Park	●				●			
26	Dauner Martin Sanctuary				●				
27	Holly State Recreation Area					●			
28	Indian Springs Metropark	●			●		●		
29	Pontiac Lake State Recreation Area	●				●			
30	West Bloomfield Woods Nature Preserve	●	●				●		
31	Orchard Lake Nature Sanctuary				●				
32	Lloyd A. Stage Nature Center			●					
33	Stony Creek Metropark	●							
34	Wolcott Mill Metropark							●	

Hike No.	Hike Name	Best Hikes with Children	Best Hikes with Dogs	Best Hikes for Birders	Best Hikes for Nature Lovers	Best Hikes for Water Lovers	Best Hikes for Wetland Lovers	Best Hikes for History Lovers	Best Hikes for Forest Lovers
35	Cranberry Lake Park				•			•	
36	Addison Oaks County Park	•			•				•
37	Bald Mountain State Recreation Area		•			•			
38	Independence Oaks County Park	•		•					•
39	Ortonville State Recreation Area		•						•
40	Metamora-Hadley State Recreation Area					•			
41	Seven Ponds Nature Center	•		•	•		•		

Detroit

There are some great places to walk in the city of Detroit. The Dequindre Cut—the old Grand Trunk Western Railroad turned into a sub-grade greenway—connects the Eastern Market with the riverfront. The paved path is well maintained and is especially popular on weekends. The Detroit International Riverwalk offers a great view of the Detroit River and takes you from the Ambassador Bridge to Belle Isle. And Belle Isle, with the reopening

The Detroit Skyline overlooks the Detroit River, as seen from Belle Isle.

aquarium and some potential state investment, becomes more and more attractive every year.

That said, there's not a lot of great hiking in the city. There are great walks, but for places where you can strap on the boots and disappear into the trees, you need to go beyond town. To the south there are parks and green spaces along Lake Erie. The miles of marshland on the lake attract millions of birds that migrate through this corridor, traveling between Michigan and Ontario, and along the Detroit River. There are paved bike-and-hike trails, rugged dirt trails, and a special breed of path known as interpretive nature trails.

Lake Erie and the Detroit River are connected to the peninsula by numerous rivers. The biggest is the Huron River. Metroparks line the

Wetlands are a critical part of the state's ecology.

Huron from the Great Lake all the way up to its headwaters northwest of Pontiac. Many of these have fine trail systems, which you would expect. Often overlooked, however, are the parks south of Detroit, across the river in Canada. The closest hike to the city (less than 5 miles away) is actually south of Windsor, Ontario.

The terrain around Detroit is relatively flat. None of the hikes listed in this section offer anything like a hill. Along Lake Erie, which was once lined with wide marshes, the view stretches out to the horizon. Farther inland, potential vistas are blocked by trees but still without hills. For more rugged terrain you will need to head over to Ann Arbor or to points north.

1 Lake Erie Metropark

Transitional areas—like the fuzzy boundary between a bog and an upland forest—are particularly fascinating to naturalists. Lake Erie Metropark straddles such a transitional area and features two hikes that together connect the shore of Lake Erie with the marshlands that once dominated the entire length of this end of the lake. This is a great hike for those who value the less-appreciated aspects of our local environment.

Start: Across the parking lot from the Marshlands Museum and Nature Center
Distance: 2.5-mile double loop
Hiking time: About 1 hour
Difficulty: Easy; widest paths around, no elevation changes
Trail surface: Wood chips, packed dirt, gravel
Best season: Spring and fall
Other trail users: None
Canine compatibility: Leashed dogs permitted on Trapper's Run loop; dogs not allowed on Cherry Island Trail

Fees and permits: Metropark Motor Vehicle Permit required
Schedule: Open daily, 6 a.m.–10 p.m.
Maps: Maps available at park office and on website; TOPO! CD: Michigan, Ohio, Indiana, disc 4
Trail contacts: Lake Erie Metropark, 32481 West Jefferson Ave., Brownstown, MI 48173; (734) 379-5020; metroparks.com

Finding the trailhead: The metropark is 20 miles south of the city in Brownstown, near the mouth of the Detroit River. From I-75 take exit 27 and drive east on Huron River Drive, which is a left-hand turn whichever direction you are coming from. (**Note:** Exit 26 is South Huron River Drive, a different road entirely.) After 2.2 miles you will come up on West Jefferson Avenue; turn left. In 0.2 mile turn right into the park and follow the signs for the Marshlands Museum. The trails start from the museum parking lot. GPS: N42 04.606' / W83 11.929'

The Hike

Lake Erie Metropark has a lot going for it, even when compared with other parks in the metropark system. In the southern half of the park you will find an eighteen-hole golf course, marina, and fishing docks. The northern half features a nature center, picnic areas, and a wave pool. Throughout the park, paddlers will find a number of boat launches and some of the best canoeing and kayaking in southeast Michigan.

Located on a marshy point where the Detroit River empties into Lake Erie, Lake Erie Metropark is perfectly situated for visitors to access the unique ecology of this region of the Great Lakes. By combining two nature hikes—Trapper's Run and the Cherry Island Trail—you get to see a great cross section of marshes, waterways, and transitional woodlands.

The hike begins near the park's Marshlands Museum and Nature Center, just across the parking lot from the building's main entrance. Trapper's Run makes an arrowhead-shaped loop, which you will hike clockwise, around a sprawling hawthorn thicket. The woods are surrounded by marshland, and the wide, even path traces the boundary between the two. Along the way you will come upon four overlooks. There are small wooden decks that jut out into the wetland. Unfortunately, large swaths of phragmites (frag-MITE-eez) block much of the view.

Also known as the common reed, this invasive wetland plant is spreading inland. A native version of phragmites is not as aggressive or as tall as the European variety. The nonnative plant grows up to 15 feet tall, outcompeting cattails and other native plants for sunlight. Its deep root system, known for efficiently filtering contaminated water, also makes it nearly impossible to eradicate by pulling or mowing.

Where the overlooks are free of foliage, you can see herons, ducks, and frogs.

The woods are described as a hawthorn

Blue lobelia is found near swamps and flood plains.

thicket. The Big Turtle Shortcut connects the first and last overlooks and will take you through the heart of the woods if you're interested. This would shorten your walk considerably, however. From the main trail the woods often seem to be overrun with all sorts of vines, from wild grape and Virginia creeper to oriental bittersweet and poison ivy. It is said that viny plants are better at processing carbon dioxide and that the gradual increase of carbon dioxide in our atmosphere has given these vines a boost.

When the trail returns to the nature center, follow the paved bike path to the Cherry Island Trail. This portion of the hike is closed to pets. The trail takes you east to the lake and follows it a ways before cutting back into the marsh and returning to the parking area. In the fall you will see avid birders contributing their eyes to the annual Lake Erie Metropark Hawk and Raptor count.

For nearly 0.5 mile the trail skirts the shore of Lake Erie. A cool breeze always seems to be coming off the water here. A long bridge takes you over open water, and for a moment you stand between inlet and lake, with views of nearby islands and, possibly, a freighter on the horizon. Returning to the paved bike path, our trail cuts through beds of American lotus. In season, the startling white flowers carpet the water on both sides of the trail. It's quite breathtaking.

The trail ends where it began, at the Marshlands Museum and Nature Center. Free to park visitors, the nature center focuses on the ecology of marshes, local

AMERICAN LOTUS (*NELUMBO LUTEA*)

The American lotus is native to the southeastern regions of the United States. So why, you might ask, are there lotus beds here on the shores of Lake Erie? The lotus produces a potato-like tuber, which was eaten by Native Americans. Tradition has it that they brought the lotus north and planted it here. This is a hard story to prove or disprove, but we do know that many of the older stands of lotus may indicate that the plant's territory reaches a bit farther north than commonly believed.

The American lotus is an "emergent aquatic plant," which means that while its roots are firmly planted in the mud under the water, its leaves and stunning flower open above water. It blooms in late July and into September, making August the best month to catch the lotus in all its glory. The blossom features wide white petals and sepals surrounding a large, almost artificial-looking yellow carpellary receptacle. This cup-shaped structure will eventually become the seedpod, which is all that will be left of the lotus by the end of its growing season.

For years the American lotus was hard to come by in Michigan. Though it's making a comeback, lotus is still on the state list of threatened species—there's a hefty penalty for messing with it.

history (ever hear of the Patriot War of 1837–38?), and the traditions of duck hunting through the years. From tanks with live aquatic specimens to vintage duck-hunting boats, the museum/nature center will add depth to your visit.

Miles and Directions

0.0   Start at the trailhead, across the parking lot from the Marshlands Museum and Nature Center. Head clockwise on Trapper's Run, the first leg of this double loop.

0.2   Riley Creek Overlook is on your left. The Big Turtle Shortcut is to your right.

0.5   Wyman's Canal Overlook is on your left.

0.7   Eagle's Way Overlook is on your left.

0.8   Sangar's Lagoon Overlook is on your left.

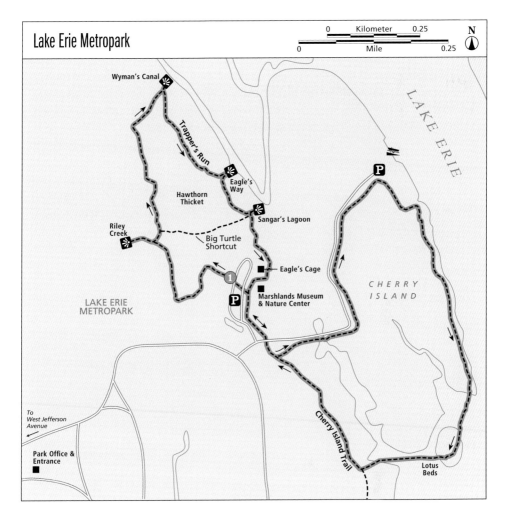

Lake Erie Metropark

0   Kilometer   0.25
0   Mile   0.25

N

Wyman's Canal

Trapper's Run

Eagle's Way

Hawthorn Thicket

Riley Creek

Sangar's Lagoon

Big Turtle Shortcut

Eagle's Cage

LAKE ERIE METROPARK

Marshlands Museum & Nature Center

LAKE ERIE

CHERRY ISLAND

Cherry Island Trail

To West Jefferson Avenue

Park Office & Entrance

Lotus Beds

0.9   A large cage on your right holds raptors. Continue on to the nature center, where the next leg of the hike—the Cherry Island Trail—begins.

1.0   Follow the paved bike-and-hike path, and cross the street.

1.1   Turn left onto the path that parallels the road. You will often see great blue herons wading in the marsh on your right.

1.5   Crossing along the edge of the woods next to the parking lot, the trail dives back into the trees on the other side. For the next 0.5 mile, Lake Erie is on your left.

1.9   A bridge leads out to Cherry Island, for which this loop is named. Stretching over open water, this is one of the best views in the park.

2.0   Lotus beds on both sides of the trail usually begin blooming in late July and last into early September.

2.2   When you get back to the paved bike path, turn right.

2.5   The trail ends back at the museum and nature center and parking lot.

Hike Information

Restaurants: 3 Hermanos, 33019 West Jefferson Ave., Rockwood; (734) 379-9600; threehermanos.com. Open for dinner, usually around 3 or 4 p.m.; closed Monday. The restaurant is just south of the metropark entrance. Not the place for the *mexicano auténtico* that purists demand, 3 Hermanos serves up that uniquely American take on Latin cuisine called Tex-Mex. Folks rave about their enchiladas.

2 Pointe Mouillee State Game Area

A coastal marsh is a unique environment, attracting thousands of birds—both regulars and those just passing through. The marshes at Pointe Mouillee are part of a large restoration project. The dikes that control the flow of water and maintain the wetlands are also your pathway to explore this exceptional nature preserve.

Start: Gate off state game road parking area, near end of Sigler Road
Distance: 7.3-mile loop
Hiking time: About 2.5 hours
Difficulty: Difficult due to length; wide and even trails
Trail surface: Gravel and packed dirt
Best season: Summer
Other trail users: Cyclists
Canine compatibility: Leashed dogs permitted
Fees and permits: No fees or permits required
Schedule: Open 4 a.m.–11 p.m.; closed Sept 15 through the end of waterfowl season—unless you have a permit

Maps: Maps available at park office and on website; TOPO! CD: Michigan, Ohio, Indiana, disc 4
Trail contacts: Pointe Mouillee DNR Wildlife Field Office, 37205 Mouillee Rd., Rockwood, MI 48173; (734) 379-9692; www.michigandnr .com/publications/pdfs/wildlife/viewingguide/ slp/107Mouillee/index.htm
Special considerations: The restrooms at Pointe Mouillee are located at the park office on the other side of the Huron River. You are very exposed to the elements in the game area. Wear a hat and sunblock, but also be aware that the wind coming off the lake can make it a bit chillier than temperatures inland.

Finding the trailhead: The preserve is on Lake Erie, 20 miles south of Detroit. From I-75 take exit 26 for South Huron Drive. From either direction, a right-hand turn takes you east. The road ends at West Jefferson Avenue (US Turnpike Road) in 2.7 miles. Turn right; in 0.3 mile turn left onto Sigler Road. Follow Sigler to its end. A dirt doubletrack continues on a few hundred yards to a parking area on your right. The gate ahead of you is the trailhead. GPS: N42 02.321' / W83 12.715'

The Hike

The wide expanse of Pointe Mouillee offers a different vista than any other you will find in the state. These are not the blowing sands of a towering dune on Lake Michigan, the craggy shores of Lake Superior, or the stony beaches of Lake Huron. This is something simpler, and yet more complex. This is a wetland on Lake Erie. In fact the Pointe Mouillee State Game Area comprises 4,040 acres of coastal wetlands. Straddling the mouth of the Huron River, it includes two islands—Celeron and Stoney—farther north in the Detroit River and is one of the best places for birding in Michigan.

The site was called Pointe Mouillee (point MOO-yay, for the uninitiated) by French traders as early as 1749. The name means "wet point." In 1875 2,000 acres of

Access to the game area, an important habitat for migrating waterfowl and other birds, is closely managed in the fall.

Pointe Mouillee were purchased to establish the Pointe Mouillee Shooting Club, and the club's wealthy members used the property for duck hunts. In 1945 the state purchased the property and created the state game area. Over the years the size of the preserve has nearly doubled.

The marshes here were once protected by a barrier beach. High water levels on Lake Erie ate away at the barrier, leaving the wetlands vulnerable to the whims of the lake. By the 1970s the marshes had been destroyed. Dikes were added to restore some of the marshes, and in the 1980s work was begun in earnest to restore the point's wetlands. According to the Department of Natural Resources, this is "one of the largest freshwater marsh restoration projects in the world."

The centerpiece of the Pointe Mouillee project, as far as civil engineers are concerned, is the crescent-shaped confined disposal facility that serves as an artificial barrier island (often called "the Banana"). When shipping channels are dredged, the material is often contaminated with toxic waste. In order to keep that toxic material from getting back into the environment, it is put here. The complex of dikes and the containment facility make Pointe Mouillee a great place to hike and bike, allowing visitors (especially birders) great access to coastal wetlands.

▶ **Water that flows into Lake Erie will stay in the lake for about 2.6 years—the shortest retention time for any of the Great Lakes. Lake Superior, in contrast, retains water for 191 years.**

The trails at Pointe Mouillee are essentially doubletrack gravel roads. Three causeways—North, Middle, and South—connect the Banana to the mainland. In between are diked marshes. The big loop, which crosses both the North and South Causeways, is over 10 miles long. A shorter loop (described here) using the North and Middle Causeways is more practical for visitors on foot. At more than 7 miles, that route is still on the long side, which is why you see a lot of bikes on Pointe Mouillee.

The trail begins at the gate to the game area and follows along the shore. To your left the Huron River empties into Lake Erie. On the other side of the river mouth is the southern end of the Lake Erie Metropark. As the trail continues around, Lake Erie stretches out to your left.

Of all the hikes in this guide, only on Pointe Mouillee do you really get a chance to take in one of the Great Lakes. Erie is the shallowest of the five Great Lakes. Its average depth of 62 feet means that the lake warms up quicker in the summer and often freezes over in winter. The coast of western Lake Erie was once rimmed by nearly a million acres of marshes and other wetlands. Early explorers describe marshes that reached to the horizon and teemed with birds—waterfowl, wading birds, shorebirds—and other

The flat terrain at Pointe Mouillee allows for long views.

wildlife. Since settlement began in earnest in the mid-1800s, 95 percent of those wetlands have been drained.

The trail continues around to the Middle Causeway, and then you make your way back to the start through a patchwork of marshes and cultivated fields. As its full name suggests, Pointe Mouillee State Game Area serves the hunting community—primarily duck hunters. (Behind wetland restoration efforts in southeast Michigan, you will often find duck hunters.) Acres of corn are planted here to attract and feed the large populations of waterfowl that make their way north and south by way of the Detroit River.

The inventory of bird species that have been spotted here is amazing and includes white pelican, brown pelican, red-throated loon, common loon, bitterns, herons, egrets, bald and golden eagles, owls, hawks, and woodpeckers of every stripe. The list of commonly sighted birds includes nearly 300 species. With binoculars you might get to see a few of them yourself.

GREEN TIP:
Go out of your way to avoid birds and animals that are mating or taking care of their young.

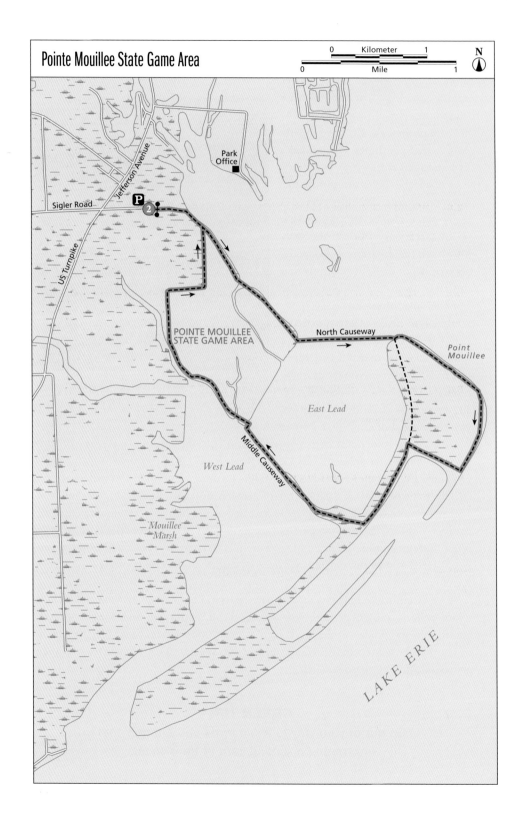

Pointe Mouillee State Game Area

0 Kilometer 1
0 Mile 1

N

Jefferson Avenue

Park
Office

Sigler Road

P
2

US Turnpike

POINTE MOUILLEE
STATE GAME AREA

North Causeway

Point
Mouillee

East Lead

Middle Causeway

West Lead

Mouillee
Marsh

LAKE ERIE

The trail ends back at the gate. During hunting season the preserve is closed to the general public, and a permit is required for entry.

Miles and Directions

0.0 Start from the parking area following the doubletrack gravel road east and through the gate.

0.4 On your right, pass a couple paths heading south. Continue straight, keeping the open water on your left.

1.3 Another intersection. Keep to the left, and continue out on the North Causeway.

2.0 Here's yet another chance to turn from the path. Don't do it. Continue to the left. Over the next mile, as you walk around the curve, you are out on the barrier that protects the marsh from the open lake.

3.2 Turn right. (To continue straight would be a dead end.)

3.6 Turn left.

4.1 Turn right here to return back along the Middle Causeway. Bring your binoculars—the marsh to your right hosts many rare birds on their annual migrations. (**Option:** If you are up for a longer, 10-plus-mile hike, continue straight and come back via the South Causeway and a series of trails along the game area's western boundary.)

5.1 A quick jog to the right and then left here will get you on the path on the other side of the channel.

5.5 Continue straight. (**Option:** You can knock more than 0.5 mile off the loop by turning right here. You will be skipping Milepoint 5.7 and approaching the intersection at Milepoint 6.5 from the opposite side.)

5.7 Turn right. The cultivated fields you see provide food for birds.

6.5 Turn left at the intersection, returning to the main path on which you began.

6.9 Turn left when you get back to the main road.

7.3 The trail ends back at the gate.

Hike Information

Restaurants: Round House BBQ, 2760 West Jefferson Ave., Trenton; (734) 671-6100; roundhousebbq.com. A bit to the north in Trenton, you will find this great local barbecue joint. Try the smoked Lake Superior whitefish for a taste of the Great Lakes.

3 Sterling State Park

Hemmed in by I-75, Dixie Highway, and industry on the River Raisin, Sterling State Park clings to a watery postage stamp of land on the shore of Lake Erie. Just outside Monroe, the park's day-use area is a popular beach and busy boat launch. The back end of the park is a patchwork quilt of man-made lagoons and an impressive marsh complex. A paved path traces the edge of the marsh and features scenic overlooks and interpretive aids that will add to your appreciation of the park.

Start: Between the hiker parking area and the nearby bridge
Distance: 3.6-mile loop
Hiking time: About 1.5 hours
Difficulty: Moderate; wide, smooth path with even grade
Trail surface: Pavement
Best season: Summer
Other trail users: Cyclists
Canine compatibility: Leashed dogs permitted
Fees and permits: Recreation Passport required
Schedule: Open 8 a.m.–10 p.m.
Maps: TOPO! CD: Michigan, Ohio, Indiana, disc 4; maps available at park office and on website
Trail contacts: Sterling State Park, 2800 State Park Rd., Monroe, MI 48162; (734) 289-2715; www.michigan.gov/sterling

Finding the trailhead: The park is located approximately 40 miles southwest of Detroit. From I-75 south of Detroit, take exit 15 for Dixie Highway. The park entrance is less than 1 mile east of the interstate. Follow State Park Road around to the large parking lot for beachgoers. Opposite this is a smaller lot for those using the trails. GPS: N41 54.669' / W83 20.321'

The Hike

For the simple reason that most people's idea of hiking doesn't include pavement, this is the only trail in the book that is completely paved. But don't be too quick to look down your nose at Sterling State Park. Sure, you will find plenty of cyclists on the path. There's a complete lack of rugged terrain, steep climbs, and switchbacks, and there are absolutely no foot-tripping tree roots. But the park does have something special: more than 3 miles of pathway surrounding a beautiful marsh.

William C. Sterling State Park is Michigan's only state park on Lake Erie. It's a rare thing these days, and it might not exist at all if it were not for a Monroe businessman who had the foresight to buy up tracts of marsh north of the River Raisin back in the 1800s. The land was later transferred to the state and set aside to preserve the wetlands that William C. Sterling realized were important to Michigan's wildlife.

Sterling State Park consists of roughly 1,300 acres tucked between the River Raisin and Sandy Creek. There was a time when the pollution pouring out of Detroit made this area unsafe for swimming and other water-related recreation (it was likely no picnic for birds and fish either), but times have changed. Today the mile-long beach at the park is its star attraction.

The south end of the park features a modern campground on Lake Erie with over 250 campsites. Behind the campground and the beach parking lot, there are three lagoons. The front two are open to kayaks and canoes (no wakes, no motors), but the far back lagoon is a nature-lover's paradise. The silhouettes of smoke stacks clustered around the mouth of the River Raisin make you realize how important and rare this wildlife habitat is.

The paved loop begins at the trailhead parking area. It circumnavigates the marsh and the northernmost lagoon before returning to the parking lot. The path is a simple one. After crossing the bridge you

Mallards, herons, and other waterfowl call Sterling State Park home.

come to a sheltered information station. Illustrated displays explain the marshland habitat and provide a great introduction to some of the birds you're likely to see on the water with photos of various herons, songbirds, raptors, and shorebirds. Situated on a cleared rise, the shelter looks out over the water, where you are likely to see white egrets, great blue herons, and ducks. Lots of ducks.

Continuing on, the loop offers two more places to stop and survey the marsh and its inhabitants. Just short of 1.0 mile into your hike, you will come to the observation tower, which offers a bird's-eye view of the wetland. At just over 1.5 miles, an observation deck affords a close-up look at the marsh's weedy shoreline.

The trail is well traveled, and on weekends you will pass a lot of people out for a walk or bike ride. Just before the turn at 2.5 miles, be sure to check out the small lagoon on your left for great blue herons. The path then continues around the final lagoon and back to the parking lot.

This part of the state, around Monroe, is chock-full of history. One of the largest engagements of the War of 1812 was fought on the banks of the River Raisin in what was then called Frenchtown. A national park has been established to commemorate the battle, which we lost, and the subsequent massacre of wounded American prisoners. An 8.0-mile paved hiking and biking path connects our loop at Sterling State

"REMEMBER THE RAISIN"

Many people forget that the end of the Revolutionary War was not the end of hostilities between the United States and Great Britain. A few decades later, loose ends were hammered out with the War of 1812. One of the most important engagements of that war was fought in Michigan, on the banks of the River Raisin.

In late January 1813 Brig. Gen. James Winchester sent troops from Fort Perry in Ohio to aid the residents of Frenchtown (present-day Monroe, Michigan). That previous summer the British had taken Fort Detroit without a shot. After a small skirmish the Americans successfully pushed the British and their Indian allies out of Frenchtown.

Several days later, however, the British returned with a greater force. The British General Procter came down from Detroit and quickly overwhelmed the Americans. General Winchester, who was captured, almost literally, with his pants down, ordered his troops to surrender. They fought on for several hours before quitting.

General Procter felt exposed in Frenchtown. Afraid that more American troops could arrive any day, he beat a hasty retreat back to Detroit. Because they would slow down his army's progress, the American wounded were left behind, told that stretchers and wagons would be returning to pick them up. Only the prisoners who could walk were taken back to Detroit.

Not long after the British left, their Indian allies began stripping the wounded of their belongings. The houses where they were sheltered were set on fire, and the wounded who tried to escape were killed. The prisoners who were marched north with the British and some of their native allies didn't necessarily fare much better. Those who faltered on the path were dispatched with a tomahawk and left beside the road. One eyewitness reported, "The road was for miles strewed with the mangled bodies."

This was a galvanizing event, and "Remember the Raisin!" became a rallying cry across the United States.

Park with the River Raisin Battlefield, historic sites in Monroe, and a recreational path west of town. It's called the River Raisin Heritage Trail System, and if history excites you (or you just want to walk to town), it's worth adding a few miles to your hike.

A paved path leads into the woods at Sterling State Park. ▶

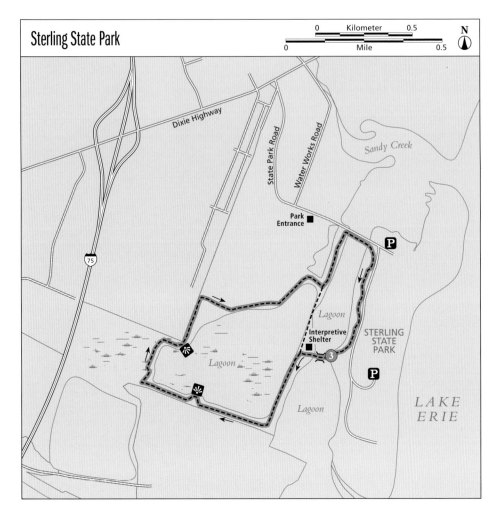

Sterling State Park

Miles and Directions

0.0 Start from the trailhead between the parking area and the nearby bridge.

0.1 Reach the interpretive shelter.

0.9 After crossing a short bridge, come to an observation tower.

1.2 Follow the trail to the right to continue around the marsh. (*Option:* The trail to the left connects with the 8.0-mile River Raisin Heritage Trail System, the River Raisin Battlefield Park, and historic sites in downtown Monroe.)

1.6 Come to an observation deck on your right.

2.5 The trail comes to a T; turn left and follow along the narrow causeway to the other parking area just off State Park Road.

2.8 Reach the main road; turn right and follow the parallel path.

3.6 The trail ends at the parking lot.

Hike Information

Local Events/Attractions: River Raisin National Battlefield Park, 1403 East Elm Ave., Monroe; (734) 243-7136; www.nps.gov/rira. This is a relatively new park; you will see this one grow and change in the future.

Martha Barker Country Store Museum, 3815 North Custer Rd., Monroe; (734) 240-7780. This is just a fun place for kids. Located in an 1860s schoolhouse, the museum is set up to look like an old store. Kids love to buy the penny candy.

Monroe County Historical Museum, 126 South Monroe St., Monroe; (734) 240 7780; www.co.monroe.mi.us/government/departments_offices/museum/index .html. Did you know that George Armstrong Custer spent much of his childhood in Monroe? The museum's General George A. Custer Exhibit will tell you that and more. You can see where he lived here, as well as learn about the town's rich history.

GREEN TIP:
If you're toting food, leave the packaging at home. Repack your provisions in ziplock bags that you can reuse and that can double as garbage bags on the way out of the woods.

4 Oakwoods Metropark

On a naturally scenic portion of the Huron River, the Oakwoods Metropark has a fine tangle of nature trails that cut through a cross section of habitat, from views of river wetlands to mature woodlands and open fields. The adjacent nature center does an excellent job of interpreting the site for you with live-animal exhibits and knowledgeable staff.

Start: Near the Oakwoods Nature Center
Distance: 2.3-mile loop
Hiking time: About 1 hour
Difficulty: Easy; very little elevation change
Trail surface: Gravel and packed dirt
Best season: Best in summer
Other trail users: None
Canine compatibility: Dogs not permitted
Fees and permits: Metropark Motor Vehicle Permit required

Schedule: Open daily, 6 a.m.–10 p.m.
Maps: Maps available at park office and on website; TOPO! CD: Michigan, Ohio, Indiana, disc 4
Trail contacts: Oakwoods Metropark, 17845 Savage Rd., Belleville, MI 48111; (734) 782-3956; metroparks.com (administered through the Lower Huron Metropark)

Finding the trailhead: Oakwoods Metropark is 30 miles southwest of Detroit, just outside Flat Rock. From the south on I-275, take the West Will Carleton Drive exit (exit 8). Turn left (west) and drive 0.5 mile to Waltz Road. Turn right onto Waltz Road and drive 2 miles to Willow Road. Take Willow Road east 2.3 miles to the park entrance, following the signs to the nature center, where the trailhead is located.

From the north on I-275, take the South Huron Road exit (exit 11). Turn right (west) and drive 1 mile to Waltz Road. Turn left and drive south for 1.5 miles to Willow Road. Then follow directions above. GPS: N42 06.357' / W83 19.063'

The Hike

The Huron-Clinton Metroparks, which are spread across five counties in southeast Michigan, are so named because the thirteen parks that make up this halo of green around Metro Detroit are all situated on the Huron or Clinton River (or on a river or stream that feeds one of these rivers). The system as a whole offers visitors a wide variety of recreational activities.

In southern Wayne County a chain of three metroparks represents more than 4,500 continuous acres on 15 miles of the Huron River. Each of the parks has something unique to recommend it. The Lower Huron Metropark has the Turtle Cove Family Aquatic Center, with waterslides, a lazy river, and a zero-depth pool. Willow Metropark has an impressive golf course, a disc golf course, and an activity center with a pool and skatepark. Oakwoods Metropark, the largest of the three, offers nature trails.

The wetlands that border the Huron River are home to numerous waterfowl.

Though larger than its neighbors, Oakwoods is much less developed. The amenities, such as they are, could use some maintenance and updating (don't even think of using the toilets at the Cedar Knoll Picnic Area), but the park's top-notch nature center and the adjacent nature trails make it especially attractive to those looking for a quiet and possibly informative walk in the woods.

All the nature trails, with the exception of the butterfly trail, begin at the nature center. One of the center's highlights—and one that's real popular with kids—is the turtle tank. This 700-gallon aquarium is home to a host of turtles. You can also see live snakes, frogs, toads, fish, etc. Outside, a large cage next to the center is the home of "Hawkeye," the center's red-tailed hawk. It's a real treat to see a raptor like this up close.

Four nature trail loops begin near the Oakwoods Nature Center. The shortest is the Split Log Trail. Only 0.1 mile long, the quick jaunt begins with a great view of the Huron River. The other three loops share a trailhead, located halfway between the parking lot and the nature center. Big Tree Trail is a short 0.75-mile hike through towering hardwoods.

The other two loops—Long Bark and the Sky-Come-Down Trails—can be combined for 2.3 miles of hiking. That's the route outlined here.

Starting on the Long Bark Trail, the path follows the Huron River. A handful of sites on the river are set aside for taking in the scenery. It's not uncommon to spot a white egret or herons wading in the shallow waters on the far side of the river. The path then turns from the river and heads into the woods. As the trail meanders back to the nature center, you will see wild cherry and shagbark hickory amid the oak. It is not uncommon to see thick poison ivy vines climbing the trunks.

At the 1.6-mile mark, you come to the junction with the Sky-Come-Down Trail. Turning to the left, you pass through field and forest and eventually come upon a charming 3-acre pond.

Another short hike you might find interesting is the butterfly-viewing trail across from the Cedar Knoll Picnic Area. This is an official monarch butterfly waystation. For a closer look at the river, bring a canoe. The Walk-in-Water Trail is for paddlers. A service drive at the far end of the parking lot leads to the riverboat launch. A map that describes what you're seeing on the water is available in the nature center.

Miles and Directions

0.0 Start from the trailhead near the nature center. Take the Long Bark Trail southward.

0.1 The Big Tree Trail, a loop of 0.75 mile is to your right. Turn left to follow the Long Bark Trail. Then on your left you will see a trail that connects to the even shorter (0.1-mile) Split Log Trail. Continue straight (east).

0.2 Come to the first of two overlooks on the Huron River. The small islands in the flow are a great place to spot some wildlife.

0.3 Reach the second overlook. The river is so wide and slow flowing here that it seems more like a marshy lake than an important river. You can spot white egrets here. The trail curves inland a bit, and though for the next 0.5 mile the river is still to your left, it's not as visible.

0.4 The connector trail on the right leads to the Big Tree Trail loop.

Oakwoods Metropark

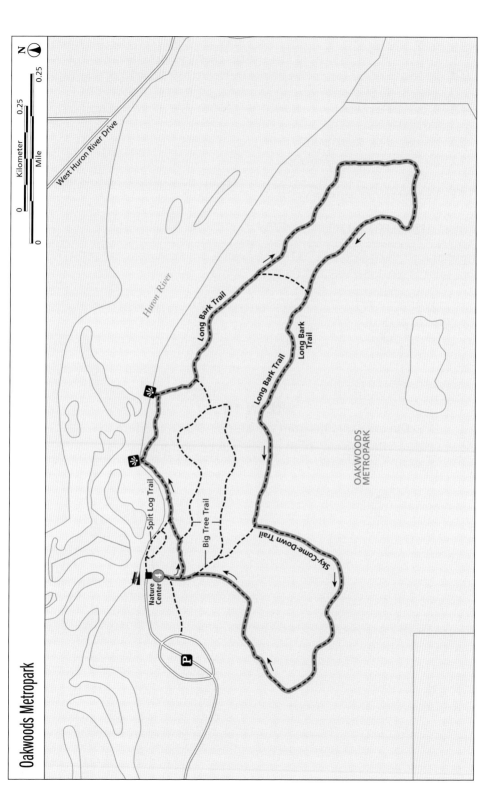

0.6 To the right is a shortcut that chops about 0.6 mile off the length of the hike. Interesting terrain, but why not stick it out for the complete experience?

1.2 The trail climbs a little as you leave the river. The shortcut from 0.6 mile back now rejoins the main loop on your right.

1.6 By itself, the Long Bark Trail is a nice hike, but turn left here to add the Sky-Come-Down Trail into the mix.

2.0 This loop passes a small pond. You'll see it here on your left.

2.2 The Sky-Come-Down Trail rejoins the Long Bark Trail, and together they head back to the trailhead.

2.3 The trail ends near the nature center.

Hike Information

Restaurants: Big Bear Lodge, 25253 Telegraph Rd., Brownstown, MI 48134; (734) 782-6600; bigbearlodge.org. The Lodge has a classic "up north" feel. The restaurant serves up American fare, with an extra bit of attention. The steaks are wood-fired, for example, and the appetizers include Maytag chips and crab cakes. The menu also includes great burgers and pizza. Be sure to try the fresh whitefish.

GREEN TIP:
Observe wildlife from a distance. Don't interfere in their lives—both of you will be better for it.

5 Crosswinds Marsh Wetlands Interpretive Preserve

Birds love wetlands, so it stands to reason that birders would also love wetlands. Hikers, hoping for dry feet, often do not. The extensive boardwalk trails at Crosswinds Marsh solve the problem of wet feet and give everyone a chance to see great blue herons, cranes, swans, and all sorts of waterfowl.

Start: Trailhead at west end of the parking lot
Distance: 3.0-mile double loop
Hiking time: About 1 hour
Difficulty: Moderate; wide level trail with no elevation changes
Trail surface: Wooden boardwalk, packed dirt
Best season: Spring through fall
Other trail users: None
Canine compatibility: Dogs permitted
Fees and permits: No fees or permits required

Schedule: Open sunrise to sunset
Maps: TOPO! CD: Michigan, Ohio, Indiana, disc 4; map posted near the trailhead
Trail contacts: Wayne County Parks, 33175 Ann Arbor Trail, Westland, MI 48185; (734) 261-1990; www.waynecounty.com/dps/dps _parks_resources_sumpter.htm
Special considerations: To protect the wetland, visitors to Crosswinds Marsh are asked to stay on marked trails.

Finding the trailhead: The preserve is west of I-275, between I-94 (to the north) and I-75 (to the south). Take the exit for Will Carleton Road and drive west to Haggerty Road. Parking is 0.5 mile north on Haggerty. The trailhead is at the west end of the parking lot. It's hard to miss the boardwalk that leads out over open water. GPS: N42 05.764' / W83 26.612'

The Hike

Since the state began addressing the problem of lost wetlands several decades ago, Michigan has gone from a state losing 0.5 million acres of wetland every year to one that is seeing an annual net gain. A big reason for this: laws that require developers to replace every acre lost during development with 1.5 acres somewhere else. So in 2005, when the Detroit Metro Airport began to look at draining property for an expansion of runways, they also began looking for other property that could be turned into marsh.

It was an ambitious project. Land was located about 6 miles southwest of the airport. Interestingly, before farmers drained the land for agriculture, the property that would become Crosswinds Marsh had been natural wetland, so a flow of water through the property already existed. Creating the marsh required removing tons of soil and planting hundreds of thousands of native aquatic plants and 10,000 seedlings. A section of the property was set aside as habitat for several rare plant species found at the airport. Not content to simply create a wetland, the site was also developed as

A long section of the trail passes over open wetlands.

an interpretive site. The result is this amazingly accessible 1,000 acres of man-made wetland in Wayne County near New Boston.

The most impressive feature of the park is the system of boardwalks. Used at other parks to help hikers over muddy ground or to protect sensitive terrain, the boardwalks at Crosswinds take hikers right over open water. From the main trailhead the board-walk leads out to a broad deck that wraps around a screened shelter. From there the boardwalk continues out to a Y and splits to the north and south.

As you walk a few feet above the water, fish are often seen schooling in the shade of the walkway above. Take a moment to scan the water's edge in the distance. Great blue herons and egrets stand very still or walk with a gentle step as they patiently look for frogs in the shallow water.

The 3.0-mile loop outlined here is a combination of several trails. By combining the Blue Heron and Bald Eagle Trails, hikers could get in a nice 4.3 miles. Our path is shorter, but it takes full advantage of the boardwalk sections of the park. The loop described below combines the Blue Heron Trail with the Mallard and Muskrat Trails, returning on a section of the Bald Eagle Trail and the Bluegill Trail.

Starting out from the parking lot, follow the boardwalk back and to the right. The trail hopscotches over an island on its way back to dry-ish land. Most of this route passes over wetlands or through fields, although toward the north end of the park, there are some impressive stands of trees—towering oaks and the like.

The westernmost stretch of the trail follows Disbrow Drain (i.e., a ditch). Sections of the drain hold still water, and as you walk through in late summer, you can hear the frogs jumping for safety just ahead of your footsteps. Stop, stay still, and look close. They don't go far and often count on stillness—rather than distance—to trick passers-by.

The trail begins as a wooden pathway, but by the end of the loop, hikers will have tromped on mown grass, packed dirt, and woodchips. The last stretch before turning back into the marsh is a doubletrack gravel drive. For the entire hike, which is punctuated with amazing opportunities for birding and nature appreciation, a steady queue of planes pass overhead. Thankfully not so close that they're loud, the planes are an ever-present reminder of what created this marsh in the first place.

Miles and Directions

0.0 Start from the west end of the parking lot; head toward the water.

0.1 Trail marker A. The first intersection is a Y in the boardwalk. Head right (north).

0.2 Trail marker B. Once on the island, the path splits again. Head right. (You will return from the left)

0.3 Come to a nice picnic area before crossing the bridge back to the mainland.

0.4 Trail marker C. Now on the Muskrat Trail, head left (north).

0.7 Trail marker D. Turn left (north) again, following the Blue Heron Trail.

0.9 Reach a picnic spot in a grassy section of the park. The trail then plunges into the woods (and some pleasant shade on hot days).

1.0 Stop and enjoy the bench.

1.2 The trail leaves the woods and parallels the power lines for a stretch.

1.3 Smaller trails break off to the left and roam the meadow. Stay straight.

1.6 A side path to the right connects with the park's Equestrian Trail.

1.7 The boardwalk skirts the edge of the Disbrow Drain. On summer days stop to see if you can find frogs hiding in the water.

1.8 The trail makes a jog here across the bridge over the drain. The trail over the bridge here is wide and is also used by folks working out of the nearby park maintenance building.

2.0 A path connecting the Blue Heron Trail with the Equestrian Trail enters from the right.

2.3 Trail marker G. You haven't seen trail markers in a bit. This one indicates the turn back to the parking lot. Turn left. (**Option:** For a longer hike, stay straight and follow the Bald Eagle Trail back to the start.)

2.4 This section of the trail is a raised boardwalk through a marshy stretch of land, which then leads out to open water.

2.5 Back at the Mallard Trail, turn right.

2.6 Instead of heading directly back to the parking lot, continue straight at trail marker A. You are now on the Bluegill Trail

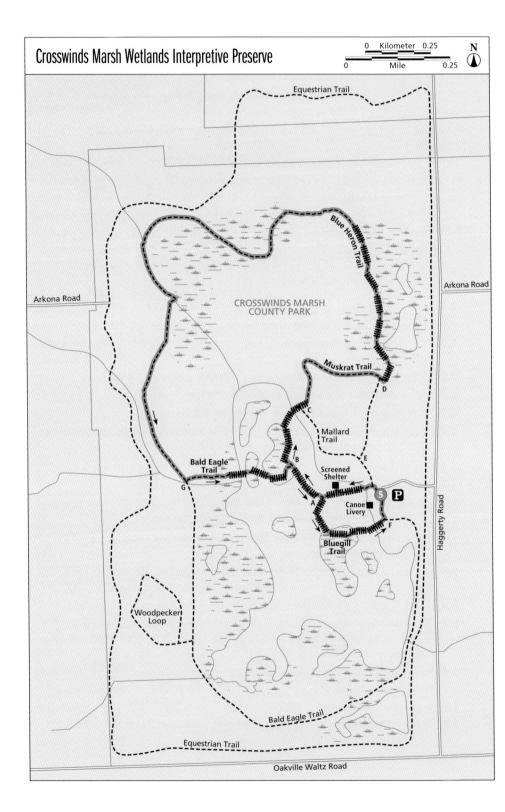

Crosswinds Marsh Wetlands Interpretive Preserve

0   Kilometer   0.25

0   Mile   0.25

N

Equestrian Trail

Blue Heron Trail

Arkona Road

Arkona Road

CROSSWINDS MARSH
COUNTY PARK

Muskrat Trail

D

C

Mallard
Trail

E

B

Bald Eagle
Trail

Screened
Shelter

5   P

G

A

Canoe
Livery

F

Bluegill
Trail

Haggerty Road

Woodpecker
Loop

Bald Eagle Trail

Equestrian Trail

Oakville Waltz Road

2.9 Back on dry land! Follow the trail left to return to the parking area.

3.0 Arrive back at the trailhead.

Hike Information

Restaurants: Twisted Rooster, 9729 Belleville Rd., Belleville; (734) 697-6201; twisted-rooster.com. Drive about 12 miles north on Sumpter Road to visit the little town of Belleville. The town sits on Lake Belleville (a dammed section of the Huron River) and has a great downtown for roaming. Just north of I-94 is the Twisted Rooster, which offers American dishes with an upscale modern twist.

Hike Tours: Crosswinds Marsh employs naturalists who give interpretive tours of the marsh. Visit the website or call (734) 261-1990 for information.

6 William P. Holliday Forest & Wildlife Preserve

The William P. Holliday Forest & Wildlife Preserve is really a handful of parks strung along Tonquish Creek. The history of the creek is rich with stories of the native Potawatomi Indians, and some of the paths here are built on their original trails. Koppernick, the farthest west of the parks, has a tangle of loops for exploring the creek and its bordering woods.

Start: Parking lot at the north end of the park

Distance: 2.3-mile loop

Hiking time: About 1 hour

Difficulty: Easy to moderate; very little climbing required, but overgrown spots make the going difficult at times.

Trail surface: Packed dirt

Best season: Summer

Other trail users: None

Canine compatibility: Dogs not permitted

Fees and permits: No fees or permits required

Schedule: Open dawn to dusk

Maps: TOPO! CD: Michigan, Ohio, Indiana, disc 4; maps available at www.hnpa.org

Trail contacts: Wayne County Parks, 33175 Ann Arbor Trail, Westland, MI 48185; (734) 261-1990; www.co.wayne.mi.us/dps/dps_parks_resources_holiday.htm

Finding the trailhead: The preserve is in Westland, approximately halfway between Detroit and Ann Arbor. From I-275 take Ford Road (M-153) 1.3 miles east to Hix Road. Drive north on Hix Road for 1.5 miles to Koppernick Road and turn left. After 0.5 mile the road makes a 90-degree turn to the left. You are now on Hannan Road. At the next 90-degree bend in the road (this time to the right), continue straight. This is the drive for the parking area. The trailhead is on the left. GPS: N42 20.463' / W83 25.760'

The Hike

Sometimes nature preserves come about because of a generous donation of land. The William P. Holliday Forest & Wildlife Preserve was the result of such a financial gift. When Detroit banker Arthur J. Richardson died in 1938, he bequeathed the means for Wayne County to establish a park, asking that this park be named in honor of his uncle, William P. Holliday. It took twenty years for all the little parcels of land to be gathered into what we have today.

The Holliday Forest & Wildlife Preserve comprises more than 500 acres of wetland and forest on Tonquish Creek, a tributary of the Rouge River. Spread out along the creek, the preserve is divided into four sections: Ellsworth, Cowan, Newburgh, and Koppernick. Each section has its own parking areas and trail loops. However, they

A few short boardwalks are meant to keep your feet dry on wet days. ▶

are all connected by the 5.0-mile Tonquish Trail. (The trail is said to go back to the days of the Potawatomi who once lived here.)

The farthest west of the four sections is Koppernick, named for the road that runs along the northern edge of the park. Koppernick is also the largest of the four, comprising nearly 250 acres. Several loops are labeled on the map (available online or at the Nankin Mills Nature Center), but you're not going to be in the woods 10 minutes before you realize the map is lacking in many respects. First of all, there are many more trails on the ground than on paper, and you'll often find two branching off where the map suggests there's just one. Also, the map isn't always clear about how trails meet. For example, the map might clearly show your trail ending in a T. But when you come to the expected intersection, you find that it's a four-way junction with a fifth trail going off at a strange angle just a few yards up the next path, and none of these seem to be going the right direction.

Thankfully, the Koppernick section of the preserve isn't a vast wilderness, so it's unlikely that anyone could stay lost for long.

The Tulip Trail starts in a dirt parking area off Koppernick Road and heads due east into the woods. The path begins quite wide. Beech and maple create a high canopy. After a short while you come to a bench in a scenic clearing. A trail here leads off to the left for the Beech Trail loop. A few yards on, the Beech Trail makes a return. You will jump on the Beech Trail and follow it for a short while. Then, by way of connecting trails and trails with names not found on the map, you will make your way to the Tonquish Trail.

If you get lost at Koppernick, the Tonquish Trail is the widest and most well worn of the paths. It runs generally east to west along the creek and then turns sharply north to connect with our original Tulip Trail. It would be hard to go far in the wrong direction before you hit the Tonquish or Tulip Trail.

THE POTAWATOMI CHIEF

Just south of Tonquish Creek on Wayne Road, a Michigan Historical Site plaque marks the burial site of Chief Tonquish and his son. The creek bears his name, and some of the trails that cut through this preserve were first trod by his people, so his story bears telling.

In 1819 conflicts between the local Potawatomi Indians and American settlers were not uncommon. One such conflict resulted in the death of a settler. The Indians involved in the killing were captured; among them was Tonquish and his son.

According to the story, Tonquish's son made a run for it. As one of the settlers raised his rifle, Tonquish told him that he would call his son back. Instead he yelled out in his own language for his boy to keep on running. When Tonquish thought his son was out of range, he told the settler that his son wasn't coming back. The man then fired, killing the son. Tonquish attacked the man in a rage and was himself killed. He and his son were buried near this spot.

Though the woods are thick, the sounds of I-275 are never far off. The hum of tires on blacktop creates an amazing din, though one that eventually fades into white noise. More romantic are the trains that pass along the park's western border. Train whistles seem as natural as birdsong here and are one of the more pleasant reminders that this sanctuary is surrounded by suburbia.

About 3 miles east of the Koppernick preserve, you will find the Nankin Mills Nature Center, also managed by the Wayne County Parks Department. They say the land here was the last farmed by the Potawatomi. In 1918 Henry Ford purchased the mill and used it to further his village industries initiative. For a time Nankin Mills produced auto parts. Today it is home to a naturalist who knows more about the Koppernick woods than most folks. This is a great place to start your adventure if you need a map—or end it if you want to interpret the experience.

▷ **Only about 6 percent of housing units in Michigan are mobile homes. In 2008 this meant that Michigan placed around thirtieth of the fifty states. South Carolina usually sits in first place, with more than 18 percent.**

Miles and Directions

0.0 Start from the parking lot at the north end of the park. The trail begins at the east end of the parking lot, just behind the metal barrier.

0.2 Two overgrown trails lead off to the left. Ignore the first; take the second. These are the ends of one of the park's many loops—in this case, the Beech Trail—and you will need to follow a stretch of this loop to reach the next section of trail.

0.3 Turn right at the intersection.

0.4 Turn left at the next intersection and pass by the "shortcut."

0.7 Here in this unnamed complex of loops is where the trail gets a bit tricky. Turn right and then make a quick left. You will know that you missed the turn if you end up in the southern parking lot.

0.8 Continuing with the tricky nature of these loops, turn left at the next intersection and then take a right onto the path that runs parallel to Tonquish Creek. (*Option:* Turning left onto this highway of a trail would eventually take you east out of Koppernick and into the next section of the Holliday Forest.)

1.0 A questionable bench and shelter here appear to be meant to offer protection from the elements. But who will protect you from the shelter?

1.3 At this intersection you find yourself back on the Tonquish Trail. Take the path to the left.

1.7 A trailer park on your left may explain the various forts and lean-tos you find as you walk through this part of the trail.

2.3 The trail ends at the parking lot.

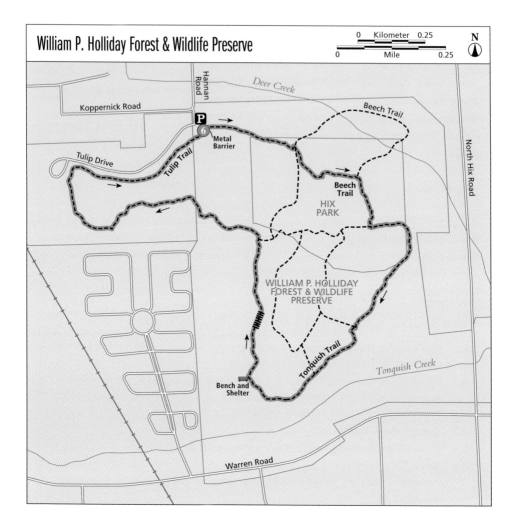

0   Kilometer   0.25

N

0   Mile   0.25

Hannan Road

Deer Creek

Koppernick Road

Beech Trail

P

6

Metal Barrier

Tulip Drive

Tulip Trail

North Hix Road

Beech Trail

HIX PARK

WILLIAM P. HOLLIDAY FOREST & WILDLIFE PRESERVE

Tonquish Trail

Tonquish Creek

Bench and Shelter

Warren Road

Hike Information

Hike Tours: Holliday Nature Preserve Association, PO Box 532243, Livonia, MI 48153; www.hnpa.org. In addition to supporting the preserve, the HNPA leads hiking tours. Check out the website for details.

Nankin Mills, 33175 Ann Arbor Trail, Westland, (734) 261-1990; www.co.wayne .mi.us/dps/dps_parks_resources_nankin.htm. Nankin Mills has lots of great historical information, and this is where you can find maps if you can't access the one online.

7 Ojibway Prairie Provincial Nature Reserve

One of the closest hikes to downtown Detroit is just across the river in Windsor, Ontario. The Ojibway Prairie complex maintains several nature units—which include prairie, wetlands, and forest—and some of the best loops are located behind the Ojibway Nature Centre. The route here combines several trails for an easy jaunt in the woods.

Start: Pin Oak Trail, at south end of the parking lot
Distance: 1.3-mile loop
Hiking time: About 30 minutes
Difficulty: Easy
Trail surface: Mostly wood chips, some packed dirt, some paved sections
Best season: Best in summer and fall
Other trail users: Joggers
Canine compatibility: Leashed dogs permitted
Fees and permits: No fees or permits required; free admission to nature center

Schedule: Open daily 10 a.m.–5 p.m.
Maps: TOPO! CD: Michigan, Ohio, Indiana, disc 4; large trail map posted near the parking lot; a more-detailed map available on the website
Trail contacts: Ojibway Nature Centre, 5200 Matchette Rd., Windsor, ON, N9C 4E8, Canada; (519) 966-5852; ojibway.ca
Special considerations: Traveling between the United States and Canada requires proper identification (passport or passport card) and money for the toll.

Finding the trailhead: The Ojibway Nature Centre is in the southwest corner of Windsor, Ontario, a few miles south of the tunnel and bridge to Detroit. From the tunnel take Wyandotte Street west for 1.6 miles to California Avenue. Turn left onto California and then take the right 1.0 mile later onto Tecumseh Road, which becomes Matchette Road when it crosses Prince Road. The park is on the right, 1.7 miles from Prince. GPS: N42 15.829' / W83 04.479'

The Hike

The closest nature hike to downtown Detroit is not in Michigan at all. Detroit is the only major city in the United States (outside Alaska) that lies north of Canada. With Windsor just a short tunnel-drive (or bridge) away, you might imagine Detroiters popping across the border for a bite to eat or to catch a show. Before 9/11 that was more likely, but the toll and often insanely long lines of drivers queuing up at customs make it harder than it sounds. It's certainly not always as easy as driving downriver to a metropark. The journey's made even more frustrating by customs officers who show a surprising amount of suspicion when you declare that the reason for your visit to Canada (or the United States, for that matter) is to "take a nature hike." Apparently that kind of behavior is suspect. Perhaps visitors should add a trip to the casino to their itinerary to justify their journey to the officials.

That said, there is good reason to cross the river. If you're Canadian there are dozens of great hikes just a short drive away. If you're from the United States, Windsor has

Purple thistle is not a native plant, but you will find a lot of it.

some great hikes you have likely been missing.

There was a time when the Detroit River was just a river, not an international border, and the ecology of this small Ontario peninsula is much more like southeast Michigan than Metro Detroit is like other parts of the state. Nature doesn't seem to recognize our political divisions. The Ojibway Nature Centre is part of a larger collection of parks, the Ojibway Prairie Complex, which includes the Spring Garden Natural Area, Black Oak Heritage Park, Tallgrass Prairie Heritage Park, Ojibway Park, and Ojibway Prairie Provincial Nature Reserve. The nature center is in Ojibway Park, and the trails take hikers through 160 acres of forest, savanna, wetlands, and tallgrass prairie.

The park's trails all begin at and return to the nature center or the adjoining parking lot. The route described here begins at the south end of the parking lot and dives right into a pin oak forest. It combines the Pin Oak Trail with the Savanna Loop and Prairie Glade Trail for an extended journey through the park. Adding the Wildlife Loop would increase the trip by nearly 1.25 miles.

Following the blue arrows (Pin Oak Trail) from the parking lot, the path curves west. At the first intersection follow the blue arrow, which points to the right (northwest). The path to the left heads off to the southwest. The park is popular with runners, hikers, and midmorning strollers. Be prepared for the soft tramp of running shoes padding up behind you as you walk.

As you walk you will see the remains of what looks like a canal on your left. In fact, it's just an old drainage ditch. The path parallels the overgrown trench for a short distance then crosses a bridge. Here the signage leaves something to be desired. Turn left, and then at the next intersection (a couple dozen yards away), turn right. This is still the Pin Oak Trail, but in 0.1 mile you will turn left onto the Savannah Loop.

Interestingly, the Savanna Loop seems to have more oak than the previous section of the route. As the name suggests, the path loops around to the pond that lies just north of the nature center. Turn right and walk around the west side of the pond, jumping back on the Pin Oak Trail. To return to the parking lot, take the first left onto the Prairie Glade Trail.

The trails on the Canadian side of the border are not so different from those in Michigan. ▶

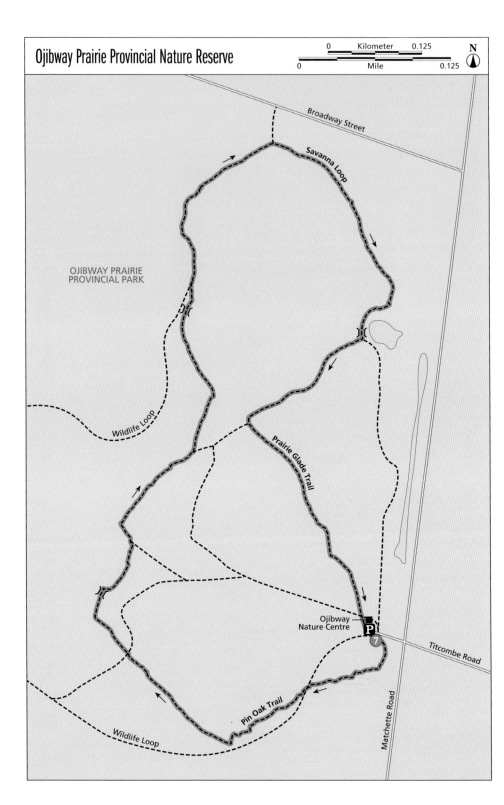

Ojibway Prairie Provincial Nature Reserve

0   Kilometer   0.125
0   Mile   0.125

N

Broadway Street

Savanna Loop

OJIBWAY PRAIRIE
PROVINCIAL PARK

Wildlife Loop

Prairie Glade Trail

Ojibway
Nature Centre

P

7

Titcombe Road

Matchette Road

Pin Oak Trail

Wildlife Loop

For more local excursions, check out the nearby trails in the complex's other units.

Miles and Directions

0.0 Start on the Pin Oak Trail, which begins at the south end of the parking lot.

0.1 The first intersection; turn right.

0.4 On the left are the remains of an old drainage ditch. Several trails lead off to the left and offer a closer look, but signs indicate this is an ecological restoration area. Cross the bridge and turn left. After about 100 feet, stay right at this intersection.

0.5 At the Y in the trail, bear left. You are now on the Savanna Loop.

0.8 Another bridge to cross. The trail is narrower than before and is now mainly packed dirt. There are many tall oaks on this section of the hike.

1.0 Another bridge to cross. The dock overlooking the water connects to a boardwalk that offers an alternate route back to the parking lot.

1.2 Turn left onto the paved section of trail to begin the Prairie Glade Trail section of the hike.

1.3 The hike ends back at the parking lot.

Hike Information

Local Information: Visit Windsor • Essex • Pelee Island, 1235 Huron Church Rd., Windsor, ON, N9C 2K6, Canada; (519) 915-7000; visitwindsoressex.com.

Local Events/Attractions: Bluesfest Windsor; bluesfestwindsor.com. The Bluesfest takes place in Canda for three days in July.

Restaurants: Frenchy's Poutinery, 361 Ouellette Ave., Windsor, ON; (519) 915-6720. Poutine is classic French Canadian fare. The basic dish is brown gravy ladled over french fries and cheese curds. Frenchy's offers some nice variations (poutine with pulled pork, for example) that make this side dish a full entree.

Ann Arbor

West of Detroit, the quintessential university town of Ann Arbor has long been the region's alternative cultural and economic center. It's also become something of an outdoor recreation wonderland. The Huron River flows from the northwest through town, pulling behind it a string of metroparks and natural areas. In town, miles of the river are bordered by bike paths, natural areas, and parks.

To the north and northwest of Ann Arbor, the flats that dominate Detroit give way to more rugged, stony terrain. A band of hills formed in the last glacial age stretch from Waterloo Recreation Area through Pinckney and Brighton, heading northeast. This terrain is a hiker's paradise. It's also a favorite with mountain bikers. Ancient glaciers dragged over the ground here, leaving behind stony, forested hills and dozens of lakes. Much of this area is state land, and there are four state parks within 15 to 20 miles of the city, including the largest in the Lower Peninsula.

The easternmost hikes in this guide are also in parks that border the Huron River. Kensington Metropark in Milford is one of the best-known parks in Metro Detroit, yet its nature trails are not close to being over-hiked. Downriver, the Island Lake Recreation Area has miles of trail looping around the river.

Even within Ann Arbor's city limits, you will find excellent nature areas. To the north, Bird Hills rises from a bend in the river, offering one of the most attractive woods around. Along the Huron River in town are several nature preserves and parks, including the University of Michigan's Nichols Arboretum. East of town, and related to the arboretum, is its sibling institution, the Matthaei Botanical Gardens.

Bees take advantage of the thistle nectar while helping to spread their seeds.

The variety offered in and around Ann Arbor means that hikers can choose from a host of experiences, including rugged

The Huron River is a sliver of nature running through Ann Arbor.

backcountry hikes, leisurely riverside strolls, and educational walks through well-managed and maintained landscapes.

8 Maybury State Park

Mountain bikers, horseback riders, anglers, and cross-country skiers all find a home at Maybury State Park.

Start: South end of the last parking loop
Distance: 3.0-mile double loop
Hiking time: About 1.5 hours
Difficulty: Moderate; some changes in elevation
Trail surface: Packed dirt
Best season: Summer and fall
Other trail users: Although there are trails for horseback riding and mountain biking, hikers encounter these folks only at the intersections.

Canine compatibility: Leashed dogs permitted
Fees and permits: Recreation Passport required
Schedule: Open 8 a.m.–10 p.m.
Maps: TOPO! CD: Michigan, Ohio, Indiana, disc 4; maps available at park office and on website
Trail contacts: Maybury State Park, 20145 Beck Rd., Northville, MI 48167; (248) 349-8390; michigan.gov/maybury

Finding the trailhead: The park is just west of Northville, about 25 miles west-northwest of Detroit. From I-275 take 8 Mile Road west for 5 miles to the Maybury State Park entrance. Follow the park road to the T; turn left. The trailhead is at the south end of the last parking loop. GPS: N42 25.849' / W83 32.108'

The Hike

Suggesting that Maybury State Park has anything in common with Andy Griffith's Mayberry would at first appear to be nothing more than a play on words, but there is something old-fashioned and quaint about Maybury State Park. Although the park's 944 acres give you a sense that you're out in the woods, far from civilization, you may pass a dozen hikers and runners on the trail. Through the trees on parallel paths, groups of young adults are horseback riding. Later, two boys carrying fishing poles and a small box of tackle walk out to the pond.

It feels a bit like an old-time summer camp at Maybury, and it couldn't be more hometown America if Opie came whistling down the trail to skip rocks on the water.

Maybury State Park seems to have been designed to get you outside on a trail. There are 10 miles of trail for cross-country skiing, 11 for horseback riding, 5 for mountain biking, and another 4 miles of paved biking and hiking trail.

Instead of beginning at trail marker 1 at the west end of the park, our route begins in the middle, using trail marker 6 as our trailhead. (Nearby is the trailhead for the park's Sanatorium History Trail—an interesting look into the history of the property.) The trail consists of two loops connected by a long out-and-back. Right from the start you're in the woods, shaded by a forest composed mainly of maple and beech. The trail begins with a gentle climb and then a long walk along the ridge of a hill.

After passing a confusing junction of trails, the hiking trail runs parallel to the equestrian path for a bit and then blazes its own route toward the pond. Along the way it traces the rim of a wooded bowl—perhaps the most scenic part of the hike. Trail marker 8 marks the beginning of the second loop, this one roughly following the shore of the pond.

The return path has you turning right at trail marker 7. This final leg is the wettest section. The trail follows the edge of a broad wetland before climbing out of the depression and back into the woods whence you began.

Mountain bikers might want to consider following up their hike with a run through the woods. The mountain bike trail here is essentially a 5.0-mile loop—not all that long for those who are used to spending time on a bike. Rated for intermediate riders, the trail includes obstacle sections for more-experienced cyclists.

Another activity to pair up with a hike at Maybury State Park would be a visit to Maybury Farm. This historic site was part of the state park and managed by the DNR until 2002. In 2003 the Northville Community Foundation took over. The barns you see here are replacements for the original buildings, which burned to the ground—livestock and all—in early 2003. Two historic barns (over 125 years old) were moved to the site in 2005. The Community Foundation uses the farm to host educational programs, including hayrides, farm tours, and maple syrup demonstrations. A general

Some visitors leave their mark on a tree at Maybury State Park.

store on the property sells fresh produce in summer, and in fall there's a corn maze. (Or should that be a "maize maze"?)

Miles and Directions

0.0 Start from the trailhead at trail marker 6. This is just a short walk south of the parking lot on a paved path. The trail begins with a fork; bear right.

0.2 A trail enters from the left. (This short connector path is not found on the official maps. It takes you right back to the start.) Stay straight.

0.4 At trail marker 7 you will see a path going off to the left. You will take this on the way home. For now continue forward into a tricky intersection. Here you have three equestrian paths coming together; one to the left, one continuing straight, and one splitting off to the right. The footpath is less obvious as it cuts through the middle. Follow the curve to the right and then, before you pass the crossroads, turn left. A narrow trail leads up to and into the woods here.

0.5 Watch your step. There's a steep sandy decline here.

0.8 Come to a fork in the path; bear right.

0.9 Here you turn left.

1.0 At trail marker 8, you've arrived at the fishing pond. The path continues to the right and follows the shoreline around. The fishing docks here are very popular with anglers who don't seem to have the need for a "secret spot." The decks are often in use.

1.1 Trail marker 10 marks the side trail that leads to trail marker 9.

1.3 For a little ways the route leaves the trail behind and takes to the road for 0.1 mile.

1.4 Turn left, and dive back into the woods.

1.5 Turn right when you come to the T, then left at the next turn. The trail meanders through the woods, with the pond just out of sight. Boy Scouts have groomed a section of trail here—a nice, wide wood-chipped path.

1.9 After passing trail marker 8, stay left at the fork. (***Option:*** An alternate route to the right meets back up with the main trail after a short detour.)

2.5 At trail marker 7, turn right.

2.8 Another trail enters from the left. This is the connector mentioned in Milepoint 0.2 above.

3.0 Arrive back at the trailhead. Turn right for the parking lot.

Hike Information

Local Events/Attractions: Maybury Farm, 50165 Eight Mile Rd., Northville; (248) 374-0200; northvillecommunityfoundation.com/mayburyfarm–c1f2v. Check their website for upcoming events.

Maybury Riding Stable, 20303 Beck Rd., Northville; (248) 347-1088; maybury ridingstable.com. If you would like to experience the park on the back of a horse, this is your chance.

Maybury State Park

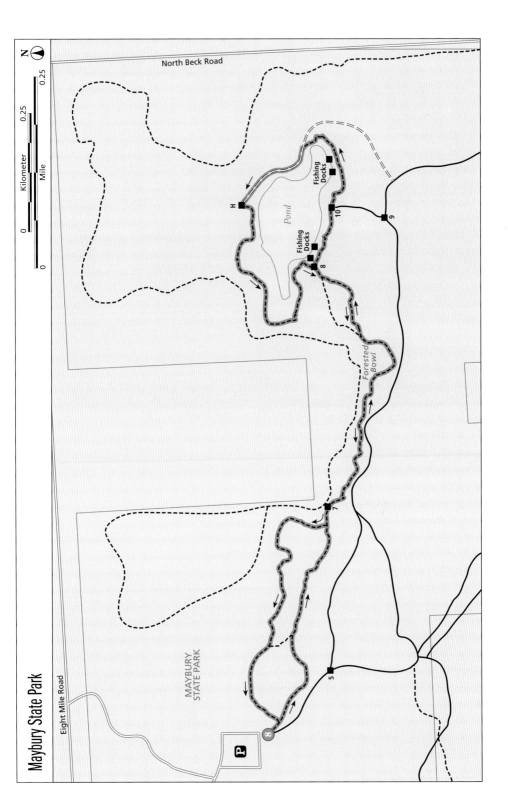

Good signage will keep you on the right path.

Mill Race Village, 215 Griswold Ave., Northville; (248) 348-1845; millracenorthville.org. Just north of Main Street, the village is a collection of historic buildings.

9 Matthaei Botanical Gardens

Gardeners come to the Matthaei Botanical Gardens to marvel at the beautifully maintained display gardens, browse books in the shop, and perhaps add a little green to their thumbs. You could spend an entire afternoon exploring the more-formal areas, but the entire property has been developed as an education in Michigan flora. Cut through the middle by Fleming Creek; the trails here wander through an exquisite collection of native trees, shrubs, and wildflowers.

Start: East end of the visitor center
Distance: 1.3-mile loop
Hiking time: About 30 minutes
Difficulty: Easy; designed for accessibility
Trail surface: Packed dirt, gravel, grass
Best season: Best in early summer, when flowers begin to bloom
Other trail users: None
Canine compatibility: No dogs permitted except service dogs
Fees and permits: Free admission; metered parking

Schedule: Grounds open daily, sunrise to sunset
Maps: TOPO! CD: Michigan, Ohio, Indiana, disc 4; maps available at the garden store and on the website
Trail contacts: Matthaei Botanical Gardens, 1800 North Dixboro Rd., Ann Arbor, MI 48105; (734) 647-7600; lsa.umich.edu/mbg
Other: Smoking is not permitted; stay on designated paths; no collecting of plants

Finding the trailhead: The botanical gardens are 1 mile east of US 23 in Ann Arbor Township. From US 23, east of Ann Arbor, take Plymouth Road (exit 41) east to North Dixboro Road. The entrance to Matthaei Botanical Gardens is 0.5 mile south, on the east side of the road. The trails begin at the east end of the main building. GPS: N42 17.984' / W83 39.659'

The Hike

The Matthaei Botanical Gardens can trace its lineage back nearly 200 years to the founding of the University of Michigan. The 1817 charter gave the school the authority to establish a number of institutions, including museums, athenaeums, and (most thankfully for this hike) botanical gardens. The first university gardens at U of M were planted in 1897 on campus. Over time the garden grew and planners became more ambitious. By 1906 the Nichols property (now the Nichols Arboretum) was being developed as a garden and arboretum.

The current property, 6 miles east of Ann Arbor, became the home of the gardens in 1957. Today the property comprises 350 acres on Dixboro Road. The gardens and conservatory make up the southern part of the site. There is a conservatory, a number of formal gardens, and a wonderful children's garden. There's also a great bookstore with lots of books on conservation and gardening with noninvasive plants.

The rest of the property is less formal, but no less intentional. More than 3 miles of trails wind through the northern section of the park, highlighting a vast collection of native Michigan species in their natural habitat. Through the middle of the preserve flows Fleming Creek. The creek shed for this tributary of the Huron River is over 30 square miles, emptying into the Huron near Geddes Road.

The trailhead for most of the nature trails is located to the left of the visitor center (when outside facing the entrance). Just past the gate for the Gateway Garden, a short bridge leads to a gazebo. Three of the park's nature trails begin here—the Fleming Creek, Dix Pond, and Sam Graham Trees Trails. The Marilyn Bland Prairie Trail is a short loop that begins and ends in the north end of the property. The Sue Riechert Discovery Trail is an even shorter loop that circles Willow Pond in front of the visitor center. The route described here combines portions of all these trails except the one that leads back to Dix Pond.

Beginning at the aforementioned gazebo, the path leads north to another short bridge and crosses to the east side of Fleming Creek. For a longer hike, the Dix Pond Trail leads off to the right. However, the trail with the scenic creek view should not be missed. Walking alongside the stream, you will see native grasses growing in the

A girl points out milkweed along the path at the botanical gardens.

low-water sandbars. Patches of wildflowers line the path, the foliage parting only here and there to allow for views of the water.

At the north end of the preserve, the Fleming Creek Trail meets the return path from Dix Pond. A bridge to the left crosses over to the west side of the creek. The Prairie Trail begins in a grove of stately oak trees. As you leave the trees, the prairie is on your right as you walk around to the Matteson Barns. The road continues in front of the barns, but the trail goes downhill behind the historic building, catching up with the dirt doubletrack on the other side. As you go along the road for a bit, the trail skirts around behind a private residence and then follows the tree line down to the Labyrinth.

There is a distinction between a maze and a labyrinth: The first is a puzzle to be solved; the second is an intricate pattern that inspires contemplation. Across from the contemplation station is the Smith Woodland Wildflower Garden. Here you find the spring ephemerals and other flowers adapted to the woodland environment. A wood-chip path leads through the garden, and there are alternate paths around this area as you head south.

You're now on the Sam Graham Trees Trail. The prairie features a number of species of trees; sections are fenced off to aid in restoration. The path then crosses the main drive and edges around Willow Pond on the way back to the parking area.

The botanical gardens are free except for the parking, so don't miss this opportunity to browse the more-formal displays—even if you only have a few minutes. The conservatory is divided into the Tropical House, Temperate House, and Desert House. Outside are the Perennial Garden, the Grower's Garden, and—a favorite with kids—the Children's Garden. A bonsai garden is currently in the works.

Miles and Directions

0.0   Start from the trailhead at the east end of the visitor center. That's on your left when you're facing the entrance. This is the Sam Graham Trees Trail.

0.1   Just past the picturesque gazebo, come to a meeting of trails and a bridge across Fleming Creek. Continuing straight on this side leads to the Sam Graham Trees Trail. Instead, cross the bridge and follow the Fleming Creek Trail to the left. (The Dix Pond Trail leads off to the right.)

0.4   Stop for a scenic creek overlook.

0.6   The Dix Pond Trail comes in from the right. Turn left and cross the creek following the Marilyn Bland Prairie Trail.

0.7   After passing the Marilyn Bland Prairie, the trail ducks behind the Matteson Barns.

0.8   Note the private residence to the right, and attempt to stifle your jealousy.

0.9   Just before you reach the 1.0-mile mark, a bench on the left and a labyrinth offer rest and contemplation, respectively. Just past the labyrinth is the Woodland Wildflower Garden, which is particularly impressive in spring. You are now on the Sam Graham Trees Trail.

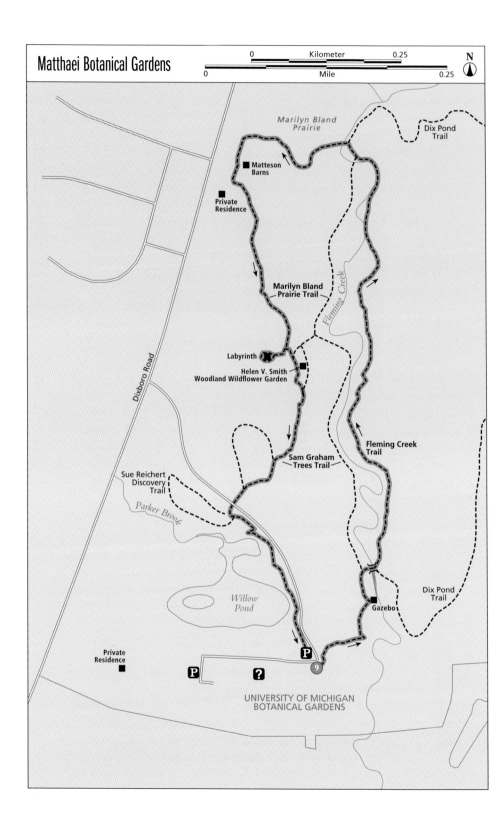

Matthaei Botanical Gardens

0 Kilometer 0.25

0 Mile 0.25

N

Marilyn Bland Prairie

Dix Pond Trail

Matteson Barns

Private Residence

Marilyn Bland Prairie Trail

Fleming Creek

Labyrinth

Helen V. Smith Woodland Wildflower Garden

Fleming Creek Trail

Sam Graham Trees Trail

Sue Reichert Discovery Trail

Parker Brook

Willow Pond

Dixboro Road

Private Residence

P

P

?

9

Dix Pond Trail

Gazebo

UNIVERSITY OF MICHIGAN BOTANICAL GARDENS

1.2 Cross the road, and turn left along the shoulder, where the path connects up with the Sue Reichert Discovery Trail.

1.3 The trail ends at the visitor center parking lot.

Hike Information

Local Events/Attractions: LeFurge Woods Preserve, 2384 North Prospect Rd., Ypsilanti; www.smlcland.org. A few miles east of Matthaei Botanical Gardens, the Southeastern Michigan Land Conservancy has cobbled together a preserve of 325 acres off Prospect Road. While the preserve is a work in progress, a nice trail system has already been developed.

10 Furstenberg Nature Area and Gallup Park

It's hard to imagine any other city of this size in Michigan that has so much natural space within its city limits as Ann Arbor. By combining a nature hike at Furstenberg Nature Center with the paved paths of Gallup Park, you can hike 2.8 miles along the scenic Huron River. The nature trails pass through wetlands and woods, oak savanna and prairie, while the park trails take you over several river islands.

Start: Northwest end of the parking lot, near the restrooms
Distance: 2.8-mile multiple loops
Hiking time: About 1 hour
Difficulty: Easy; wide path on level ground
Trail surface: Pavement and gravel
Best season: Summer
Other trail users: In-line skaters, runners, and cyclists on paved paths
Canine compatibility: Leashed dogs permitted

Fees and permits: No fees or permits required
Schedule: No posted hours, although daylight hours best for safety
Maps: Map available on website and posted on the trailhead kiosk; TOPO! CD: Michigan, Ohio, Indiana, disc 4
Trail contacts: City of Ann Arbor, Natural Area Preservation, 1831 Traver Rd., Ann Arbor, MI 48105; (734) 794-6627; a2gov.org/nap

Finding the trailhead: The park is located off Geddes Road in east Ann Arbor. From US 23 take exit 39 for Geddes Road west. The natural area parking lot is 1.7 miles west on the left. (The road becomes Fuller Road when it crosses Huron Parkway.) The trailhead is at the west end of the parking lot. GPS: N42 16.849' / W83 42.467'

The Hike

Ever since John Allen's gristmill, the Huron River has played a central role in the development and character of Ann Arbor. The city was born on the Huron's banks and spread southward. Several city-owned dams provide electricity for the town, and the resulting ponds have become great places for paddling and other outdoor recreation. In fact, much of the land around the river has been left in a relatively natural state—or at least developed for recreational use. For example, Fuller Park, just east of town, is a 60-acre bend in the Huron River with soccer fields and a huge public pool. Downriver from that, you have the university's Nichols Arboretum.

All told, parkland borders about 3 miles of the Huron River. East of downtown, the Furstenberg Nature Area sits on the north side of the river. And next to that is Gallup Park. A great hike that combines the natural charms of the nature area with stunning views of the Huron River begins with a walk through Furstenberg and then, by way of a footbridge, connects to Gallup Park. By combining the wooded nature trails with the paved hike-and-bike paths, you can create a fine 2.8-mile loop that traces both sides of the river and explores some of the several small islands in Geddes Pond.

The trail begins at the Furstenberg Nature Area. (The parking lot is on Fuller Road, across from Huron High School.) The area comprises 38 acres of mixed habitat, with a mile or so of paved and gravel paths. There are restrooms and a large trail map at the northwest end of the parking lot. The trails begin there, looping north through prairie and oak savanna edged by wetlands. The return path follows the Huron River, which can be seen through the trees. With the river on your right, the trail continues to the southeast. Passing through wetlands, the gravel path becomes a boardwalk, and then a beautiful wooden footbridge leads you up and over the water to Gallup Park.

Gallup Park is 69 thin acres along two sides of Geddes Pond (a widening of the Huron River). The park has a fishing pond for kids, a canoe livery, and a butterfly and hummingbird garden. This is the city's most popular park, and hikers share the paved paths with in-line skaters, cyclists, and runners. Following the river downstream, you

The University of Michigan Medical Center Campus rises above the Huron River.

GREEN TIP:

For rest stops, go off-trail so that others won't have to get around you. Head for resilient surfaces without vegetation.

come to Gallup Park proper, which has a parking area, playground, and the aforementioned fishing pond. There are a dozen park benches and enough barbecue grills for any Smith family reunion. From this small peninsula, bridges allow you to leapfrog across three islands to the other side of the river. This may be the most scenic part of Gallup Park; and in terms of really feeling the river, walking this section is second only to renting a canoe at the livery and paddling through this stretch of water.

All along the path there are places to rest, picnic areas, and restrooms. Once past the canoe livery, the trail turns to the left and heads toward the bridge back to Furstenberg. If you need more of an island fix, continue left for the bridge opposite the nature area bridge. Since these islands are not part of a loop, there are fewer people on this short section of path.

Crossing back over to Furstenberg, a short side trail to the right loops through some wetlands. Once you regain the main trail, your route takes you right back to the parking lot.

The Gallup Park trails are part of the county's Border-to-Border Trail, which follows the Huron River and is planned to eventually traverse Washtenaw County. Completed portions of the trail already allow cyclists to pedal from Ypsilanti to Ann Arbor.

Miles and Directions

0.0   Start from the trailhead at the northwest end of the nature area parking lot. There is a large posted trail map next to the restrooms; this is where the trails begin.

0.1   The trail begins as pavement. After a short walk to a prairie, often blooming with wildflowers, turn right onto a gravel path through an oak savanna. As the path turns to the left, there is a picturesque swamp on your right.

0.2   To the right, a trail leads down to a bench on the Huron River.

0.3   The right turn here is easy to miss. It looks like just a path down to the river, but this is the way.

0.6   The paths on the left are for the alternate side trail you will take on the return back to the parking lot.

0.7   A footbridge leads over the water. Be sure to check for fish swimming under the bridge. Once across the water, follow the paved path to the right. Cross the Huron on a road/pedestrian bridge and turn left.

1.1   The path along the river goes under the Huron River Parkway. Ahead at the parking lot, stay on the path as it bends to the left, hugging the shore.

1.4   A footbridge at the north end of the park leads to a series of three islands. There are no side paths for quite a while.

1.7   Back on land, the trail heads upriver, along the opposite shore.

1.8   On your right is the Elizabeth D. Dean Grove & Butterfly and Hummingbird Garden.

Furstenberg Nature Area and Gallup Park

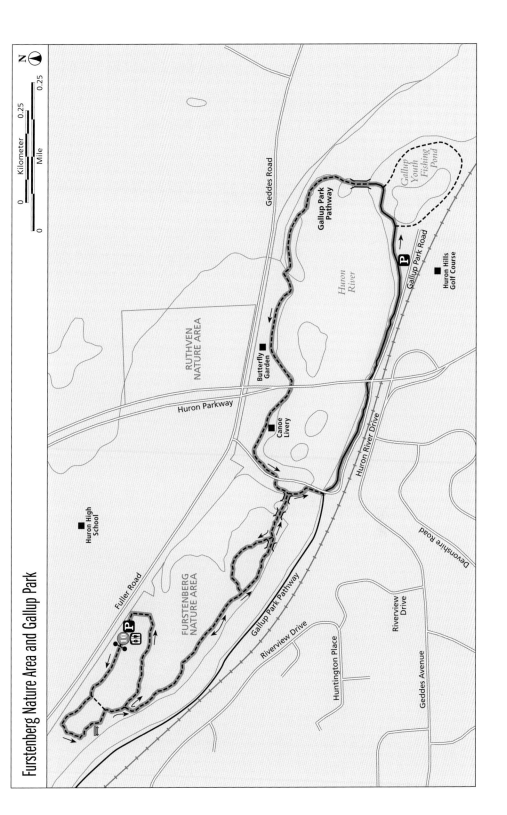

2.0   Pass under the Huron River Parkway again; the canoe livery is on your left.

2.1   Turn left onto Gallup Park Road, and take the footbridge back to Furstenberg.

2.2   Turn right at the first path.

2.4   Back on the main trail, turn right again.

2.8   Turn right. From here you can see the parking lot, where the hike ends.

Hike Information

Local Events/Attractions: Gallup Canoe Livery, 3000 Fuller Rd., Ann Arbor; (734) 794-6240; a2gov.org. There's no better way to see the river than to rent a canoe and paddle it. The livery is open daily, 10 a.m.–7 p.m.

Restaurants: Krazy Jim's Blimpy Burger, 304 South Ashley St., Ann Arbor; (734) 663-4590. You know you've made it when your burger joint is featured on *Diners, Drive-Ins, and Dives*, but I think Krazy Jim knew long before that. This has been a student favorite for years.

11 Nichols Arboretum

For a short, rugged hike close to Ann Arbor, the Nichols Arboretum on the Huron River has a few miles of trails with steep climbs, scenic overlooks, a formal garden, and riverside picnic areas. The trails pass through prairie, wetlands, and hardwood forest. In addition to a fine collection of native Michigan trees, this "living museum" features species from around the world.

Start: Gate on Nichols Drive
Distance: 2.6-mile loop
Hiking time: About 1 hour
Difficulty: Easy, though some climbing
Trail surface: Dirt path
Best season: Summer
Other trail users: None
Canine compatibility: Leashed dogs permitted

Fees and permits: No fees or permits required
Schedule: Open sunrise to sunset
Maps: TOPO! CD: Michigan, Ohio, Indiana, disc 4; map available on website and posted at the trailheads
Trail contacts: Nichols Arboretum, 1600 Washington Heights, Ann Arbor, MI 48104; (734) 647-7600; lsa.umich.edu/mbg

Finding the Trailhead: The arboretum is east of the University of Michigan campus in Ann Arbor. From US 23 take exit 41 for Plymouth Road west. Drive 3 miles to Maiden Lane and turn left. The road becomes East Medical Center Drive; take the first left onto Nichols Drive. The trailhead is at the gate. GPS: N42 17.047' / W83 43.594'

The Hike

Touted as a living museum, Nichols Arboretum (or the Arb, as the locals call it) was established in 1907 as the University's botanical garden and arboretum. Less than ten years later, the botanical garden and the arboretum went their separate ways. The garden moved to a new location on Iroquois Street. Nearly fifty years later, the garden moved again, to its current site on Dixboro Road. (See the Matthaei Botanical Gardens hike description.)

The arboretum comprises 123 hilly acres tucked between the University of Michigan, Geddes Road, and the Huron River. What began as an 80-acre site has grown significantly in the past hundred years. Considering the future of Nichols Arboretum, in 1934 a task force affirmed the preserve's mission when it reported that the arboretum would "become a haven of quiet one hundred years from now." It also made the dire prediction that "our rich native flora will have become a thing of the past in most places."

So far the arboretum has lived up to these expectations. The park has the Peony Garden, the Dow Prairie, wetlands, and woody uplands. While special care is taken to nurture a collection of trees native to Michigan, the arboretum also features a collection of nonnative species from around the world.

Parking is the first challenge of a hike at Nichols Arboretum. During the week, the University of Michigan uses the two closest lots and a window sticker is required for parking. If you don't have a sticker (and even if you do), you're not going to get a spot. Your best bet, other than hiking on a weekend, is to park at the University of Michigan Health Center—there are a few parking structures on East Medical Center Drive near Ann Arbor Arboretum Road. From there it's a short walk to the trailhead.

This loop begins at the Nichols Drive parking lot (that's the university's lot M-29, just east of the medical center). For the first 0.1 mile, the Huron River is on your left. Then your route departs the wide path and, following a trail on the right, takes you up a steep rustic trail. With grades over 45 percent, you climb nearly 100 feet to a scenic

The Huron River hems in the northern end of the arboretum.

overlook of the Huron River valley. The forest here is primarily oak and hickory. The woodlands have been harvested here a couple times, and the trees you see are second- and third-growth trees—most about one hundred years old.

Connecting back up with a primary trail, you are on the main path back to the arboretum's Gateway Garden entrance. Turn left to avoid leaving the park. Continuing south, you come to two more scenic overlooks. The trail is tracing the top of a long ridge, on its way to the Geddes entrance. At the third scenic overlook, you are at the highest point of the loop. Turn left onto another rustic trail, which quickly descends, regains a main trail, and passes between the caretaker's residence and the arboretum office.

A little more than 1.0 mile into the hike, the trail you're on is about to return to Nichols Drive. A dozen yards or so before that happens, turn right onto a side trail for the Dow Prairie. Passing the amphitheater on your left, the trail follows along the southern edge of the prairie. Turning north and beginning the return loop, you can stay with the prairie or take a right and continue along the Nichols Drive path. The railroad tracks slip in between the trail and the river, and it's not uncommon to hear a train's horn.

Whichever path you choose, they join together and then follow the river back to the parking lot.

Miles and Directions

0.0 Start from the trailhead at the gate on Nichols Drive. There's a large posted trail map and a dirt doubletrack alongside the Huron River.

0.1 Before you get too comfortable on this easy, wide path, take the rustic trail to the right and start climbing. About 100 feet above you, there's a scenic overlook of the Huron River valley.

0.3 Return to the main path; turn left. You will shortly come to an intersection. Continue straight. (*Option:* Take a short side trip to the right to see the arboretum's Peony Garden.)

0.4 Reach another scenic overlook. Take in the view and then continue straight ahead.

0.7 At the next scenic overlook, take a left down the steep stairway. At the bottom of the stairway, take a left.

0.8 The trail passes between the caretaker's residence and the arboretum office.

1.2 Just before you rejoin the trail you came in on, turn right for the Dow Prairie. Pass the amphitheater on your left, and walk along the southern edge of the prairie.

1.7 At the other end of the prairie, you have some options. When the trail splits, you can go left and continue with the prairie or turn right and jump back onto the Nichols Drive path. Both trails end up at the same spot.

2.6 The trail ends back at the Nichols Drive parking lot.

Nichols Arboretum

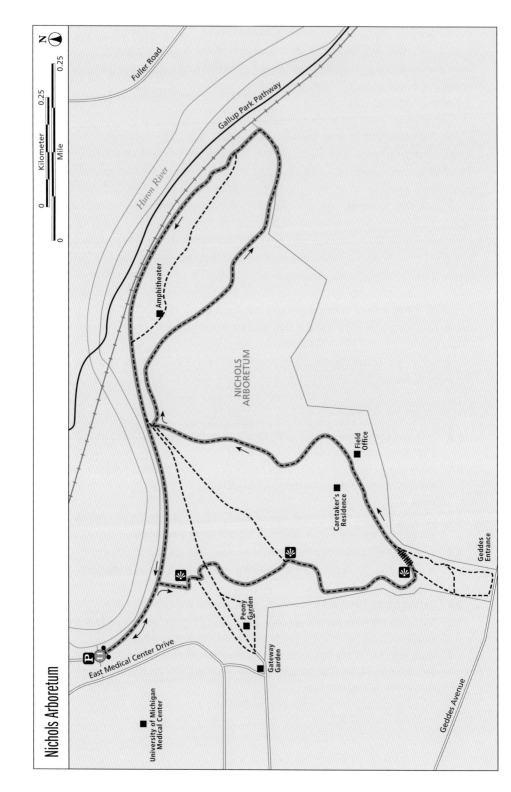

Hike Information

Local Information: Ann Arbor Area Convention and Visitors Bureau, 120 West Huron St., Ann Arbor; (734) 995-7281; visitannarbor.org.

Restaurants: Zingerman's Delicatessen, 422 Detroit St., Ann Arbor; (734) 663-3354; zingermans.com. Zingerman's has grown from a small deli in downtown Ann Arbor to one of the most respected eateries in the state. The deli has great sandwiches, and lines often wrap around the outside of the building. West of town, a more-formal dining experience can be had at Zingerman's Roadhouse.

12 Bird Hills Nature Area

Without a doubt one of the most stunning forests in the area, the Bird Hills rise up 200 feet from the Huron River below. The forest is a mix of maple, poplar, oak, ash, and other hardwoods. The trees reach arrow straight to a high canopy, allowing hikers an incredible view of the terrain in all directions. Rustic log benches, ancient oak on hilltops, trails winding after thin streams all combine to give these woods a rich primeval feel.

Start: Gate on Bird Road, across the street from the parking area
Distance: 1.6-mile double loop
Hiking time: About 1 hour
Difficulty: Difficult; some very steep climbs
Trail surface: Packed dirt
Best season: Spring and fall
Other trail users: None
Canine compatibility: Leashed dogs permitted

Fees and permits: No fees or permits required
Schedule: No posted hours, although daylight hours best for safety
Maps: TOPO! CD: Michigan, Ohio, Indiana, disc 4; map available on website and posted on the trailhead kiosk
Trail contacts: City of Ann Arbor, Natural Area Preservation, 1831 Traver Rd., Ann Arbor, MI 48105; (734) 794-6627; a2gov.org/nap

Finding the trailhead: The nature area is north of Ann Arbor, tucked between M-14 and the Huron River. From M-14 north of Ann Arbor, take exit 3 for North Main Street. Take the first sharp right onto West Huron River Drive. Drive 1.1 miles and turn left onto Bird Road. The parking lot is a dirt pull-off on the right, about 0.1 mile in. The trailhead is directly across the street. GPS: N42 18.491' / W83 45.560'

The Hike

A large wooded hill is wedged in the crook between M-14 and the Huron River at the north end of Ann Arbor. This is the Bird Hills Nature Area, which has one of the most beautiful forests in the region. Walking beneath the high canopy of oak and maple, it might surprise you to know that most of the trees you see here are second growth. Back in the 1800s this area was logged over. The bald hill that was left was used to pasture livestock—presumably because the land wasn't level enough or rich enough to till for crops. The area's natural ravines were left exposed and over the years were sharpened by erosion.

By the early 1900s the property was owned by the Graves family, who thought that planting trees on the hill would make the property more attractive to developers. You would typically find a mixed hardwood forest here, but thanks to proactive planting, there's a surprising mix of trees—from ash and sassafras to Douglas fir and Scots pine. The Graves family held onto the property until 1967, when they sold it to the city.

The wide forest paths and high canopy give the woods at Bird Hills a fairy-tale aspect.

The hill itself is part of the Fort Wayne Moraine—marking the southern edge of an ancient glacier. The Huron River bends around the base of the promontory and, along with Huron River Drive, marks the east boundary of the nature area. To the south is M-14; to the west are Newport Road and some residential neighborhoods. Across the top is Bird Road, although the property does poke a finger north to connect with Barton Park.

Looking at the preserve map, you might think the best place to park your car is at Barton Park, but be aware. The path from Barton to the trailhead is often a swampy mire and not well traveled. Fallen trees, soggy grass, and muddy tracks await the hiker here. Instead, park on Bird Road, just west of Huron River Drive. A small pull-to-the-side dirt lot is on one side of the road; a gate into the park is on the other.

The nature area trails can be confusing. For example, there are well-trodden paths that you won't find on the map. The hill runs north to south. Two main trails follow the line of the hill along its base on the east and west sides. A third trail follows right down the middle, across the top of the hill. At the south end of the nature area, these trails are blended into tracks heading more west to east.

From the gate take the path on your right. The trail follows down the west edge of the hill. To your right a stream flows north to the river. About 0.3 mile in, you come to a T of sorts. This junction is not on the official map. Turn left and climb to the top of the hill. This is a steep hike on loose ground. At the top of the hill, an old oak spreads its branches wide. Turn right and continue along the ridge of the hill.

Come to an intersection; continue south. When you reach a fork in the path, veer to the left. The forest here is stunning. The canopy is high, the tree trunks are arrow-shaft straight, and the understory is wide open. Continue straight at the next trail crossing, and then make a right. This section of the trail continues south to where the sound of M-14 becomes a bit distracting.

When you come to a T, take a left. This path runs parallel to the highway. Follow it a short ways, and then take the second trail on your left to complete the loop and return north. On the return path you retrace old ground. At the second intersection of trails, veer to the right. This route takes you along the east side of the hill and ends back at the gate on Bird Road.

Miles and Directions

0.0   Start from the gate at the north end of the nature area on Bird Road. Once inside the fence, take the path to your right.

0.2   The stream on your right winds through this side of the park, keeping west of the hill to your left.

0.3   Taking a left here, you take on the steepest hill of the hike, climbing 65 feet in short order. At the top of the hill, there's a huge oak tree. Turn right and follow the ridge of the hill south.

0.5   Continue straight through the first intersection of trails.

0.6   At the next intersection you face four options. Ignoring the paths to the immediate right and left, you essentially are left with a fork in the road. Take the right tine.

0.7   Getting closer to M-14, you can hear the traffic. Continue straight ahead.

0.8   Here at the south end of the nature area, you are at the highest point of the hike, 150 feet above the trailhead. Turn left, and ignore the first path on your left.

0.9   Take this second left, and loop back to the big intersection you came to earlier.

1.1   At the second intersection, take the trail on the right. This path follows along the eastern slope of the hill.

1.5   Come to a T in the trail; turn right, back toward the trailhead.

1.6   The loop ends at the gate on Bird Road.

Options: There are a dozen loops you could make here. You can also park at the south end of the nature area, off Newport Road or Beechwood Drive, and explore the trails nearer M-14, but any hike at the Bird Hills Nature Area should include a walk down that middle ridge.

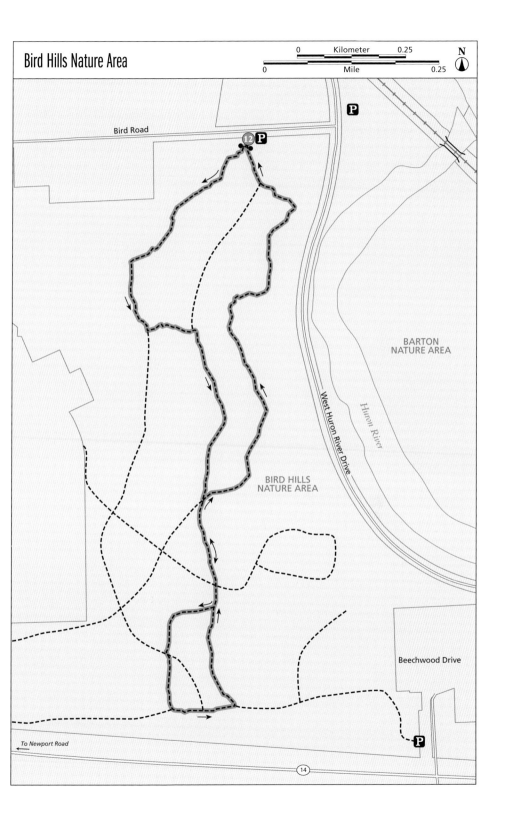

Bird Hills Nature Area

Bird Road

BARTON
NATURE AREA

West Huron River Drive

Huron River

BIRD HILLS
NATURE AREA

Beechwood Drive

To Newport Road

Hike Information

Local Information: Ann Arbor Area Convention and Visitors Bureau, 120 West Huron St., Ann Arbor; (734) 995-7281; visitannarbor.org

Restaurants: Frita Batidos, 117 West Washington St., Ann Arbor; (734) 761-2882; fritabatidos.com. The tag line here is "Cuban inspired street food," and they don't lie. A *frita* is a chorizo burger served with shoestring fries on top. You'll find all sorts of variations on that theme here. The restaurant is just 2 miles south of the Bird Hills Nature Area, 1 block west of Main Street.

13 Brauer Preserve

Offering a quiet, secluded hike, Brauer Preserve is one of the more unusual natural areas around. Its 226 acres feature upland forests, hardwood swamps, and a small lake; 85 acres are maintained as an active farm. The 2.0 miles of trails here skirt the edges of farm fields—ripe with corn and soybeans—on the way to the more "natural" sections of the property.

Start: West end of the dirt parking lot off Parker Road

Distance: 1.8-mile lollipop

Hiking time: About 45 minutes

Difficulty: Easy

Trail surface: Grass and packed dirt

Best season: Summer

Other trail users: None

Canine compatibility: Dogs not permitted

Fees and permits: No fees or permits required

Schedule: Open sunrise to sunset

Maps: TOPO! CD: Michigan, Ohio, Indiana, disc 4; map available on website and posted at the trailhead

Trail contacts: Brauer Preserve, PO Box 8645, Ann Arbor, MI 48107; (734) 971-6337; ewashtenaw.org/government/departments/parks_recreation/napp/preserves/brauer.html

Finding the trailhead: The preserve is west of Ann Arbor, about 6 miles south of Dexter. From I-94 west of Ann Arbor, take exit 167 for Baker Road. Turn south and take a right (west) onto Jackson Road. Drive 1.1 miles and turn left onto South Parker Road. Drive 3.7 miles. The preserve is on your right, just past Waters Road. The trailhead is at the end of the parking area. GPS: N42 14.238' / W83 53.800'

The Hike

Some of the most underappreciated natural spaces around are farmland. In some circles agriculture is seen as the enemy of the environment—and in many places it can be. But we need agriculture, and we need healthy farm environments. So there's an effort afoot in the conservation community to preserve farmland.

Local land conservancy groups would like to see old family farms stay in the community. Since this is often difficult when residential and commercial growth make it more profitable to sell a farm to a condo developer than to keep it as a farm, organizations are raising money to help farmers establish agricultural conservation easements. This allows the owner to take advantage of the property's increased value but also preserves the land for agricultural use in perpetuity.

The Brauer Preserve is not a conservation easement, but it does include agricultural land in its conservation plans. Of the preserve's 226 acres, 85 are farmed. Crops are rotated, and the edges of the fields have been planted with native grasses to protect waterways from runoff. The rest of the property is composed of a hardwood swamp, a

A portion of the Brauer Preserve is set aside for agriculture.

forest pond, and wooded uplands. The preserve attracts all sorts of wildlife, especially birds. And through it all run 2 miles of trails.

The trails are roughly divided into three hikes: the Lake Isabelle Trail, the Woodland Loop Trail, and the Oak Knoll Loop Trail. Individually these are all 15-minute hikes. This is great for birding, because the best viewing spots are just minutes from the parking lot. Our hike, however, will combine all three trails into one 1.8-mile walk.

The hike begins at the parking lot. To your right, across a field of soybeans, is the farm at the corner of Waters and Parker. The trail passes through two farm fields, which have been planted with soybeans and corn. As you head west, the next few acres of corn are set beyond the Zahn Drain.

▷ **Conservation easements can be used to protect the natural beauty of your property, protect it from future development, and save you money on property taxes.**

When the trail comes to a T, turn left and continue south. As you enter the woods, there is a hardwood swamp on your left. At the end of the trail is Lake Isabelle, which is surrounded by wetlands. This whole route is the Lake Isabelle Trail, a simple out-and-back. Follow the trail back to the farm fields and turn left for the Woodland Loop Trail. The

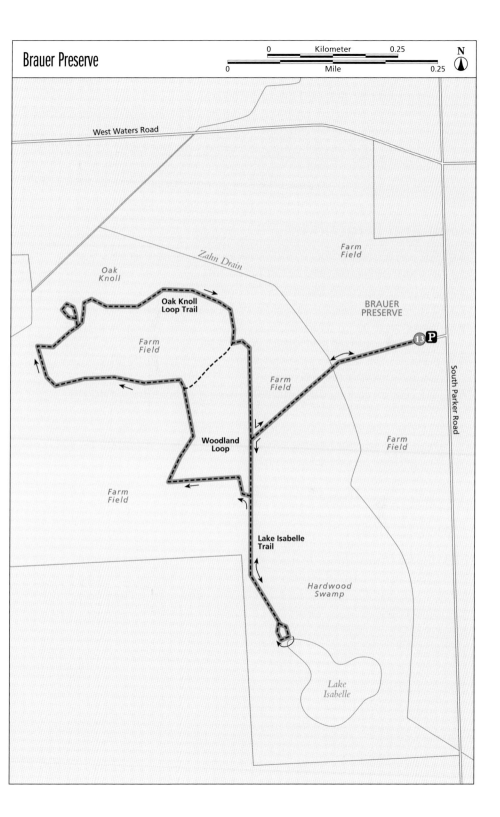

Brauer Preserve

West Waters Road

Zahn Drain

Oak Knoll

Oak Knoll Loop Trail

Farm Field

Farm Field

Farm Field

BRAUER PRESERVE

South Parker Road

Woodland Loop

Farm Field

Farm Field

Lake Isabelle Trail

Hardwood Swamp

Lake Isabelle

13 P

0   Kilometer   0.25

0   Mile   0.25

N

route follows the edge of the field and then crosses north through a forest of mixed hardwoods.

Come to a T in the path. The Woodland Loop Trail continues to the right. Instead turn left for the Oak Knoll Loop Trail. Again following along the edge of a farm field, the trail deposits you on an oak knoll at the northwestern corner of the preserve. The trek through woods includes an extra little loop before heading out to the farm fields again. At the east end of this field, you join back up with the Woodland Loop Trail, cross a narrow band of trees, and essentially head out the way you came in.

The trail to Lake Isabelle is particularly wet in spring; be sure to wear appropriate footgear.

Miles and Directions

0.0 Start from the trailhead at the west end of the dirt parking lot off South Parker Road. The lot is small, and you can't miss the Lake Isabelle Trail.

0.2 Cross over the Zahn Drain and come to a T. Turn left.

0.3 Continue straight ahead. You will come back to the trails on your left on the return trip.

0.5 The trail passes through a hardwood swamp. The route is often lined with ferns. At Lake Isabelle turn around and head back the way you came.

0.7 Back at the farm fields, turn left and follow the path that heads into the woods. You are now on the Woodland Loop Trail.

0.9 Back out in the open, the Oak Knoll Loop Trail heads off to the left. Follow it along the south edge of this farm field.

1.2 As the trail takes you into the oak knoll, there's a small loop off to the left.

1.5 Return to the Woodland Loop Trail and turn left through the trees. The trail then heads to the right. Follow the path along the field.

1.6 Turn left and head back to the parking lot.

1.8 The trail ends at parking lot.

Hike Information

Local Events/Attractions: Motawi Tileworks, 170 Enterprise Dr., Ann Arbor Charter Township; (734) 213-0017; motawi.com. In the tradition of Pewabic Pottery in Detroit, Motawi Tileworks creates beautiful handmade tiles. The studio is open every day but Sunday.

14 Scio Woods Preserve

Scio Woods Preserve has a 2-mile loop through forest and wetlands. It's an easy escape for folks living in Ann Arbor and a great hike for families with younger children. Keep an eye out for the barred owls and pileated woodpeckers that call Scio Woods home.

Start: At the north end of the parking area on Scio Church Road

Distance: 2-mile loop

Hiking time: Less than an hour

Difficulty: Easy

Trail surface: Packed dirt

Best season: Year-round

Other trail users: None

Canine compatibility: No dogs

Fees and permits: None

Schedule: No hours posted

Maps: Map available on preserve website

Trail contacts: Washtenaw County Parks and Recreation Commission, Scio Church Rd., Ann Arbor; (734) 971-6337; ewashtenaw.org/government/departments/parks_recreation/napp/preserves/scio-woods-preserve

Finding the trailhead: The trailhead is located at the north end of the preserve parking lot. GPS: 42 15.358' / W83 48.491'

The Hike

Scio Township in Washtenaw County straddles I-94 west of Ann Arbor. The town of Dexter, on the Huron River, sits in the northwest corner of the township. The Huron River attracted many early American settlers, and communities like Dexter and Dehli Mills along the river can trace their histories to those early days of the republic. There are also stories of the communities that either faded into memory or were absorbed by larger neighbors.

While the river was the center of local industry, business, and transportation, land farther afield was cleared and settled by farmers. The land here is still being farmed, generations later. The Huron River runs through the northern portion of the Scio Township. The Scio Woods Preserve, on the other hand, is close to the township's southeast corner. The preserve was established in 2008 with the acquisition of 91 acres of woodlands and wetlands just 4 miles southwest of downtown Ann Arbor.

The Washtenaw County Natural Areas Preservation Program partnered with Scio Township and the City of Ann Arbor Greenbelt Program to acquire and preserve the property. Washtenaw County has created a number of preserves for the benefit of the public. A sister to Scio Woods is the Brauer Preserve (hike 13 above).

The city of Ann Arbor has a few nature areas of its own as well. Just to the north of Scio Woods on South Wagner Road are the Dolph Nature Area and the adjacent Lakewood Nature Area (the two parks are connected by a trail).

Remember that bikes on not allowed on the trails at Scio Woods.

Scio Woods features over 2 miles of trails. On the official trail map, these are divided into two sections: the inner loop, a shorter loop that keeps close to the parking lot, and the outer loop, which connects the inner loop to the rest of the preserve. Together, these two loops roughly trace the shape of the preserve itself. There are also several connecting trails that can be used to vary the length of your hike quite a bit, a great feature for hikers on a schedule.

Visitors can expect to find oak-hickory hardwood forest as well as areas of maple-beech forest. The east side of the preserve features wetlands

Leaves frozen in a Scio Woods stream

(or, a swamp, if you prefer). Most of the trails are packed dirt, but as the path winds through more swampy areas, boardwalks will keep your feet dry.

Visitors can, of course, choose their own path, but following the trail markers, you will make a counter-clockwise tour of the preserve. The numbers trace the outer loop. (The inner loop is unnumbered.) To stay on the correct path, always choose the path on the right when given an option. Every left-hand turn from the main loop is a connector that cuts off a portion of the hike.

Scio Woods is a pleasant hike no matter the season. In the summer, the trees provide a nice cover from the heat. In the spring, the woods are smattered with wildflowers. In the fall, the variety of trees adds depth to the field of reds and oranges.

Miles and Directions

0.0 Start from the trailhead at the north end of the parking lot and take the path on the right.

0.1 Here you come to the first cut-back trail. Turn left for a very short loop.

0.2 At trail marker 1, there's another opportunity to shorten the hike. Stay to the right.

0.5 At trail marker 2, there's an opportunity to cut off the northeast section of the loop. Stay to the right to experience the preserve's wetlands.

0.8 If you had taken the shortcut at trail marker 2, you would have popped out here at trail marker 3.

1.2 Trail marker 4 offers hikers a chance to cut off the southwest portion of the loop. Continue to take the right path.

1.7 Trail marker 5 is the end of the shortcut offered at trail marker 4. Continue to the right.

1.8 Trail marker 6 is the last of the official markers. Head left to do the loop again, or turn right to head back to the parking area.

2.0 The loop ends where it began in the parking area on Scio Church Road.

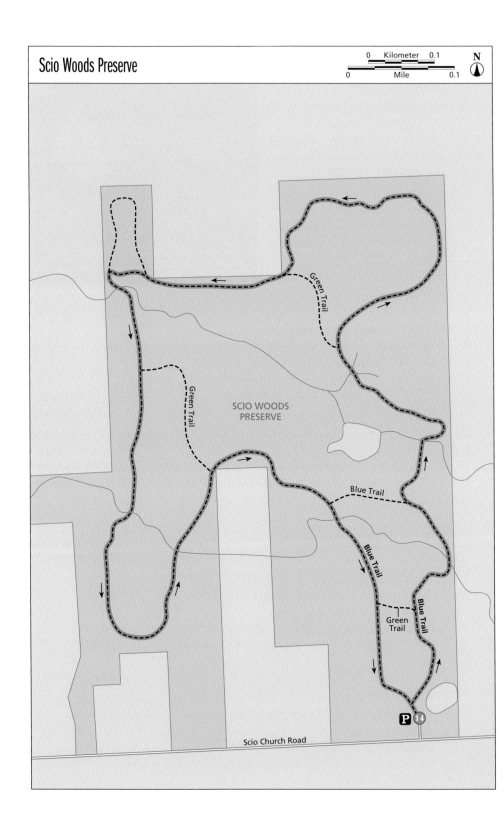

Scio Woods Preserve

0 Kilometer 0.1

0 Mile 0.1

N

Green Trail

Green Trail

SCIO WOODS
PRESERVE

Blue Trail

Blue Trail

Blue Trail

Green
Trail

P 14

Scio Church Road

Boardwalks keep feet dry during the spring melt.

Hike Information

Local Events/Attractions: Downtown Ann Arbor is just 4 miles northeast of Scio Woods. Museums, restaurants, bookstores, and the University of Michigan are just a stone's throw away.

15 Waterloo State Recreation Area

The Hickory Hills Trail at Waterloo State Recreation Area is a long walk to a steep loop. Along the way you pass wetlands and lakes, climbing into a dense hickory and oak forest. Several side trips can be added to include views of Mill Lake or the bog near the park's Discovery Center.

Start: To the left of the Gerald E. Eddy Discovery Center
Distance: 4.2-mile lollipop
Hiking time: About 1.5 hours
Difficulty: Difficult; long hike with steep climbs
Trail surface: Packed dirt
Best season: Fall
Other trail users: None
Canine compatibility: Leashed dogs permitted
Fees and permits: Recreation Passport required

Schedule: Open 8 a.m.–10 p.m.
Maps: TOPO! CD: Michigan, Ohio, Indiana, disc 4; map available at the Discovery Center, the park office, online, and on the trail markers
Trail contacts: Waterloo State Recreation Area, 16345 McClure Rd., Chelsea, MI 48118; (734) 475-8307; michigan.gov/waterloo
Special considerations: Portions of the trail pass through land open to hunting.

Finding the trailhead: The recreation area is in Washtenaw, west of Chelsea. From I-94 west of Ann Arbor, take exit 157 for Pierce Road and go north on Pierce for 2.5 miles. Turn left onto Bush Road. Drive a little over 0.5 mile and turn left into the entrance for the Discovery Center at Waterloo Recreation Area. The trailhead is located in the lower parking lot, the one by the Discovery Center. GPS: N42 19.319' / W84 05.221'

The Hike

With more than 21,000 acres, Waterloo State Recreation Area is the biggest park in Michigan's Lower Peninsula. Even Pinckney, which weighs in with 9,000 acres, is overshadowed by this giant. The park has 47 miles of hiking trails, 12 miles of interpretive nature trails, four campgrounds (two modern, one rustic, and one equestrian), eleven lakes for fishing, rustic cabins to rent, numerous boat launches, and a swimming beach. The Waterloo–Pinckney Trail, which threads its way 31 miles through both recreation areas, is southeast Michigan's only backpacking trail, offering campers an actual multi-night backpacking experience close to Metro Detroit. In winter there's cross-country skiing and snowmobiling.

The nature trails at Waterloo Recreation Area all begin at the Gerald E. Eddy Discovery Center. The center itself is worth a visit. You'll find a large interactive relief map of the park, a huge display of arrowheads that were found nearby, and a hands-on exhibit area for the kids. With staff on hand to answer questions and indoor restrooms, it's the perfect starting place for your hike.

Unnamed wetlands and a distant pond are visible from the path.

There are a number of trails you can take from the discovery center. The Old Field Trail, the Bog Trail, and others are off to the east. West of the center you have the Oak Woods, Lakeview, and Hickory Hills Trails. And through the middle runs the 31-mile Waterloo–Pinckney Trail.

The Hickory Hill Trail is essentially a lollipop—a lollipop with a long stick. The 4.2-mile round-trip begins at the discovery center. The trail meanders north and a bit west, taking you all the way up to the Waterloo Recreation Area park office on McClure Road. The particularly scenic route passes close to Crooked Lake, the view of which is stunning in the fall, and then climbs steeply through an oak and hickory forest. The trees part for a moment to offer a scenic overlook before descending again, this time approaching the park office from behind.

The trailhead is at the west end of the discovery center's lower parking lot. Heading into the woods, primarily oak, the trail follows a forested strip of land between wetlands. To your right, out of sight, is Mill Lake. To the left an open marsh is visible through the trees. The trail is packed dirt. To the right you pass other trail loops, including the Oakwoods Trail and, much later, the Lakeview Trail. As you pass the legs of this latter trail, Spring Lake is off to your left. For the next 0.75 mile, the path slowly climbs. You cross Ridge Road and approach the park office on McClure Road from the south.

GREEN TIP:
Pack out your dog's waste, or dispose of it in a trash can.

▷ The Chelsea Milling Company has been in business for more than 120 years. They make and sell the "Jiffy" Mixes you see at the grocery store. From storing wheat to the little blue box on the shelf, the company does it all here in Chelsea, shipping their mixes to all fifty states.

The Hickory Hills Trail, the goal of all this hiking, begins at trail marker 12. If you don't have time for the 4.2-mile trek but want to experience this little loop, you can park at the office and knock 3.2 miles off the hike. From trail marker 12 the trail dips to the south and touches the north shore of Crooked Lake before turning back north. The lake is intensely beautiful in the fall, surrounded by orange and red.

Climbing up from the lake, you cross McClure Road and are deep in a forest of hickory and oak. All this while the trail you've been hiking has been part of the Waterloo–Pinckney Trail. That splits off to the left at trail marker 13 and continues on its winding path west toward its final destination at Portage Lake Campground. The Hickory Hills Trail continues north and then east, back toward the park office.

This is the payoff. The hills are steep and wooded. There's plenty of climbing. Just before the end of the loop, you reach the highest point of the hike. Atop this hill a portion of the trail has been paved, and there's a scenic lookout toward the north. Descending once again, you come out of the woods near the park office, cross the road, and return to trail marker 12.

The return trip is simply the first third of the hike in reverse. The general disposition of the entire hike is a long walk uphill followed by a long walk back down. The elevation change is gradual. You may not notice, especially with all the little ups and downs that keep the hike interesting.

Miles and Directions

0.0 Start from the trailhead, to the left when facing the discovery center.

0.3 The trail that leads off to the right at trail marker 8 is the Oak Woods Trail, a short loop out to Mill Lake. Continue straight.

0.9 At trail marker 9 is the return path for the Lakeview Trail. This loop follows the western shore of Mill Lake before cutting back through the woods. Continue straight.

1.0 Trail marker 10 is the outward-bound path for the Lakeview Trail. Between trail markers 9 and 10, you pass a private home on Spring Lake, perhaps the choicest piece of real estate in the area.

1.4 As you continue northward to the Hickory Hills Trail, you cross Ridge Road.

1.6 On the other side of McClure Road is the park office. At trail marker 12 turn left, staying on this side of McClure for a bit.

1.9 The view of Crooked Lake is fantastic. This also should be a heads-up that you are about to start climbing. The Hickory Hills are the hilliest part of the route.

2.1 Cross McClure Road.

2.2 The hike so far has been on part of the Waterloo-Pinckney Trail. At trail marker 13 it's time to part ways. Waterloo-Pinckney heads left (west); you continue straight head (north).

Waterloo State Recreation Area

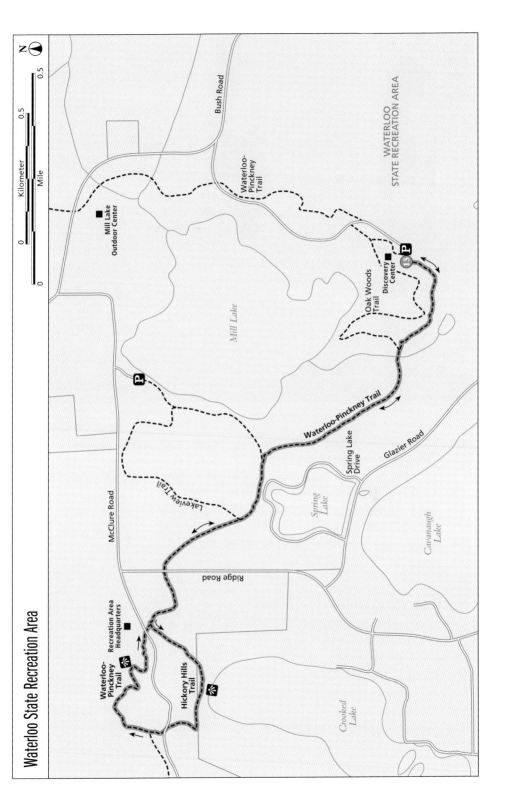

The path hugs the northern shore of Crooked Lake.

2.6 This is the highest point on the hike. Though it's only about 130 feet above the lowest point, the hills do add up. By trail's end you will have climbed and descended about 620 feet. The scenic overlook here is worth a quick stop before heading down to the park office and across the street.

2.7 Back at trail marker 12, take the path to the left. The return route is as simple as going back the way you came, ignoring side trails along the way.

4.2 The trail ends back at the parking lot near the discovery center.

Hike Information

Local Events/Attractions: Chelsea Milling Company, 201 West North St., Chelsea; (734) 475-1361; jiffymix.com. You can take a 1-hour tour of the mix plant in Chelsea on weekdays. Reservations required.

Chelsea Teddy Bear Co. and Toy Museum, 400 North Main St., Chelsea; (734) 433-5499; chelseateddybear.com. Factory tours available on Saturday, call for times. Store and museum open daily.

Restaurants: Mike's Deli, 114 West Middle St., Chelsea; (734) 475-5980; mikesdeli chelsea.com. Great sandwiches featuring Zingerman's bread. The Reubenesque, at the very least, is worth a visit.

16 Pinckney State Recreation Area

Glaciers turned what's now Pinckney State Recreation Area into one of the most rugged places you will find in Michigan. By combining two loops, you can hike 5.3 miles of the park's moraine-strewn mixed hardwood forest. Along the way the trail touches on three named lakes—Silver, Crooked, and Pickerel—as well as a number of unnamed lakes and kettle ponds.

Start: Far north end of the Silver Lake day-use area

Distance: 5.3-mile loop

Hiking time: About 2.5 hours

Difficulty: Difficult; lots of steep climbs

Trail surface: Packed dirt

Best season: Fall

Other trail users: Mountain bikers

Canine compatibility: Leashed dogs permitted

Fees and permits: Recreation Passport required

Schedule: Open 8 a.m.–10 p.m.

Maps: Trail map available at the park office, the old welcome kiosk near park entrance, and online; TOPO! CD: Michigan, Ohio, Indiana, disc 4

Trail contacts: Pinckney State Recreation Area, 8555 Silver Hill Rd., Pinckney, MI 48169; (734) 426-4913; michigan.gov/pinckney

Finding the trailhead: The recreation area is 15 miles northwest of Ann Arbor. From Metro Detroit take US 23 to North Territorial Road (exit 49). Drive west for 3.6 miles and turn right (north) onto Dexter Townhall Road. After 1.1 miles come to Silver Hill Road on the left; this is the entrance to the park. Follow the road 0.5 mile to the Silver Lake day-use area. The trailhead is at the far end of the second parking lot. GPS: N42 25.043' / W83 57.852'

The Hike

Pinckney State Recreation Area is 11,000 acres of challenging moraine-and-kettle country. The park features rolling hills, mature forests, wetlands, and one of the most extensive networks of trails in the state. Two trails here—the Crooked Lake and Silver Lake Trails—can be combined for a decent 5.3-mile loop. Other options include the 17.5-mile Potawatomi Trail and the multiday backpacking route known as the Waterloo–Pinckney Trail.

The trail begins at the Silver Lake day-use area. A beach with restrooms makes it the perfect launching pad for the nearly 5.0-mile trek. The trailhead, at the far north end of the day-use area, is easy to find. There's a large wooden map of the recreation area trails right next to trail marker 1. From here the footpath crosses a boardwalk, taking you through the marsh at the west end of Silver Lake and into the woods.

The first intersection you come to, at trail marker 2, is both the start of the Silver Lake Trail and the return path for the Crooked Lake Trail. If you choose to cut the trip short later on, this will be your return path. These two loops are used by mountain bikers as well as walkers. To keep order, cyclists make a clockwise circuit of the

THE WATERLOO-PINCKNEY TRAIL

Most hikers looking to go on a backpacking trip in Michigan look beyond the Detroit–Ann Arbor area. In the northern Lower Peninsula, the High Country Pathway, an 80-mile loop, connects seven state forest campgrounds. The North Country Trail threads its way north from the Ohio border, up the west side of the Lower Peninsula, and across the Superior shore of the Upper Peninsula. The most ambitious backpackers shoot for Isle Royale, that remote island national park in north Lake Superior. Very few realize there's a decent multiday trip in their backyard.

The Waterloo-Pinckney Trail is southeast Michigan's only legitimate backpacking trail, traversing 36 rugged miles from Portage Lake Campground in the Waterloo Recreation Area to the Silver Lake day-use area in the Pinckney Recreation Area. Hikers usually take the trail west to east—the timing seems to work better. Traveling west to east, a long day's hike brings you to Sugarloaf Lake Campground. The second day is somewhat shorter, ending at Green Lake Campground. Day three sees you all the way through Pinckney.

The trail passes through a lot of different country—woods, marsh, and meadow. In summer the fields are full of wildflowers. In fall the leaves turning colors on all those hills can be stunning.

trails and go left at trail marker 2; hikers go counterclockwise (unless you're taking the Silver Lake Trail, in which case you have to watch your back for a ways until the trail splits). For the first 1.25 miles the trail climbs steadily. The trail continues to the top of Crooked Lake, where there's a scenic overlook. (There's a rustic campground on the east shore of the lake tucked into the woods, a great place for tent camping.)

The rugged terrain here is consistent: Pinckney offers a lot of ups and downs. The hills at Pinckney are primarily moraines: huge deposits of glacial till. You can see the loose rocks mixed in with the dirt of the trail. This isn't gravel; it's what you find whenever you take a shovel to the soil here. The kettles between the moraines often hold water, creating wetlands. And over it all is the mixed hardwood forest.

Though you will only hit 1,005 feet one time on the hike, you will bounce between 900 and 950 feet so many times that you'll find you've climbed more than 550 feet in less than 5 miles. Of course that also means you've descended more than 550, and as every hiker knows, going down is often as difficult as going up. Mountain bikers love this stuff. Climbs mean drops, and often they can carry momentum

GREEN TIP:
Consider the packaging of any snacks you bring. It's best to properly dispose of packaging at home before you hike. If you're on the trail, pack it out with you.

The western end of Silver Lake is shallower than the rest.

from the drop into the next climb—it's a regular roller coaster out here.

At trail marker 9 the Crooked Lake Trail meets up with the Potawatomi Trail. Continue to your left unless you're feeling up for a 17.5-mile hike. After trail marker 8 the path passes north of Pickerel Lake, crossing the stream that connects Pickerel with Crooked Lake to the north. At trail marker 3 you have a choice. Continuing straight on the Crooked Lake Trail will cut nearly 1.0 mile from your trek. To continue on the described hike, turn right onto the Silver Lake Trail.

At trail marker 4 turn left. To the right, the Waterloo–Pinckney Trail wanders 30-some miles to the west. Straight ahead puts you onto the twisty portion of the Potawatomi Trail and extends the trip to no good end. A little ways past the trail marker, there's a remnant of a homestead, a chimney, and a cellar.

At trail marker 5 you meet up for the third time with the Potawatomi–Waterloo-Pinckney Trail. This time you hike a portion of it, continuing straight back to the Silver Lake parking lot. Walking down to the beach area and cutting north brings you full circle back to the trailhead.

Miles and Directions

0.0 Start from trail marker 1, at the far north end of the Silver Lake beach/picnic area. This is the Silver Lake Trail.

0.3 Come to trail marker 2; one-way traffic on the trail begins. Mountain bikers go left and follow the loop clockwise; hikers go right and follow the loop counterclockwise.

0.7 The trail crosses Silver Hill Road, leaving the lake behind.

1.0 The road you cross here leads to Crooked Lake Campground—rustic sites tucked into the woods on Crooked Lake. This portion of the trip follows the Crooked Lake Trail, although there aren't many views of the water.

1.5 The jogs in the path here take you around the fingers of marsh that creep out from Crooked Lake.

2.3 Trail marker 9 marks the junction with the Potawatomi Trail. Because of its length, the 17.5-mile loop is primarily used by mountain bikers. Stay left here.

2.6 The trail to the right here at trail marker 8 leads to the beach on Halfmoon Lake.

3.5 At trail marker 3 turn right for the Silver Lake Trail. (**Option:** If the hike has become too much, now is your opportunity to cut bait. The Crooked Lake Trail continues straight, leading in almost a straight line back to trail marker 2 and the beginning of the loop.)

3.9 At trail marker 4 you meet up with the Waterloo-Pinckney Trail. The first trail on the right leads off toward Waterloo State Recreation Area. The second will take you back to Silver Lake by way of a long and winding route.

4.5 At trail marker 5 you meet up with the Waterloo-Pinckney Trail again.

Pinckney State Recreation Area

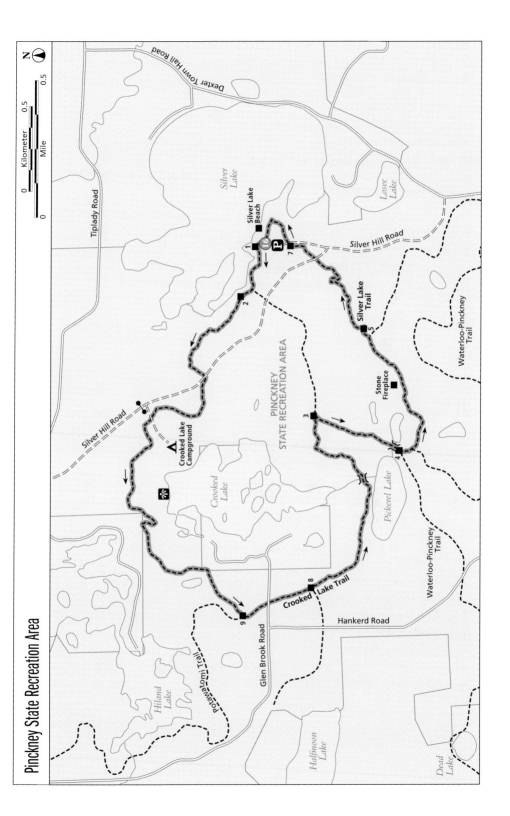

4.9 Trail marker 7 at the southernmost corner of the Silver Lake parking area is the end of the line. From here follow the parking lot toward the lake. Turn left at the restrooms.

5.3 The hike ends at the trailhead, trail marker 1.

Hike Information

Restaurants: Hell in a Handbasket. Hell's Kitchen, 4025 Patterson Rd., Hell; (734) 648-0456; gotohellmi.com. The stuffed burgers here will certainly compensate for calories burned on the trail.

GREEN TIP:
Before you start for home, have you left the woods as you'd want to see them?

17 Hudson Mills Metropark

When you want the getting there to be half the fun, consider the Acorn Trail at Hudson Mills. This low-key nature loop is located in north Washtenaw County, just north of Dexter on the Huron River. In summer there's a lot going on along the river. In autumn the woods practically glow. And in any season the trip up Huron River Drive sets the mood for a great hike.

Start: Behind and to the right of the activity center
Distance: 1.7-mile loop
Hiking time: About 45 minutes
Difficulty: Easy; level path
Trail surface: Gravel and dirt
Best season: Fall
Other trail users: None
Canine compatibility: Leashed dogs permitted
Fees and permits: Metropark Motor Vehicle Permit required

Schedule: Open dawn to dusk
Maps: Maps available at park office and on website; TOPO! CD: Michigan, Ohio, Indiana, disc 4
Trail contacts: Hudson Mills Metropark, 8801 North Territorial Rd., Dexter, MI 48130; (734) 426-8211; metroparks.com
Special considerations: Jogging is prohibited on the nature trails.

Finding the trailhead: Hudson Mills is on the Huron River in Dexter. From US 23 north of Ann Arbor, take exit 49 to North Territorial Road and drive west for 8 miles. The park entrance is on your left. Once in the park follow the signs for the activity center. The trailhead is behind the activity center to the right. GPS: N42 22.548' / W83 54.504'

The Hike

Huron River Drive is one of the most scenic drives in the state, especially in fall when the leaves have begun to turn. Beginning at Bird Hills Nature Area in Ann Arbor, the drive follows the river upstream, passing a handful of parks on the water along the way. Dexter-Huron Metropark, for example, is a small (122-acre) site with a great view of the water where you can rent canoes and kayaks for exploring by paddle. The drive also takes you through Dexter, a great little town for a lunch break, and ends several miles north at Hudson Mills Metropark.

Hudson Mills is one of ten metroparks on the Huron River that stretch from Indian Springs at the river's headwaters to the park on Lake Erie at the river's mouth. The north boundary of the metropark is North Territorial Road. Few people realize the historical significance of this road. Way back in 1829, eight years before Michigan would declare statehood, three overland routes were established to connect Detroit with points west. The Territorial Road was one of them. By 1835 the route had been surveyed all the way across the second-tier counties through Van Buren County, connecting Detroit with St. Joseph on Lake Michigan. The road still exists. In the west

part of the state, it's called the Red Arrow Highway. From Metro Detroit out to Dexter, it's simply called North Territorial Road.

A small hamlet called Hudson Mills was established at the intersection of the Territorial Road and Dexter–Pinckney Road in the early 1800s. There's little left of the town now, which never got all that big to start with, and the park that bears its name sees more visitors every day than ever lived here at one time. This is to be expected—the original Hudson Mills didn't have a golf course.

▷ All that remains of one of the mills that gave the one-time town its name is a stone foundation. Head over to the west side of the river by way of the bike path and look for the foundation near the Rapids View.

The metropark comprises 1,549 acres of forest and meadows along more than 3.5 miles of the Huron River. More than any other park in the area, Hudson Mills is dedicated to the sport of disc golf. Near the park's activity center, surrounding the nature trails are two disc golf courses where various tournaments are held throughout the season.

There is only one nature trail at Hudson Mills, the Acorn Trail—a 1.7-mile loop through forested wetlands and along the wooded banks of the Huron River. The trail begins behind the activity center. Numbered stations along the route provide information about the local environment, answering questions including "What's going on in that rotting log?" and "What's a tamarack swamp?" The woods at the start are mixed hardwood. In fall the maples turn a rich red and carpet the trail in crimson.

It can be tricky to navigate what is essentially a pretty simple loop, since the nature trail overlaps, and at times parallels, the park's dirt service drives. At 0.6 mile in, a trail leads off to the south. This is the shortcut. As it cuts south toward the return leg of the loop, it passes just west of a wooded swamp. The shortcut shortens the loop by 0.7 mile, but it does so by bypassing the best part of the hike, the portion near the Huron River.

Just before you get to the river, the trail crosses the paved bike path that makes a 5-mile loop through the park. Then, with the river on your right and the bike path on your left, the trail heads south for a bit. For less than 0.25 mile, you walk along the river. The trail veers east and then north before returning to the trailhead.

Miles and Directions

0.0 Start from the trailhead behind and to the right of the activity center. Take the path to the right, and quickly cross over the paved bike path.

0.4 The path joins with the service drive for a short stretch and then splits off back into the woods.

There are amazing fall colors at Hudson Mills.

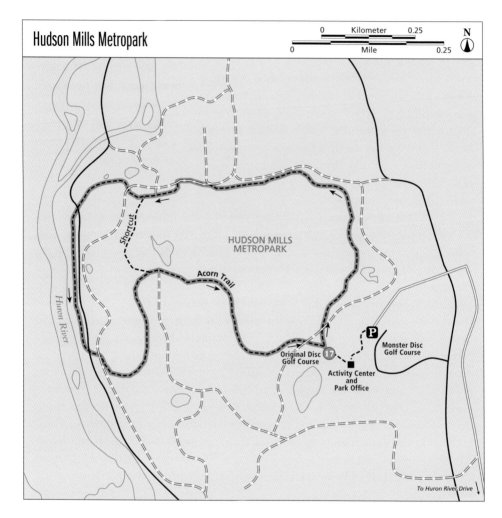

0.6 The trail to the left is the shortcut. Continue straight. (**Option:** Taking the shortcut bypasses the river and makes this a 1.0-mile hike.)

0.8 The trail crosses the paved bike path and then turns to the south, keeping the bike path on the left and the river on the right.

1.0 The trail crosses back over the paved bike path and heads north.

1.3 This is the other end of the shortcut.

1.7 The trail ends at the trailhead behind the activity center.

Options: The paved path and the service drives can both be used to add mileage to your hike. The bike path continues south along the river a ways, loops back to the north, and finally approaches the activity center from the east. Another option is to jump on the bike path and, just as it leaves the river, take one of the service drives back to the parking lot.

Hike Information

Local Events/Attractions: Dexter Bakery, 8101 Main St., Dexter; (734) 426-3848; thedexterbakery.com. There's no better place around to load up on a few carbs before a hike.

Dexter Cider Mill, 3685 Central St., Dexter; (734) 426-8531; dextercidermill .com. Cider mills are all the rage in the fall, and since Hudson Mills makes for a great fall hike, a visit here is the perfect activity to round out an autumn afternoon.

GREEN TIP:
Be green and stylish too—wear clothing made
of organic cotton or recycled products.

18 Brighton State Recreation Area

With two metroparks and two state recreation areas within a short drive, the village of Brighton enjoys an abundance of green space that draws hikers and nature lovers from all over southeast Michigan. One of the closest trails to town is the Penosha Hiking Trail, which loops through Brighton Rec's hilly woodlands, meadows, and wetlands.

Start: Off the parking lot, just east of Bishop Lake
Distance: 5.0-mile loop
Hiking time: About 2 hours
Difficulty: Difficult; mostly due to the changes in elevation
Trail surface: Packed dirt
Best season: Summer and fall; can be muddy in spring
Other trail users: None
Canine compatibility: Leashed dogs permitted
Fees and permits: Recreation Passport required

Schedule: Open 8 a.m.–10 p.m.
Maps: Maps available at park office and on website; TOPO! CD: Michigan, Ohio, Indiana, disc 4
Trail contacts: Brighton State Recreation Area, 6360 Chilson Rd., Howell, MI 48843; (810) 229-6566; michigan.gov/brighton
Special considerations: Sections of this trail pass through land open to hunting. It's not uncommon to hear the report of hunting rifles in the fall. Hikers should wear bright orange during hunting season.

Finding the trailhead: The recreation area is just southwest of Brighton, 15 miles north of Ann Arbor. From downtown Brighton take Main Street west to Bauer Road. Turn south and drive 2 miles to Bishop Lake Road; turn west again. The park entrance is a little more than 1 mile, on the south side of the road. Take the first right, which goes to the parking lot. The trailhead is on your left as you enter the lot. GPS: N42 30.044' / W83 50.097'

The Hike

The town of Brighton, halfway between Detroit and Lansing, has established itself as one of the nicest commuter towns in southeast Michigan. Situated strategically near the junction of US 23 and I-96, it's an easy commute to both Ann Arbor and the heart of Metro Detroit. Grand River Avenue, which was the main thoroughfare before the interstate, runs right through town. This road, in fact, was built on the old Grand River Trail, one of the Native American trails that traversed the Lower Peninsula. A nice way to explore Michigan is to pick up Grand River Avenue in Detroit and follow it out to Lansing. (After Lansing the name is dropped, but you can follow the roads that run parallel to the Grand River all the way out to Lake Michigan.)

The trail at Brighton State Rec Area passes through mixed hardwood forest.

Brighton is more than just a bedroom community. The city has an active business community and a vibrant downtown. Of course it's all about location, location, location; and when you look at a map, Brighton sits in a swath of green that begins with Indian Springs Metropark in northern Oakland County and ends with Waterloo State Recreation Area in eastern Jackson County. That green means parks, and there are a ton of them on and around the Huron River and its tributaries. This means there is seemingly no end to the outdoor recreation opportunities within an easy drive of Brighton.

The closest park to the city is the 4,947-acre Brighton State Recreation Area. Anywhere else, it would be unimaginable that this park could be overlooked, but you seem to hear much less about Brighton than you do its popular neighbors. Island Lake Recreation Area to the east has paddling on the Huron River; Pinckney to the south offers incredible mountain-bike trails and an overnight hike that connects with Waterloo; and Huron Meadows Metropark, right next door, has a golf course and a decent swimming lake.

While it may not have the hype, Brighton is anything but ignored. Its nearly 5,000 acres are chock-full of forests, fields, lakes, and streams. The waters here feed the Huron River to the south by way of South Ore Creek and Ore Lake. There are miles of trail for hiking, biking, and horseback riding. Campers have their pick of two rustic campgrounds, one modern campground, and a campground especially for those who like to sleep with their horses. There are even a number of rustic cabins spread throughout the park for a different kind of overnight experience.

The hiking trails are found at the park's Bishop Lake day-use area. The trailhead is off the parking lot, just east of Bishop Lake. There are two loops, both of which cut through acres of rolling, forested hills. The 2.0-mile Kahchin Trail is the shorter of the two. The Penosha Trail makes a wide 5.0-mile sweep. It is said the trail names mean "short" (kahchin) and "long" (penosha) in the Chippewa language.

Our path is the longer one. For the first 0.5 mile, the two loops overlap. When Kahchin turns south, Penosha continues on, marked with a blue dot. Teahen Road cuts through this section of the park, and a subdivision and some homes are nestled in between state land. The trail does a good job of avoiding the residential area. Except for a portion of the trail that makes use of Teahen to cut through a section of private land, the nearby homes are invisible.

Thousands of years ago, glaciers scoured this region of Michigan and left behind these hills. You will often hear them called moraines, which is a mound of glacial drift. (The hike at Huron Meadows is the Moraine Fen Trail. Same glacier, different result. In that case, a hunk of glacier broke off and created a wetland.) The Penosha

GREEN TIP:
Carry a reusable water container that you fill at the tap.
Bottled water is expensive, lots of petroleum is used to make
the plastic bottles, and they're a disposal nightmare.

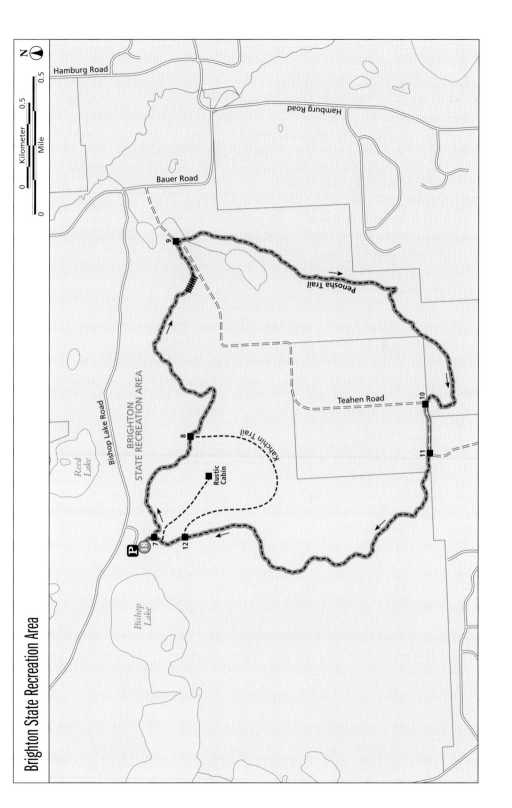

Brighton State Recreation Area

Trail wanders around, between, and up and over these moraines, nearly all of which are covered by a forest of mixed hardwoods.

Miles and Directions

0.0 Start from the trailhead at the east side of the parking lot, next to the outhouse. When you come to the first Y in the path, stay to the right.

0.1 Turn left at trail marker 7 (toward trail marker 8). Cross the road and pick up the trail on the other side. This first section of the Penosha Trail Loop overlaps the shorter Kahchin Trail between trail markers 7 and 8.

0.6 Turn left at trail marker 8.

0.8 Take the left trail at the next Y.

1.5 The trail seems to offer an option: Go straight or take the stairs. Take the stairs. Erosion has eaten away at the hill, and the stairs seem a great solution.

1.6 Come to trail marker 9.

2.1 Take the path to the right.

2.5 Prepare for a long climb. There are a few on this route, but this is the longest.

3.0 Take the right trail at the next Y. (The path to the left leads to private property.)

3.1 Trail marker 10. Turn left and follow Teahen Road for a stretch.

3.3 The trail picks up and leaves the road behind and then quickly comes to trail marker 11.

4.8 At trail marker 12 the Kahchin Trail connects from the right. The two loops overlap back to trail marker 7.

5.0 The trail ends at the parking lot.

Hike Information

Restaurants: The Wooden Spoon, 675 West Grand River Ave., Brighton; (810) 588-4386; woodenspoonmarket.com. Instead of bringing a lunch for the trail, stop by the Wooden Spoon and carry out the Lunch Box of the Day—a much-better-than-the-usual-feedbag picnic lunch.

19 Huron Meadows Metropark

If your idea of a perfect hike is upland oak forest, rolling hills, and wide scenic vistas, there are trails at Huron Meadows you will like. The Moraine Fen Trail, however, is not one of them. This one is for the adventurer, the bushwhacker. This narrow, often-overgrown dirt path offers hikers an experience altogether different from the usual. Here you have the unique chance to explore the fringes of a hardwood swamp.

Start: Southwest corner of the parking lot
Distance: 2.3-mile loop
Hiking time: About 1 hour
Difficulty: Moderate. Sections of the hike are slippery, and there are often fallen trees to climb over and brush to beat through.
Trail surface: Packed earth, grass
Best season: Fall for the best chance to miss the bugs, but spring reveals a lot about fens.
Other trail users: None
Canine compatibility: Leashed dogs permitted
Fees and permits: Metropark Motor Vehicle Permit required

Schedule: Open 7 a.m.–10 p.m. Apr–Oct; 7 a.m.–8 p.m. rest of the year
Maps: Maps available at park office and on website; TOPO! CD: Michigan, Ohio, Indiana, disc 4
Trail contacts: Huron Meadows Metropark, 8765 Hammel Rd., Brighton, MI 48116; (734) 426-8211; metroparks.com. The park is administered through the nearby Hudson Mills Metropark.
Special considerations: This trail is more difficult when it's wet. Be sure to wear long pants to protect against the swaths of poison ivy.

Finding the trailhead: Huron Meadows Metropark is west of US 23, just south of Brighton. From US 23 take Winans Lake Road (exit 55) west 0.5 mile to Rickett Road. Drive north 1.2 miles and turn left (west) onto Hammel Road. The south park entrance is on your left after almost 0.5 mile. Follow the park road to its end at a parking lot. The trailhead is on your right, near the southwest corner of the parking lot. GPS: N42 28.503' / W83 46.953'

The Hike

Huron Meadows Metropark, comprising 1,540 acres, is named for the Huron River that passes through the southern section of the park. The park's two main attractions are the par-3, eighteen-hole golf course and an extensive complex of trails for cross-country skiers (more miles of trails than hikers have in summer, since the golf course is converted to a cross-country ski course in winter).

The park is roughly divided in half by Hammel Road. To the north of the road you have the golf course, a softball diamond, picnic areas overlooking Maltby Lake, and a fishing pier. South of the road you have a large wetland, hardwood forest, and the Huron River. The river here is popular with paddlers, and a canoe takeout at Huron Meadows seems to be the

▶ Paddling maps measure portages in rods. A rod is 16½ feet (5.5 yards). This is roughly the length of a canoe, making this old unit of measurement quite useful for paddlers.

bane of canoeists, who need to carry their boats 50 rods (275 yards) to the parking lot from the river. (One paddling guide advises its readers to skip this section of the river, seemingly because there are no convenient takeouts. Of course if 50 rods is a hard carry, then perhaps the issue isn't the takeout but the weight of the boat or the fitness of its crew.)

When folks visit Huron Meadows to hike, they typically tackle one of the more attractive sounding trails. Beech Alley, for example, is nearly 2.0 miles of hardwood forest. Maltby Vista offers 1.7 miles of lake views and passes close to the golf course. Fewer people opt for the 2.2-mile Moraine Fen Trail, which is just as swampy as the name suggests. At least the first half of the trail is.

The trail begins at the south parking lot. After a cheerful start in the woods, the trail quickly becomes overgrown. Right from the outset, the path is skirting the edge of the extensive wetland that sits between the park and Ore Lake to the west. The woods are mixed hardwood, with a good spattering of beech and lots of oak. The trail, even in a dry year, is dark black with groundwater. In some low spots, the tree roots crossing the path act as stepping-stones over wetter sections of the trail. The wettest sections, however, get a boardwalk.

Unlike a marsh, the terrain here isn't simply flat. Scattered hillocks give the hike character and keep it from being a long slog. Trail maintenance doesn't seem to be a priority

The canopy of trees creates beautiful lighting on warm days.

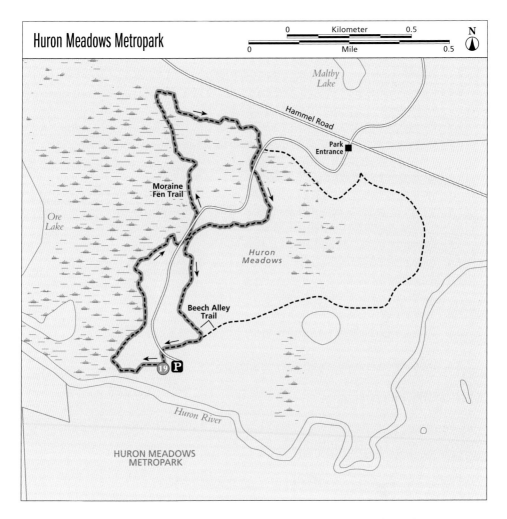

0   Kilometer   0.5

0   Mile   0.5

N

Maltby Lake

Hammel Road

Park Entrance

Moraine Fen Trail

Ore Lake

Huron Meadows

Beech Alley Trail

19 P

Huron River

HURON MEADOWS METROPARK

on this loop. Fallen trees must be climbed over, and care must be taken when traversing broken boardwalks. Of course if the trail were more used, the general grind of foot traffic would make the path more accessible. In some sections the overgrowth was so out of control it met in the middle of the trail. Sometimes you are wading through thigh-high plants, hoping there isn't much poison ivy in the mix.

After the first 1.0 mile of the hike, the trail climbs to higher ground. By the time you cross the road, you are sharing the path with the more kindly Beech Alley Trail.

For all the trials and tribulations, however, the Moraine Fen Trail offers some beautiful surroundings. Wooded wetlands are a rare locale for a hike, and this one gives you the feeling that you're actually going somewhere few people dare.

Miles and Directions

0.0 Start from the southwest corner of the parking lot on the Moraine Fen Trail.

0.1 The trail comes out on a wide doubletrack. Turn right.

0.2 The trail narrows and then splits. Take the path to the right. It will just get wetter and wetter the other way.

0.6 The trail seems to disappear for a moment. Keep an eye focused on the beaten path.

0.7 The trail leaves the woods. Turn to the left and walk between the road and the woods. The trail continues on your left just a short way up the road.

1.1 The halfway point. You are at the far north edge of the hike. From here on out, your path lies to the south and back to the parking lot, and the path overlaps the Beech Alley Trail.

1.4 The rest of the trail is east of the road. You can cross here or cross later. Turn right; in about 0.1 mile you will see the path pick up and head into the woods on your left.

1.5 Back in the woods, the path is wide and sandy.

1.6 Come to a three-way intersection and a picnic table. Take the path to the right.

1.8 The trail leaves the woods for a short stretch. The path isn't clear; just walk the grass until you see a break in the trees on your left.

1.9 The trail returns to the woods. Turn left and into the trees.

2.1 Coming out into a field, the trail turns to the right, skirts the woods, and then cuts through a corner of trees.

2.3 The trail crosses the road and ends where it began.

Hike Information

Restaurants: Zukey Lake Tavern, 5011 Girard Dr., Pinckney; (810) 231-1441; zukey laketavern.com. Located at the eastern end of the Huron Chain of Lakes, the tavern has been around since the end of Prohibition.

20 Island Lake State Recreation Area

Short of hauling a canoe to the park (or renting one from the livery), there's no better way to explore the Huron River at Island Lake State Recreation Area than to hike the 6-mile Yellow Loop. As it passes through mixed hardwood forest, the trail crosses the river twice and offers both scenic overlooks and places to stop and dangle your feet.

Start: Southeast corner of the parking lot, opposite the outhouses
Distance: 5.9-mile loop
Hiking time: About 2 hours
Difficulty: Difficult due to length and elevation changes; a rugged trail in places
Trail surface: Packed earth (singletrack); sandy in spots
Best season: Best in spring and fall; very buggy in summer
Other trail users: Mountain bikers
Canine compatibility: Leashed dogs permitted
Fees and permits: Recreation Passport required

Schedule: Open 8 a.m.–10 p.m.
Maps: Maps available at park office and on website; TOPO! CD: Michigan, Ohio, Indiana, disc 4
Trail contacts: Island Lake Recreation Area, 12950 East Grand River Ave., Brighton, MI 48116; (810) 229-7067; michigan.gov/islandlake
Special considerations: These trails are multiuse, and mountain bikers love the two loops. Keep an ear open for the sound of tires and the much appreciated "On your right!" that announces their presence.

Finding the trailhead: Island Lake is southeast of the interchange between I-96 and US 23, about 15 miles north of Ann Arbor. From I-96, just east of the US 23 interchange, take exit 151 for Kensington Road. Drive south 0.5 mile to the park entrance. Once past the gatehouse, take a right onto Kent Lake Beach Road and follow it 1 mile. A short drive to the trailhead parking area is on your right. The way is well marked. The trail begins in the southeast corner of the lot, opposite the outhouses. GPS: N42 30.494' / W83 42.510'

The Hike

Water is a big part of Island Lake State Recreation Area. The park is named for a small lake that touches on its northwest boundary. Island Lake has, as you might suspect, a pair of islands. Only part of the lake is within the park borders, however, and the opposite shore is crowded with homes. At the other end of the park is Kent Lake, which was created by impeding the flow of the Huron River. Connecting these lakes, the river, and several smaller bodies of water are State Park Road and several fine trails.

At 5.9 miles long, the Yellow Trail is the shorter of the park's two hiking loops. It encircles a section of the Huron River in the eastern half of the recreation area. The 9.0-mile Blue Trail navigates a course through the western half of the park. (A third trail is shown on the park maps: 4.0 miles of paved path for hiking and biking.)

This old bridge was built for heavier traffic than pedestrians and cyclists.

The trailheads for the Yellow and Blue Trails begin in the same parking area. Their paths cross a couple times in a forest of pine before crossing the Huron River and parting ways. The Blue Trail circles wide and passes close by Island Lake and Spring Mill Pond. The Yellow Trail meanders, one tight curve after another, north and east.

You might think from all this talk of water that the trails at Island Lake would be particularly wet. On the contrary, in summer the trails are high and dry. One minute you're standing on a cement bridge—one built for something more substantial than foot traffic—and looking at the river. A few moments later the path is cutting across the edge of a steep drop looking down at the water far below.

It's these elevation changes that make the trail so popular with mountain bikers. On a bike the payoff of every steep climb is a rapid descent. For hikers the elevation changes add variety, not an adrenaline rush.

When the trail approaches Kensington Road, it crosses the Huron River and returns west. As you follow the trail back on its meandering route to the parking lot, you cut along the forested edge of a wide meadow and through high-roofed woods.

Mountain biking is a popular activity on both loops. While most cyclists tend to ride on the weekends, even on a weekday morning you will encounter a bike or two on your hike. Some hikers may find this a distraction. The only real danger, however, is a collision. The trail is a narrow singletrack, so keep an ear open to the sounds of tires on dirt. Most cyclists are overly courteous and will slow down and give you a heads-up as they pedal near.

In addition to pedaling, another popular activity at Island Lake is paddling. The Huron River was once a crucial transportation route. A short 8-mile portage connects the Huron to the Grand River and thus offers a water route between Lake Erie and Lake Michigan. Many people still paddle the Huron for recreation, some even making the cross-state journey. Others simply begin upstream for a multiday paddling trip, going with the flow. For those paddlers, Island Lake maintains two campsites on the Huron River. These sites are only accessible from the water (and an unmarked service drive).

The trail hugs the line between prairie and forest.

Island Lake State Recreation Area

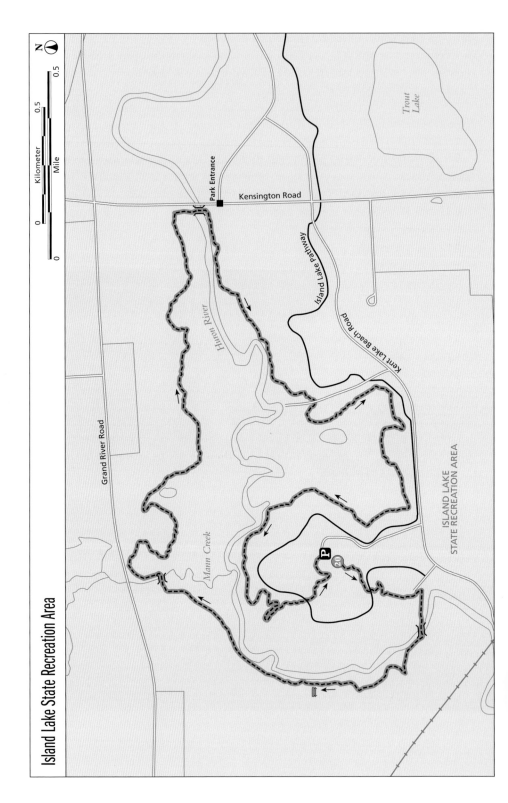

Miles and Directions

0.0   Start at the trailhead in the southwest corner of the parking lot, opposite the outhouses. Follow the loop in a clockwise direction.

0.2   The trail crosses a paved path.

0.3   A trail enters from the right; continue straight.

0.4   Side trails here connect to the parking lot.

0.5   Cross a long cement bridge over the Huron River.

0.6   Turn right.

0.7   A trail to the right leads to a river overlook.

0.8   The bench here is a nice place to rest from recent climbs.

1.5   A wooden bridge crosses Mann Creek.

2.9   Turn right onto the gravel doubletrack.

3.0   Bridge over the Huron; the path parallels Kensington Road.

3.3   The trail skirts the edge of the woods next to a large open meadow.

3.6   Turn left.

3.7   Cross the road.

3.9   Continue straight at the intersection of trails (right leads to a small pond).

5.5   Cross the paved path again.

5.9   The trail ends at the parking lot.

Hike Information

Restaurants: Brown's Root Beer & Sandwich Shop, 399 South Lafayette St., South Lyon; (248) 437-6376; brownsrootbeer.com. Brown's has been around for decades; this classic drive-in was the first in South Lyon. Closed on Sunday.

21 Kensington Metropark

The nature trails at Kensington Metropark may not look like much on a map, but 6.0 miles of trails wind through the property behind the nature center. The less-traveled paths that loop through the park's upland forest add some ruggedness and variety to less-strenuous paths closer to the trailhead. Because running and jogging are prohibited, the trails tend to attract nature lovers and dedicated hikers as opposed to the iPod-and-running-shoes crowd.

Start: Across from the nature center
Distance: 3.3-mile loop
Hiking time: About 1 hour to 1.5 hours
Difficulty: Moderate; some hills to climb on the back half
Trail surface: Packed gravel
Best season: Great in all seasons
Other trail users: None
Canine compatibility: Dogs not permitted
Fees and permits: Metropark Motor Vehicle Permit required

Schedule: Open daily 6 a.m.–10 p.m.
Maps: Maps available at park office and on website; TOPO! CD: Michigan, Ohio, Indiana, disc 4
Trail contacts: Kensington Metropark, 2240 West Buno Rd., Milford, MI 48380; (810) 227-8910; metroparks.com
Special considerations: The nature trails are for walking only; running and jogging prohibited.

Finding the trailhead: From I-96, just east of the US 23 interchange, take exit 151 for Kensington Road. The park entrance is just north of the interstate. The nature center parking area is on the north side of Highridge Drive, 1.3 miles from the park entrance. The trailhead is across from the doors to the nature center. GPS: N42 31.788' / W83 40.226'

The Hike

The most popular park in the Huron-Clinton Metropark system is Kensington Metropark near Milford. It is also the largest park in the system. (Its 4,481 acres beat out Stony Creek by just 20 acres.) The park has a golf course, a nature center, a farm center, boat rentals, a disc golf course, a beach, and a water park, but the centerpiece is 1,600-acre Kent Lake. Kensington is also connected to Proud Lake State Recreation Area by way of mountain bike and equestrian trails and to Island Lake State Recreation Area via a trail under I-96.

Two and a half million people visit Kensington each year. To put that into perspective, that's a visit about every 8 seconds—assuming of course that no one is visiting when the park is closed. And yet there are times you can walk the nature trails at Kensington and not run into another person. Maybe this is because bikes and pets are prohibited on the nature trails; so are jogging and running.

The nature center overlooks the Kingfisher Lagoon at the west end of Kent Lake. A long, narrow marsh stretches out behind the nature center, connecting the lagoon

You can get close to the sandhill cranes, but don't get too close, especially when there are younger cranes around.

with Wildwing Lake. There are seven named trails and loops, as well as several connecting paths that wind around the marsh and wetlands and into the adjacent upland forest. Each describes just a portion of the 6.0-mile trail system, and by combining routes you can create a decent hike.

The loop described here follows the Deer Run Trail to the Fox Trail, connecting up with the Chickadee Loop, Tamarack Trail, and Aspen Trail for a 3.3-mile hike. This route takes you through a good cross section of the property, but grab a map at the nature center for other options. Adding the Wildwing Loop, for example, can tack on nearly 2.0 miles.

The Deer Run Trail starts out behind the nature center and follows the southern edge of the marsh. In about 1.0 mile the trail begins to climb, and for the next 1.0 mile you wander through hardwood forest and meadow. The effect of invasive species on the environment is sadly all too clear here. A few clearings are choked with autumn olive, and acres of woods have been overcome by oriental bittersweet. It's sad to see green blankets of vines draped over dead trees; however, much of the forest remains free from bittersweet, so there's still hope.

Returning to the Tamarack and Aspen Trails, the trail continues west, making a loop north of Wildwing Lake. On the return to the nature center, the path passes

SANDHILL CRANE

Named for the Nebraska Sandhills, which they seem to love, the sandhill crane is one of the largest birds you will find in Michigan. Almost all gray, the crane has white cheeks and a vibrant splash of red on its head. It can stand nearly 4 feet tall.

The crane's distinct call is an unpleasant trumpeting that resembles a loud American crow. You might be lucky to see two mated cranes standing together performing their duet. This is known as "unison calling," and there's a pattern to their patter. The female will call twice for every call the male makes.

When trying to identify the bird in flight, it is somewhat easy to confuse the crane with a great blue heron. Take note that the sandhill crane flies with its neck extended, while the heron pulls its neck back.

the remnant of the one-time summer retreat of the Labadie family. Jo Labadie sought to build a getaway for workers without the means to leave the city during the hot summer months. The retreat was called Bubbling Waters. (Jo's brothers bought land adjacent to his and built a film studio, the Labadie-Detroit Motion Picture Company.) The Labadies spent time here from 1912 until 1933, when Jo died. In 1941 his children gave the property to the county for parkland.

From here the trail cuts across the marsh and returns to the nature center. The wide, straight-as-an-arrow path that cuts the property down the center was once Labadie Road. It's not uncommon to see families here feeding songbirds, many of which will hop up on your hand to peck seeds from your palm.

Another delight for birders is the large number of sandhill cranes wandering the grounds. Places farther west, like the Platte River in Nebraska, see nearly half a million sandhill cranes pass through during the annual migration. Michigan doesn't see anything like those numbers, but you will see quite a few cranes at Kensington throughout the summer months.

Miles and Directions

0.0 Start at the trailhead across from the nature center.

0.2 The marsh behind the nature center drains into the Kingfisher Lagoon. A bridge crosses this edge of the marsh. Just past the bridge the Tamarack Trail leads off to the left; continue straight on the Deer Run Trail.

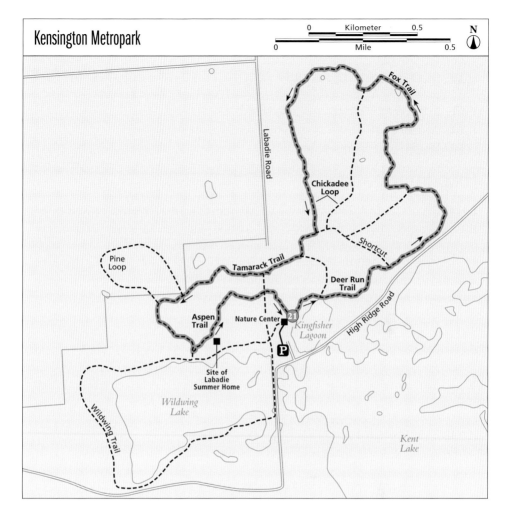

Kilometer
0   0.5
0   Mile   0.5

N

Fox Trail

Labadie Road

Chickadee
Loop

Pine
Loop

Tamarack Trail

Shortcut

Deer Run
Trail

Aspen
Trail

Nature Center

21

Kingfisher
Lagoon

High Ridge Road

P

Site of
Labadie
Summer Home

Wildwing
Lake

Wildwing Trail

Kent
Lake

0.4 The path crosses a couple boardwalks on the way to the next trail junction. Another trail leads off to the left. This is a shortcut back to the nature center. It is too early in the walk for this to tempt you, so continue straight.

0.8 Here the trail starts to get steeper. You are beyond the wide, gentle paths most used by the meandering public. Turn right for the Fox Trail.

1.2 An unofficial connector trail here links to the park's West Trail, an equestrian path that originates in the northernmost corner of the park. Stay to the left.

1.4 You are now on the Chickadee Loop. Take the right path to follow the longer leg of the loop.

2.1 Come to an intersection; turn right.

2.2 Turning right again, you are now on the Tamarack Trail.

2.3 Continue past the wide path to your left. This was once part of Labadie Road. You are now on the Aspen Trail.

2.5 The Pine Loop begins on your right. Continue straight.

2.6 The Pine Loop ends on your right.

2.8 Stay to the left.

2.9 Two paths on the left lead back to the nature center. Take the first path, the Aspen Trail. The second is the Wildwing Trail. From this junction, Wildwing Lake should be in view.

3.1 This is the site of the Labadie summer home.

3.2 Continue straight through the intersection to return to the nature center.

3.3 The trail ends at the nature center.

Hike Information

Local Events/Attractions: Kensington Metropark Farm Center, 2240 West Buno Rd., Milford; (248) 685-1561; metroparks.com. It wasn't that long ago that much of this area was still farmland. In fact, a local man who was raised and lived all his life on a nearby farm still visits the farm center at Kensington. He knew the family that lived here and has all sorts of stories to tell about the place. But even if you don't run into this friendly stranger, there's a lot to learn about farming here. There's also a concession stand, as well as restrooms and water.

22 Lyon Oaks County Park

Its size and noble bearing make the great blue heron a favorite among birders (and non-birders) here in Michigan. Lyon Oaks County Park features a heron rookery, which gives you the chance to see these birds in their nesting habitat. The long loop trail includes a walk around a wetland-creation project, a mixed hardwood forest, and transition wetlands.

Start: Parking area across from the interpretive center
Distance: 2.3-mile lollipop
Hiking time: About 45 minutes
Difficulty: Easy; wide, even path with no elevation changes
Trail surface: Gravel doubletrack; gravel through the woods as well
Best season: Beautiful in fall
Other trail users: Bikes permitted but not common; cross-country skiing in winter
Canine compatibility: Leashed dogs permitted
Fees and permits: Daily vehicle permit (reduced price for Oakland County residents)

Schedule: Open daily, 30 minutes before sunrise to 30 minutes after sunset
Maps: Maps available at park office and on website; TOPO! CD: Michigan, Ohio, Indiana, disc 4
Trail contacts: Lyon Oaks, 52221 Pontiac Trail, Wixom, MI 48393; (248) 858-0906; www.destinationoakgov.com/parks/parksandtrails/Lyon-Oaks/Pages/default.aspx
Special considerations: Sections of the park are open to deer hunting during archery season.

Finding the trailhead: Lyon Oaks is on Pontiac Trail, between Kensington Metropark and Wixom. From I-96 take exit 155 for Milford Road (if you're coming from the west) or exit 159 for Wixom Road (if you're coming from the east), and follow either of those roads north to Pontiac Trail. The park is halfway between them. After you enter the park, ignore the turn for the golf course. When you come to a T, turn right and then park. The trailhead is at the top of the intersection. GPS: N42 31.148' / W83 33.671'

The Hike

This is the second of the three Oakland county parks featured in this guide. The county parks all have the word "Oaks" in their name: Independence Oaks, Groveland Oaks, Addison Oaks, etc. Lyon Oaks is not the largest of the group, but at 1,204 acres (800 of which are wetlands) it's certainly not small. The park features an eighteen-hole golf course, its main attraction, as well as picnic areas and a nice dog park.

The setting could hardly be more urban. To the south the park is bordered by I-96. To the north is a portion of Pontiac Trail dedicated to light industry. The center of Wixom is only 1.5 miles away. Nonetheless, the park's rich wetlands and hardy woods support a lot of wildlife, including the nesting grounds for some of Michigan's more impressive birds.

> **See the trees with bark that looks like burnt potato chips? Those are wild black cherry. Every part of the tree, except for the cherry flesh, is poisonous.**

Along the Coyote Corridor you can access three of the park's loops—the Heron, Turkey, and Fawn Loops. These were once connected by a trail now called the Red-Tail Run. Using this connector, you used to be able to plan a much longer hike through the park. That trail, however, has been severed by wetlands, creating two sections of trail and requiring a few there-and-back treks if you want to add on the miles.

The trail begins near the parking area, across from the nature interpretive center. As you walk down the Coyote Corridor, here a gravel doubletrack road, to your left is a huge dog park and one of the county's wetland-mitigation projects. Wetland mitigation is the requirement that developers replace acres of wetlands lost during building. This even applies to the county road commission. In order to compensate for wetlands lost to a number of planned road projects, the county is creating wetlands here.

The first trails you come to on the Coyote Corridor are the two paths that connect with the Heron Loop. Heading south into the woods, you pass through a forest of wild cherry, maple, poplar, and shagbark hickory. There are even a few beech trees scattered about. With 800 acres of wetlands (about two-thirds of the park's area), if you take away the picnic areas, the dog park, and the golf course, it's a wonder you can find a dry patch to walk on. The woods here border wetlands to the west and north.

This artificial heronry attracts the great blue heron.

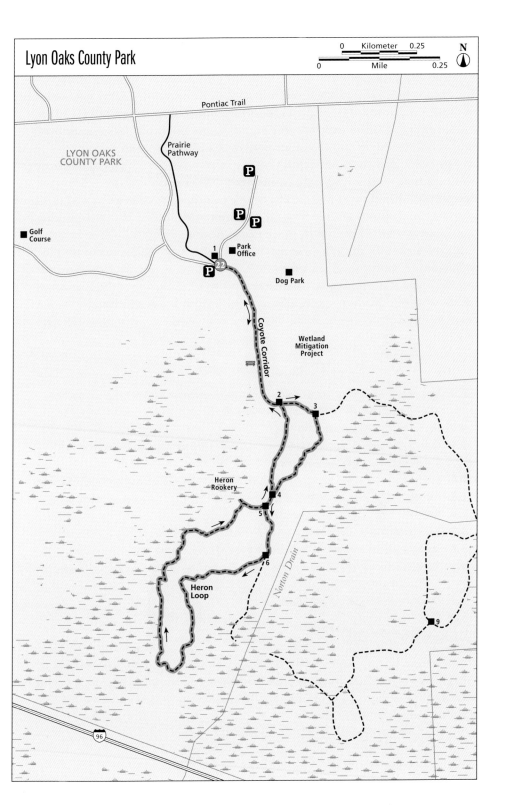

Lyon Oaks County Park

One of the most unusual features of this hike comes on the return journey. On the left (about 1.7 miles into the hike) is a trail for the heron rookery. Herons tend to nest in colonies. They look for tall trees with vertical branches near the top to support their nests, which are typically about 3 feet across. The trees they prefer tend to be on islands or surrounded by water. It's also a big bonus if that water supports food for them to eat. The rookery (or, more properly, the heronry) at Lyon Oaks is an artificial one—the first in Michigan—but it meets all the birds' requirements.

The family that once owned this property reports that herons had been nesting here as far back as the early 1900s. Typically they nested in tall, dead trees. When the trees fell over, the herons moved on. The nesting poles here are utility poles with nesting platforms and were erected with the intention of restoring a traditional nesting spot. It's really a great opportunity to see herons nesting.

At the end of the loop, the trail rejoins the Coyote Corridor and returns to the parking area. A short enough trail, the whole route can be done in 45 minutes, which includes a stop at the rookery. Or add some distance by trying one of the other loops farther down the way. It's a great hike in the fall, when leaves are changing. If you come in summer, be sure to bring bug spray. With all these wetlands, mosquitoes thrive.

Miles and Directions

0.0 Start from trail marker 1, across from the interpretive center, and follow the gravel double-track into the park. This is the Coyote Corridor Trail.

0.3 There's a clearing here with a bench.

0.4 Pass the first trail on your right (trail marker 2), which is a connector to Heron Loop. That's the return path. Instead, turn right at the second connector, trail marker 3.

0.6 Continue straight at trail marker 4, and then bear left at trail marker 5 onto Heron Loop.

0.8 A trail to the left here, at trail marker 6, once passed through to the other section of trails. It appears to be blocked by wetlands now.

1.7 A short side trail to your left leads out to a view of the park's heron rookery.

1.8 Two lefts in a row here get you back on the finishing stretch of the loop.

2.0 The loop is complete; turn left onto the Coyote Corridor Trail to follow the lollipop handle back to the parking area.

2.3 The trail ends back at the parking lot.

Hike Information

Restaurants: Burrito King, 30950 Beck Rd., Novi; (248) 960-6566; burritoking novi.com. This great little Mexican place has gathered quite a following in a few short years. The menu hints at a hybrid of sorts, with some guests seeing a bit of Texas on the plate and others seeing SoCal.

Metro Detroit and Points North

The trails in this section of the guide are spread out across four counties. While most are in north Oakland, there also are hikes in Genesee, Lapeer, and Macomb Counties. The Huron River flows through all three sections covered in this book. Here in north Oakland County, it flows out of the Indian Springs Metropark, where you can explore the Huron's headwaters. Though it begins small, by the time it reaches Proud Lake Recreation Area the river is easily navigable by canoe or kayak. The trails at Proud Lake follow portions of the river and explore its neighboring wetlands.

Trails are not always this nicely posted.

With so many wetlands, boardwalks become a reliable way to create usable trails.

The moraine terrain that begins northwest of Ann Arbor continues here and is the highlight of parks like the Holly, Ortonville, and Bald Mountain Recreation Areas. A bird's-eye view of this part of the state reveals a swath of lakes—as well as ponds, impoundments, rivers, creeks, and streams—spread out in a broad arch over Metro Detroit.

Waterways to the west flow into the Huron River, but the wetlands at Independence Oaks in Clarkston (and points east) feed another waterway altogether. The Clinton River flows from north Oakland County east through Macomb County, emptying in Lake St. Clair in Mount Clemens. The river is fed by Stony Creek, which runs through Stony Creek Metropark north of Rochester. This metropark has miles of nature trails, certainly more than you can hike in one visit. To the east, Wolcott Mill Metropark on the North Branch of the Clinton River tells the story of how early Michiganders used these waterways to carve out a living on the frontier.

Many of the parks in this section don't fall under the usual state, county, and metropark categories. Dauner Martin Preserve in Fenton, for example, is owned and managed by the Michigan Nature Association. The Lloyd A. Stage Nature Center in Troy is run by the Troy Nature Society, and the Seven Ponds Nature Center in Dryden has its own not-for-profit organization. Each, however, offers something unique for local hikers.

23 Proud Lake State Recreation Area

This loop at Proud Lake State Recreation Area follows the Huron River, crosses the river next to Proud Lake, and then explores the woods northwest of the lake. On the return is an extensive boardwalk through a dense river marsh. The trails are semi-rugged, and the woods will give you that deep sense of solitude, even when you pass the occasional day campers on the trail.

Start: Parking lot just east of the Wixom Road entrance

Distance: 4.6-mile bow-tie loop

Hiking time: About 2.5 hours

Difficulty: Difficult due to length

Trail surface: Predominantly packed earth, at times sandy or mucky; boardwalks over wetlands

Best season: Best in summer; fewer bugs and nice colors in the fall

Other trail users: None

Canine compatibility: Leashed dogs permitted

Fees and permits: Recreation Passport required

Schedule: Open 8 a.m.–10 p.m.

Maps: TOPO! CD: Michigan, Ohio, Indiana, disc 4; maps available at park office and on website

Trail contacts: Proud Lake State Recreation Area, 3500 Wixom Rd., Commerce Township, MI 48382; (248) 685-2433; michigan.gov/proudlake

Special considerations: Wet weather makes the trail more of a challenge, with muddy spots and slippery roots and stones.

Finding the trailhead: The recreation area is north of I-96 east of Milford. From I-96 take Wixom Road (exit 159) north. Drive exactly 6 miles north to the recreation area entrance, and turn right. The parking lot for the trailhead is the second one on your left (the first is the park office). The trailhead is at the far end of the lot. GPS: N42 34.246' / W83 33.235'

The Hike

Proud Lake State Recreation Area comprises more than 4,700 acres of rolling woods and wetlands. The Huron River pours out of the eponymous Proud Lake at the east end of the park and flows many miles through a chain of lakes before emptying a short distance from Kensington Metropark at the west end. Less than 9 miles away, as the crow flies, the Huron River wells up from the ground and is little more than a trickle. By the time it gets to Proud Lake, it's a respectable river, but nothing like it is downriver of Ann Arbor. Here at Proud Lake the river is the perfect size for recreation. Deep enough for trout and the draft of a canoe, yet shallow enough for the water to riffle on the surface and for you to see the riverbed. Wide enough to look down and see what waits ahead, but narrow enough for two neighbors to chat amiably from opposite banks.

Throughout the year, a quick peek at the river picnic area just off Wixom Road reveals a handful of anglers in hip-high waders casting their lines. Fishing and paddling

Dead trees on the river are regularly cleared for canoe traffic.

are popular activities here, as are hiking, biking, and horseback riding. The park also features a modern campground and canoe rentals.

The hiking trails at Proud Lake can be roughly divided between those south and west of the Huron River and those to the north and east. The complex system of trails can be confusing at times, and this situation is only made more baffling if you attempt to consult the park's trail map. One feature, however, is easily understood: The hiking trails are all east of Wixom Road; the biking and bridle paths are all on the west side.

The hike outlined here is composed essentially of the Blue Trail, which overlaps with the Red Trail loop for a stretch. During the hike you will find blaze marks to this effect. The adventure begins in the parking lot just east of the Wixom Road entrance. You will be following the trail markers as you go. At the beginning the trail is often sandy, and you pass a plantation of pine trees. The trail meets up with the state park road, and after a quick walk through the day camp area, you come to the bridge at the Proud Lake Dam. On this side of the bridge are the toilets. On the other side you will see a sign for the Huron River Water Trail, marking the first portage in the 104-mile trek to Lake Erie.

GREEN TIP:
Shop for fleece clothing that is made from recycled pop bottles.

Once across the bridge, the bigger Blue Trail loop still awaits. Skirting the wetlands north of Moss Lake, the trail can be wet here, even during dry years. Ferns line the trail, and from time to time you see a woodland swamp to your left. Eventually the trail begins to climb, and soon you're in a hardwood forest full of beech and oak. As you walk east, the trail primarily passes through wetlands. On the return west, upland forest is more prominent, although there is a bit of a mix in both directions.

The loop brings you back to the bridge. The final leg of the hike follows the southern bank of the Huron River and ends with an amazing walk through a river marsh. Here an elevated boardwalk gets you up above the grasses and cattails. Wildflowers lean in over

Path heads up into the woods from the canoe put-in.

the path. It's a unique experience walking through such a dense habitat.

The trail ends at the parking lot, shortly after you step off the boardwalk.

Miles and Directions

0.0 Start from the trailhead at the east end of the parking lot. This is just a connector that will lead you back to trail marker 1.

0.1 Trail marker 1; stay to the right.

0.2 Trail marker 2; follow the arrow left in the direction of trail marker 20.

0.3 Trail marker 20; turn right.

0.5 When you come to trail marker 8, turn left and follow the dirt road back into the park. You will pass a number of buildings, some used for day camps in summer. Just before the road comes to an end, turn right toward the bridge.

0.8 Trail marker 9 is off to your left. Cross the bridge to trail marker 10, and continue to the right. You are now on the Red/Blue Trail loops.

0.9 Take a left at trail marker 11. The next stretch is bordered by ferns.

1.0 Trail marker 12; continue on to marker 13. The path is a bit drier here.

1.3 Trail marker 13; continue straight on the Blue Trail. (**Option:** A left here will take you on a shortcut, the Red Trail, to trail marker 17.

1.6 The trail crosses underneath the power line.

HURON RIVER WATER TRAIL

For ambitious paddlers hoping to put a notch in their yoke for paddling the entirety of a major river, no other in Southeast Michigan but the Huron River will do. The official Huron River Water Trail includes the section of the river that is generally considered navigable: from the boat launch on Proud Lake, 104 miles to Lake Erie. Of course you can try your luck upstream, but at some point it becomes more like trailblazing than canoeing.

This epic route hasn't always been paddler friendly. For those hoping to make it in one go, there weren't always enough places where you could overnight. And even for day trips, portages around the several dams on the river weren't always well marked or maintained.

Now several parks along the way allow paddlers to set up camp for the night—even some that don't have campsites will make an exception for the Huron River traveler. In addition, in great part due to the council's RiverUp! program, communities are investing resources in updating portages and making the journey a tad bit easier.

1.7   Once across the clearing, enter the woods and come to trail marker 14. Turn left; you're going to bypass trail marker 15 and head straight for marker 16.

1.8   The trail merges with a dirt road. To the right, this road dead-ends at a boat launch on the Huron River. Instead go left and look for the next trail marker about 0.3 mile up on your left.

2.1   At trail marker 16 the trail once again regains the forest.

2.2   This section of the trail seems little used. The small bridge here is buried at times in branches and leaves.

2.4   The trail crosses back underneath the power lines.

2.7   Trail marker 17; turn right.

3.2   There's a cornfield on the right, and you can see a large dead tree in a field a little ways off the trail.

3.4   Trail marker 19; turn left and follow the wide sandy path.

3.5   Trail marker 18; turn right.

3.7   You've returned to trail marker 10. Turn right and cross the bridge.

3.8   Bear right at trail marker 9, and follow the path alongside the Huron River. The trail here is part of the Chief Pontiac Trail.

4.1   Trail marker 21; stay to the right to follow the River Trail.

Proud Lake State Recreation Area

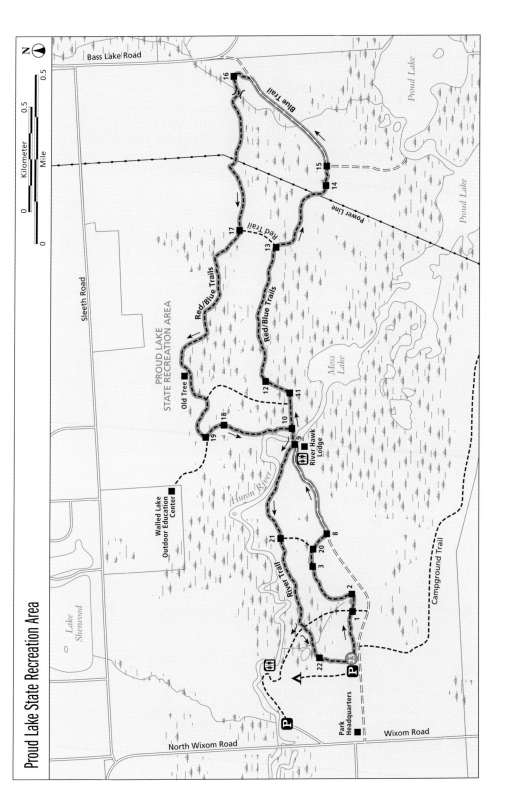

4.5 After crossing a lengthy raised boardwalk, you are back on dry ground at trail marker 22. Turn left; at the next fork go right. This will take you back to the parking lot. (Left goes back to trail marker 1.)

4.6 The trail ends at the other end of the parking lot.

Options: Consider trying a few of the other trails at Proud Lake; most are simple additions to this one. For one short add-on, walk the path west along the river out to Wixom Road. This is a scenic out-and-back. If you bring a bike, the trails in the west side of the park connect with the mountain bike trails in Kensington, significantly increasing your two-wheeled options.

Hike Information

Local Events/Attractions: Huron River Water Trail; www.hrwc.org/our-work/ programs/huron-river-water-trail. The Huron River Watershed Council maintains resources for paddling the length of the Huron River, from the launch on Proud Lake to Lake Erie.

24 Highland State Recreation Area

A simple 4.3-mile loop through Highland State Recreation Area is the perfect introduction to the "highlands" region of Oakland County, which is named for the moraines that dominate the landscape. The trail skirts kettles and climbs moraines, passing through dense hardwood forest and some boardwalked marsh. The property once belonged to Edsel Ford, who built an estate on nearby Haven Hill as a retreat from life in the city.

Start: To the right (west) of the barn, heading off toward the campground
Distance: 4.3-mile loop
Hiking time: About 1.75 hours
Difficulty: Difficult; long route with plenty of hills
Trail surface: Packed dirt
Best season: Summer and fall
Other trail users: None
Canine compatibility: Leashed dogs permitted
Fees and permits: Recreation Passport required
Schedule: Open daily, 8 a.m.–10 p.m.

Maps: Maps available at park office and on website; TOPO! CD: Michigan, Ohio, Indiana, disc 4
Trail contacts: Highland State Recreation Area, 5200 Highland Rd., White Lake, MI 48383; (248) 889-3750; michigan.gov/highland
Special considerations: The hike passes entirely through land closed to hunting. However, just before it enters the Haven Hill Natural Area, the trail passes close to state land open to hunting. The boundaries are not always clear in the woods, and bright orange clothing is recommended during hunting season.

Finding the trailhead: Highland is in White Lake, west of Pontiac. From Woodward Avenue in Pontiac, take M-59 west for 13.5 miles to the park entrance. Follow Haven Road, which becomes Moraine Road if you stay on the main thoroughfare. The parking area in front of the historic barn is 1.4 miles from the entrance. The trailhead is to the right of the barn, heading off toward the campground. GPS: N42 38.071' / W83 33.080'

The Hike

The Ford family has influenced the progression of southeast Michigan in many ways, the most obvious being that Henry Ford was the father of the automobile industry that has driven this region's economy for over one hundred years. Ford founded the Henry Ford Health System, and the family's charitable giving supported a number of important cultural institutions. Looking for a retreat from the city for himself and his wife, Eleanor, Henry's son, Edsel, began buying property around White Lake in the 1920s.

On and around Haven Hill—at 1,120 feet, one of the tallest in the area—he built a gatehouse, carriage house, riding stable, and a lodge. There was a pool and tennis courts; south of the hill he built a large barn, part of a working farm. At 15,000 square feet, the barn was one of the biggest east of the Mississippi River. It has been noted that the design is similar to early Ford factories—in particular, the height allowing for windows that let in natural light. Most of the barn blew down in a windstorm in 2008. Plans are under way to restore the remaining portion and add a covered porch to extend the length of the original building.

Edsel Ford died in 1943, and his wife donated Haven Hill and the property's 2,422 acres to the state. This was the start of the Highland State Recreation Area, which has grown to 5,903 acres. In 1976 the Haven Hill Natural Area—the park within the park, so to speak—was designated as a National Natural Landmark. The most beautiful sections of the hike here pass through the natural area.

Highland has 17 miles of foot trails. There are also equestrian trails, and another portion of the park has 16 miles of trails dedicated to mountain biking. The hiking trails are all east of Duck Lake Road, the portion of the park that includes Haven Hill, Haven Hill Lake, the Haven Hill Natural Area, and the Haven Hill Barn. (Interestingly, the hill used to be called Heaven Hill, but Ford changed it.)

There are three named loops: Red, Blue, and Green. With Red being the shortest and Green the longest, the happy middle is the 4.3-mile Blue Loop, described here. These loops are not on the official park map. Your best bet for direction is the map printed on the trail marker signs. Every important junction is marked, so you can hike map to map to map without carrying one in your pocket.

All three loops share the trailhead just west of the historic barn. The first section of the hike joins up with the bridle paths, but once past the Chief Pontiac Trail (at trail marker 10), you're back on foot trails until the very end of the loop. The Chief Pontiac Trail is used by Boy Scouts, who hike the path from Highland Recreation Area all the way to Kensington Metropark. You can see the trailhead—a rusty arrowhead pointing east—as you walk through the campground at the start of the hike.

Soon after passing trail marker 10, you enter the natural area of the park, where you're asked not to mess with the vegetation. The trail traces the edge of a kettle. On your left, if you stand still and look carefully, you may see dozens of frogs sitting just feet from shore, counting on their camouflage to hide them. For the next mile or so, the path climbs a handful of small hills.

At the north end of the park, 0.25 mile of trail follows an elevated boardwalk through the heart of a marsh. The route is overgrown with phragmites, but it's an interesting habitat nonetheless. From here the trail skirts east of Haven Hill Lake and returns to the parking area. Close to trail marker 23, you're at the highest point of the route, which at 1,028 feet is only 50 or so feet higher than the lowest point along the route.

Highland Rec boasts a network of boardwalk paths. ▶

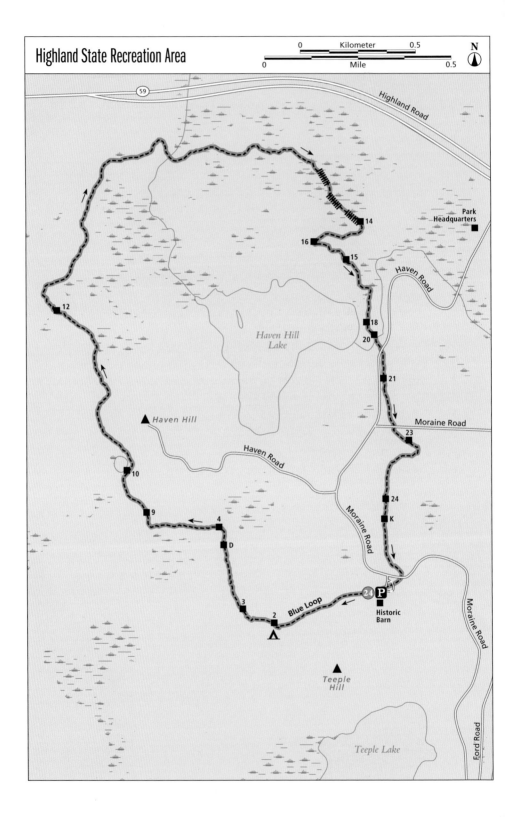

Highland State Recreation Area

59

Highland Road

Park
Headquarters

Haven Road

Haven Hill
Lake

14

16

15

18

20

12

21

Haven Hill

Moraine Road

23

Haven Road

10

9

4

24

D

K

3

2   Blue Loop

24   P

Historic
Barn

Moraine Road

Teeple
Hill

Moraine Road

Ford Road

Teeple Lake

Miles and Directions

0.0 Start from the trailhead at trail marker 1, to the right (west) of the barn at the west end of the parking lot.

0.3 The trail begins with a walk out to the park's group campground and continues into the woods near the outhouses. Trail marker 2 is just a short ways along the wooded path.

0.4 Turn right at trail marker 3.

0.5 For a short stretch the route joins up with one of the bridle paths.

0.6 At trail marker D continue straight on the path. Then turn left at trail marker 4 (also E).

0.9 Stay straight at trail marker 9. The trail begins a steep climb.

1.0 At trail marker 10 turn right toward marker 12, finally leaving the bridle path.

1.6 At trail marker 12 cross the bridge and continue straight.

2.1 The trail flattens out here. At the northern limit of the loop, you can hear traffic on M-59. During rush hour it creates quite a din.

2.7 The boardwalk here passes through 0.25 mile of marsh. Along the way the deck widens, giving you a chance to stop and check out the scenery. Unfortunately the marsh is almost completely inundated with phragmites. There is still some variety right next to the board-walk, but the tall reed blocks most of your view.

2.9 Back on dry land! At trail marker 14 turn right toward marker 16.

3.1 Bear left at trail marker 16.

3.2 At trail marker 15 continue straight. The terrain gets hilly, and there's a big descent down to lake level as you approach marker 18.

3.4 Bear left at trail marker 18.

3.5 Continue straight across the road at trail marker 20.

3.6 Continue straight at trail marker 21.

3.7 Cross the gravel utility road, and then take the path to left.

3.8 At trail marker 23 turn right for marker 24. (When in doubt, follow the sign with the cross-country skier on it.)

4.0 At trail marker 24 continue straight ahead for marker 26.

4.1 Along the way you will pass trail marker K, a sign that the path is also open to horses here.

4.2 Cross the road at trail marker 26. Just beyond is the horse staging area.

4.3 The trail ends at the equestrian trail staging area, next to the parking lot.

Option: Consider heading over to the Haven Hill hike to explore what remains of the old Ford estate.

Hike Information

Restaurants: Root Restaurant & Bar, 340 Town Center Blvd., White Lake; (248) 698-2400; therootrestaurant.com. Root is one of the most talked-about restaurants in north Oakland County. "Regional, seasonal cuisine" is the big attraction. This is a pretty classy place and perhaps best for lunch before you get all tousled on the trail.

25 Seven Lakes State Park

Seven Lakes is one of the newer parks in Michigan's state park system. The park boasts a variety of ecosystems, but for hiking, the forested Green Trail Loop can't be beat. The trail winds through rolling woodlands between Dickinson, Little Seven, and Big Seven Lakes, passing the shores of the first and offering scenic overlooks of the latter two.

Start: Far end of the Dickinson Picnic Shelter parking lot
Distance: 2.0-mile loop
Hiking time: About 1 hour
Difficulty: Moderate
Trail surface: Packed dirt
Best season: Fall
Other trail users: Mountain bikers
Canine compatibility: Leashed dogs permitted

Fees and permits: Recreation Passport required
Schedule: Open 8 a.m.–dusk
Maps: Maps available at park office and on website; TOPO! CD: Michigan, Ohio, Indiana, disc 4
Trail contacts: Seven Lakes State Park, 14390 Fish Lake Rd., Holly, MI 48442; (248) 634-7271; michigan.gov/sevenlakes

Finding the trailhead: The park is between Holly and Fenton, 50 miles northwest of Detroit. From I-75 take Grange Hall Road (exit 101) west toward Holly. After you pass through town (4.3 miles from the interstate), turn right onto Fish Lake Road. The park is 1 mile up, on the left. Once in the park, follow signs for the Dickinson Shelter (take the first left, then the first right, and then the first left). GPS: N42 48.640' / W83 39.718'

The Hike

Count them on a map. There are six lakes at Seven Lakes State Park. Once upon a time this property was slated for development. Nestled in these wooded hills were seven lakes, but the developers had a dream. Building a dam, they created one large lake. There is still a dam at the north end of Big Seven Lake. In 1969 the state bought the property, and in 1992 the park was opened to the public. All told the property comprises 1,434 acres of rolling hills and forest. The park has a modern campground on Sand Lake, boat launches and fishing piers on Dickinson and Big Seven Lakes, a swimming beach, and miles of trails for hiking and biking.

Several miles of trails wander through the woods. Nature trails to the southeast pass close by the park's fens and make a loop between Spring and Mud Lakes. A much longer path uses the access roads to circle Big Seven Lake. Of the named trails here, the Green Trail loop has the most to offer. With the optional short out-and-back addendum, you have a chance to see three of the park's lakes. In between, the trail passes through mixed hardwood forest and some wetlands, over moderately challenging terrain.

A picture-perfect overlook of the lake.

The trailhead for the Green Trail is at the far end of the parking lot for the Dickinson Picnic Shelter. From trail marker 14 the path descends to the level of Dickinson Lake. Less than 0.25 mile into the hike you come to trail marker 10, which has to be the most confusing meeting of trails on the hike. The map suggests a simple four-way intersection, but coming to the post you see not four but five trails, counting the one that led you here. To the right and left is the Dickinson Nature Trail. The two other trails actually meet up at the fishing pier, so either will do.

Past the fishing pier, walk by the boat launch on Dickinson Lake and cut through a small prairie full of wildflowers before diving back into the woods on the other side. At trail marker 8 the Red Trail breaks off to the left. So far the hills have been short, but at marker 7 the trail begins to climb steadily. A short path to your left leads out to a scenic overlook of Big Seven Lake.

At the 1.0-mile mark (trail marker 6), the Yellow Shortcut breaks to the right. Continue straight ahead. The trail descends and then rises again as it approaches the narrow strip of land between Big Seven and Little Seven Lakes. It's easy to miss the lakes for the trees here. At trail marker 5 there's another overlook to the left, and straight ahead will take you north on the Red Trail. Your path is to the right, heading southeast back toward the start of the loop.

Your path will come to two more shortcuts before making it out to the road. The first is the back end of the Yellow Shortcut. From this direction it's not a shortcut at all but an invitation to a *Groundhog Day*–like loop, dooming you to keep repeating the same trail over and over. The second is the Red Trail. Not really labeled a shortcut, this one does get you back to the start a tad quicker. Continuing left at both of these junctions takes you north through some wooded wetlands. Some rough boardwalks make a valiant—and successful—effort to keep your feet dry.

For the final bit, the path crosses the park road. To your left you can see the drive for the parking lot. A tunnel has been punched through the shrubs between you and the Dickinson Shelter and follows a mowed path to the picnic tables. There always seem to be flies here—even in years when there have been very few flies. Perhaps it's leftovers from picnickers. If you want to avoid the flies, you can cut to the left and follow the pavement back to your car.

Miles and Directions

0.0 Start at the trailhead at the far end of the parking lot, just before the turnaround circle. The hike starts with trail marker 14.

0.2 At trail marker 10 things get a little dicey. The Dickinson Trail crosses the Green Trail, and there seem to be more options than there should be. The hard turn to the right returns to the Dickinson Picnic Shelter. The hard turn to the left heads out to a nature loop on the Dickinson Trail. The other two options take you to the next trail marker near the fishing pier.

0.3 Trail marker 9 marks the fishing pier.

0.4 The trail comes out at the boat launch for Dickinson Lake. Across the paved drive the trail passes through a portion of field that is full of wildflowers throughout the season.

0.6 At trail marker 8 stay to the right.

0.8 At trail marker 7 a path heads left to a nice overlook of Big Seven Lake. The out-and-back trip is about 0.25 mile. To continue on the loop, bear right.

1.0 At trail marker 6 the Yellow Shortcut to marker 17 leads off to the right. Continue to the left.

1.2 Trail marker 5 offers several options. In the end you will want to make a hard right toward marker 17.

1.5 Trail marker 17 is the other end of the Yellow Shortcut. Continue to the left.

1.6 At trail marker 16 there's another alternative path. This is the Red Trail, a short spur that leads out to the road. It's a quicker path back to the parking lot but not terribly scenic. Instead turn left and finish out the Green Trail.

1.9 At trail marker 15 you're back at the road. All that's left is a short hike through shrubs and you're home.

2.0 The trail ends at the Dickinson Picnic Shelter.

Seven Lakes State Park

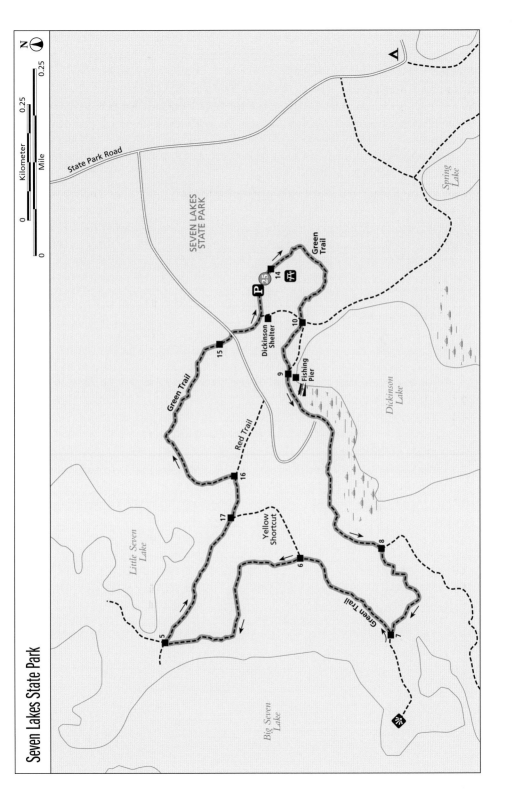

Hike Information

Restaurants: Beale St. Smokehouse BBQ, 2461 North Rd., Fenton; (810) 750-0507; bealestreetsmokehouse.com. Southeast Michigan isn't known for its barbecue, so it's a real treat to find a place that does it right. The Smokehouse is tucked in the most unlikely of places—attached to a gas station near exit 80 off M-23.

The Laundry, 125 West Shiawassee Ave., Fenton; (810) 629-8852; lunchandbeyond .com. Serving some of the finest food in the area, The Laundry is best known for great breakfasts and killer sandwiches.

Hike Tours: Hiking Michigan; hikingmichigan.com. The folks at Hiking Michigan are often heading out to Seven Lakes to check out the fens. This is a great opportunity to see Michigan's carnivorous pitcher plant, found only in area bogs and fens.

26 Dauner Martin Sanctuary

It's rare to find a Michigan Nature Association sanctuary within any city limits. Dauner Martin in Fenton is one of the fine exceptions. With 155 acres of forest, field, and wetland and 4.5 miles of trail meandering through this lightly managed preserve, Dauner Martin is a great way to get away from the hustle and bustle without having to drive beyond the reaches of civilization.

Start: Parking lot off North Leroy Road
Distance: 2.4-mile loop
Hiking time: About 1.25 hours
Difficulty: Easy to moderate; small elevation change but trail overgrown in places
Trail surface: Packed earth
Best season: Summer and fall
Other trail users: None
Canine compatibility: Leashed dogs permitted
Fees and permits: None

Schedule: No hours posted
Maps: Maps available at the kiosk near the parking lot; TOPO! CD: Michigan, Ohio, Indiana, disc 4
Trail contacts: The Michigan Nature Association, 326 East Grand River Ave., Williamston, MI 48895; (517) 655-5655; http://michigan nature.org/home/sancts/daunerMartin/ daunerMartin.shtml

Finding the trailhead: The sanctuary is located in Fenton, approximately 40 miles north of Ann Arbor. From I-75 take the exit for Grange Hall Road (exit 101). Drive west for 7.3 miles and turn right (north) onto Leroy Street. Continue on Leroy for 1.2 miles. The parking lot is behind the small office building that's just past the grocery store on your right. Drive behind the office and follow the dirt drive to the small parking area. The trailhead is right there. GPS: N42 52.138' / W83 26.288'

The Hike

Although no more than 155 acres, the Dauner Martin Sanctuary offers a fine natural setting with 4.5 miles of trails. The sanctuary is owned and operated by the Michigan Nature Association, which oversees dozens of similar properties throughout the state. The MNA was given the property by the Martin family, whose grandparents once owned the farmland and woods.

Located behind a prime commercial strip on North Leroy Street in Fenton, it was unimaginable that this property would escape development. But the Martins saw a different future for the land, and the resulting preserve is a significant natural asset for the city.

There are two parking areas for Dauner Martin. One is on Dauner Road, about 0.5 mile east of Leroy. The other is on Leroy Street, next to a grocery store. The trail begins at the far end of the small parking area on Leroy (but the hike can be done from either parking area). A kiosk marks the trailhead with a somewhat faded map and a list of the sanctuary rules.

The path outlined here is a combination of loops and trails. You will follow the Western Run to the Northern Loop to the Eastern Loop, taking in a section of the Prairie Trail before walking the White Loop to the final return along the Red Loop. This path takes in the whole of the sanctuary, from woodlands to wetlands.

On your first visit it's not unnatural to feel a little disappointed at the outset of the hike. Where are the woods? Where are the trees? The path seems to be a tunnel carved through a thicket of autumn olive. Soon, however, the bushes pull back and you're walking through straight planted rows of tall pine. (Another pine plantation awaits you later in the hike as well.) Not the pristine forest you might have been hoping for, but it's a vast improvement on invasive woody bushes.

The hike doesn't start to get really interesting until you're about 0.5 mile in. Here the woods are more mature—full of maple, cherry, hickory, and oak—and the trail skirts a bright green swamp. Several places along the path offer a peek at the swamp through the trees. Coming around from the northeast corner of the park, the path is wet at times; short boardwalks help in wet weather.

These pine plantation rows are a common sight around Michigan.

Then you begin to climb a little. Just as you jump on the Prairie Trail, a large tree stands in your path. The tree appears to be dead, but it is impressive nonetheless. You can tell from the stretch of its branches that this was an oak. What's less obvious is that more than 300 years ago it was an acorn. The sheer mass of this tree makes it hard to believe that trees essentially pull their building material from the air.

Continuing along, pass through the pine plantation mentioned before, and then come to an intersection marked with a short sign pointing to the parking area on Dauner Road. Turning right, the path continues back into the heart of the sanctuary. Heading due west from anywhere along this stretch of path would lead back to the parking area. It would also lead through a long wetland that stretches from the middle of the park all the way down to Dauner Road.

▶ Squirrels fail to retrieve 74 percent of the acorns they bury to eat later. Because of this, scientists think that squirrels may be responsible for the spread of oak trees across North America.

Walking around the wetland brings you back close to the trail you came in on. But instead of making this a lollipop path, you eventually cut back south and return on the Red Loop Trail.

The MNA attempts to maintain sanctuaries with a minimum of development. The trails here are often confusing, and less-used paths are more overgrown than you would expect at a state or county park. While it would be difficult to get lost in Dauner Martin, it would be very easy to get turned around. So be sure to print out a map ahead of time, and wear long pants if you're worried about ticks and prickers.

Miles and Directions

0.0 Start from the parking lot off North Leroy Street. In less than 0.1 mile take a left at the first fork onto Western Run. Stay to the left past the next side trail.

0.3 As the trail opens up a little, you come to a clearing with one of the nice benches that are scattered throughout the sanctuary. Just beyond the clearing you find yourself in the planted pine forest.

0.5 On your right is a connector trail that leads to the Valley Trail. Keep left, now on the Northern Loop.

0.7 At the split in the trail, continue to the left on the Eastern Loop.

0.8 Off to your left you should be able to see the swamp through the trees.

1.0 After a wide, roundabout route, come back to the swamp again, this time from the east.

1.3 Standing in the path is the trunk of a 300-year-old oak tree. Pictures do a poor job of relating the size of this tree, the trunk of which measures 6 feet in diameter. You're now on the Prairie Trail.

1.4 The Valley Trail enters from the right, and then you come to an intersection. Turning left (the White Trail) will take you to the Dauner Road parking area. Turn right onto the White Return.

1.7 Following the White Return north, come to a T in the road. Turn left, and then make another left at the next fork.

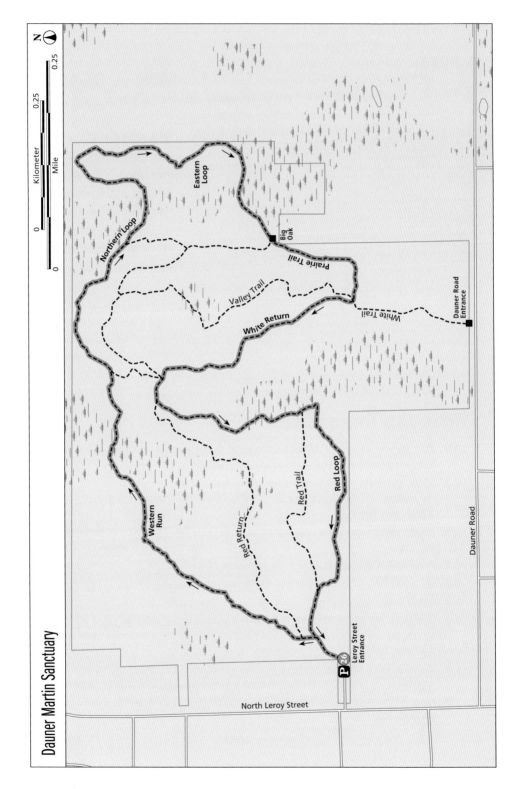

Dauner Martin Sanctuary

1.9 The Red Loop enters on your right. Continue straight, and follow the Red Loop home. The trees part on your left for a view of the wetland.

2.3 As you make your way back to the parking area, all the other loops are coming to an end here. Two enter from the right. Just stay to the left and you should be fine.

2.4 The trail ends back at the parking lot.

Hike Information

Restaurants: Halo Burger, 1355 North Leroy St., Fenton; (810) 750-1952; halo burger.com. If you're coming from outside Genesee County, there's a good chance you've never had a Halo Burger. This local chain began in Flint in 1923 as the original Kewpee restaurant. The founder is credited with being the first to serve burgers with a flat-bottomed bun. Be sure to order your burger "deluxe" with olives. (See other hikes in the area for listings of more upscale dining.)

27 Holly State Recreation Area

Nearly 8,000 acres of park straddle Dixie Highway and I-75 east of Holly. This park is a popular destination for swimming, camping, mountain biking, paddling, fishing, and disc golf. Hikers know it as a great place for a walk in the woods, with rolling hills, woodland lakes, and open prairies.

Start: Parking lot near the causeway between Heron and Wildwood Lakes

Distance: 2.5-mile loop

Hiking time: About 45 minutes

Difficulty: Moderate; an easy trail with several steep climbs

Trail surface: Packed dirt, gravel

Best season: Spring through fall; trails groomed for cross-country skiing in winter

Other trail users: Hunters in season

Canine compatibility: Leashed dogs permitted

Fees and permits: Recreation Passport required

Schedule: Open daily in summer, 8 a.m.–10 p.m.; closed at dusk in winter

Maps: TOPO! CD: Michigan, Ohio, Indiana, disc 4; trail map available at the park office, at the old welcome kiosk near park entrance, and on website

Trail contacts: Holly State Recreation Area, 8100 Grange Hall Rd., Holly, MI 48442; (248) 634-8811; michigan.gov/holly

Special considerations: Sections of this trail pass through land open to hunting. It's not uncommon to hear the report of hunting rifles in the fall. Hikers should wear bright orange during hunting season.

Finding the trailhead: The park is about 45 miles northwest of Detroit. From I-75 take exit 101 at Grange Hall Road and drive east. The entrance to the park is 2.3 miles from I-75. Just before the park, Grange Hall turns sharply to the north. Continue straight on McGinnis Road—the signs are pretty clear. The trailhead for the Lakeshore Trail is found at the parking lot near the causeway between Heron and Wildwood Lakes, about 0.8 mile from McGinnis. GPS: N42 48.492' / W83 31.014'

The Hike

Woodward Avenue starts in downtown Detroit and heads north-northwest, almost in a beeline toward Bay City. Along the way the name changes to Dixie Highway, connecting it with the much larger old highway system of that name. This is an old route. Native Americans first blazed the trail, creating a shortcut across the Thumb and connecting Lake Erie with settlements near the base of Saginaw Bay.

In 1830, when Alexis de Tocqueville traveled through this region looking to experience the American frontier, he and his traveling partner followed this trail from Detroit to Saginaw Bay. Along the way they rode their horses through these woods and saw many of the lakes and ponds that are scattered between Pontiac and Grand Blanc. They may have looked down upon Heron Lake as the trail they followed cut along its western edge.

Where the woods open to prairie, you will find wildflowers in summer.

Holly State Recreation Area is stunningly scenic in spots. The park is split into north and south sections by McGinnis Road. To the north are McGinnis Lake and a large campground. The south section features Heron, Valley, and Wildwood Lakes. A beach on Heron Lake makes it the most popular destination in the park during summer. Other visitors come to fish on the smaller lakes, play a round on the park's rugged twenty-four-hole disc golf course, or hike in the woods.

The park maintains a host of trails. There are a couple short nature trails that can be walked in less than 20 minutes, as well as a more-ambitious Wilderness Trail that draws a 6.4-mile loop around the northern half of the park.

The Lakeshore Trail, highlighted here, cuts a line down the middle. Less than 3.0 miles long, the loop circumnavigates Wildwood and Valley Lakes in the southern section of the park. Beginning in a parking area near the causeway that separates Wildwood Lake from Heron Lake, the trail passes through stunning oak and maple forests, keeping within sight of the water.

The first stretch of the trail stays so close to the water that hikers run the risk of getting their feet wet, especially in spring. As you walk along the northeastern shore of Wildwood Lake, the terrain rises quickly away from the water's edge. Atop the rise is the park's Overlook Picnic Area.

The trail hugs the edge of Wildwood Lake, with great views of the water.

As the trail rounds the southeastern corner of the lake, the forest clears and hikers cross an open beach. This was once a semipopular picnic and bathing area; now two new rental cabins dominate the scene. Heading back into the woods, the trail passes close to wetlands. Listen careful for the kerplunk of turtles leaping from their perches on sun-soaked logs as you pass. Keep your eyes open: A blue heron may be standing in the water just across the way.

The unique quality of this hike becomes evident as the trail begins to rise. Once following close to the shore, south of the lakes the trail climbs to the bluffs above the water. The trail connects several picnic areas and boat launches that provide tables for resting, drinking water, and restrooms.

▶ For a longer hike—6 to 8 miles—try the Wilderness Trail in the northern section of the park. The trail winds around McGinnis Lake and features rolling moraines and high-roofed forest.

The trail continues around to our starting point. From the causeway, as you walk back to the car, you can see the beach on Heron Lake in the distance. If you've thought ahead and brought your bathing suit, a dip in the lake is a great way to cool off from the hike.

For your next visit, consider bringing a canoe or kayak. Valley and Wildwood Lakes are connected by a short channel, and both lakes have numerous inlets

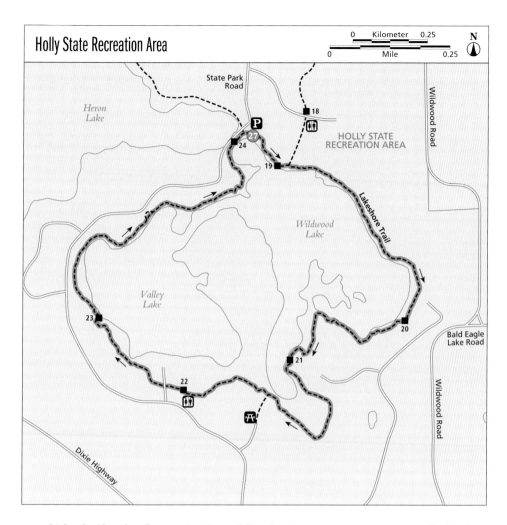

and islands. Shortly after putting in, paddlers begin to experience a sense of solitude unexpected on these smaller lakes.

Miles and Directions

0.0   Start from the parking lot on the northeast side of the causeway that separates Heron and Wildwood Lakes.

0.1   Trail marker 19 indicates the path that leads up to the Overlook Picnic Area.

0.4   The path diverges from the shoreline, heading into the woods before coming to the old beach area on Wildwood Lake.

0.6   Pass trail marker 20 as the trail heads back into a woods of towering oaks.

0.8   A path to the right is a scenic dead end, leading across a spit of land that connects a false island to land. Continue straight.

1.3 Trail marker 21 indicates another picnic area. As the path follows the southern shore of the lake, it is noticeably higher and drier than the first stretch of the hike.

1.5 The trail presents a Y; continue to the right, or go left for another picnic area.

1.7 Near trail marker 22 are restrooms and drinking water. The woods after this point become predominantly maple, though you will also find birch trees and sassafras.

1.9 Before trail marker 23 is the steepest climb of the hike. It's followed by another in short order.

2.1 The trail splits. When the ground is wet, take the detour to the left. Under drier conditions continue straight along the lakeshore.

2.4 This side of the causeway is trail marker 24. The trail follows the road and cuts between Heron and Wildwood Lakes. The parking lot is in sight.

2.5 Arrive back at the parking lot.

Hike Information

Local Events/Attractions: Michigan Renaissance Festival, 12600 Dixie Hwy., Holly; (248) 634-5552; michrenfest.com. Held annually on weekends from late August through September, the Renaissance Festival celebrates medieval culture. Just a few miles north of the recreation area on Dixie Highway.

Restaurants: Red Devil Restaurant, 104 South Broad St., Holly; (248) 634-4422; www.facebook.com/RedDevilRestaurant. A long hike sometimes calls for a plate of hearty carbs. When that happens, head to Holly for some of the best Italian in the area.

Mountain Biking: Holdridge Lakes Mountain Bike Area. Drive west on Grange Hall Road past I-75 to Hess Road; turn north and look for the signs on the left after 1.4 miles. Over 23 miles of dedicated mountain-bike trails are maintained by the Holly/Flint Chapter of the Michigan Mountain Biking Association (mmba.org). The loops are nicely separated into three sections for beginner, intermediate, and advanced riders.

28 Indian Springs Metropark

You will find the headwaters of several important rivers in north Oakland County. The Huron River, which eventually empties into Lake Erie south of Detroit, springs up from the wetlands in Indian Springs Metropark. In early spring the woods around the park's nature trails are blanketed with skunk cabbage, one of the most interesting of our wetland plants. Later in April and May, the woods are splashed with spring ephemerals.

Start: Behind the park office, at the end of the main park road

Distance: 3.1-mile loop

Hiking time: About 1 hour

Difficulty: Moderate; wide, even path with no real changes in elevation

Trail surface: Dirt

Best season: Early spring

Other trail users: None

Canine compatibility: Dogs not permitted

Fees and permits: Metropark Motor Vehicle Permit required

Schedule: Open 7 a.m.–10 p.m. Apr–Oct; 7 a.m.–8 p.m. Nov–Apr

Maps: TOPO! CD: Michigan, Ohio, Indiana, disc 4; maps available at park office and on website

Trail contacts: Indian Springs Metropark, 5200 Indian Trail, White Lake, MI 48386; (248) 625-7280; metroparks.com

Special considerations: Jogging is prohibited on the nature trails. Also, the eastern Massasauga rattlesnake makes its home in wetlands just like these; stay on the path.

Finding the trailhead: As it passes through Pontiac, US 24 changes from Telegraph Road to Dixie Highway. Driving west on Dixie Highway for 4.6 miles, turn left onto Andersonville Road. Continue 2.7 miles and turn left onto White Lake Road. The entrance to the park is 3.3 miles farther on the right. Turning into the park on Indian Trail, follow the road until it ends at the park office. The trailhead is just behind the office on the left. GPS: N42 42.473' / W83 29.239'

The Hike

All the Huron-Clinton Metroparks sit on land that somehow contributes to or participates in the flow of the Huron and Clinton Rivers. The springs for which Indian Springs is named feed the Huron Swamp, which in turn forms the headwaters of the Huron River. This park is important to the life cycle of the river. As a metropark, its biggest draw may be the Indian Springs Golf Course, though the kids' Spray 'n' Play Park pulls in quite a few families. The nature hikes at the park don't see nearly the traffic of either of these more popular attractions, although it's harder to sell a swamp than a giant bucket that periodically dumps gallons of water on giggling heads.

The nature trails are all at the very end of Indian Trail near the park office (restrooms available during park hours). The Woodland Trail is a 3.1-mile loop through the Huron Swamp, with an optional short out-and-back to Timberland Lake. Three shortcuts along the trail allow you to customize the hike—creating alternative 0.75-,

The level paths at Indian Springs make one large loop with a few optional connectors to cut the walk short.

1.25-, and 2.0-mile loops. In addition to these swampland walks, the Farmland and Pondside Trails present different habitats.

The essential difference between a marsh and a swamp is that swamps are woody environments, while marshes are shallow, grassy extensions of a lake, pond, stream, or river. The Huron Swamp is just that—a wooded wetland. You can put the images of the Okefenokee Swamp aside, though there is some of that here. Mostly you're looking at a soggy forest environment. The trail follows a path of high ground that is usually dry. Where it crosses a low spot, wide boardwalks have been installed.

Leaving from the park office, the trail heads north and then west, tracing the loop counterclockwise through the swamp. Crossing over a stream, the trail heads into the woods. You will see standing water and moss growing up trees—and

▷ Among folks who are concerned about our environment, there's a lot of talk about invasive species—garlic mustard, oriental bittersweet, and phragmites in particular. Interestingly, the eastern skunk cabbage, a North American native, has been exported to the UK for planting in bog gardens. Both American and Asian skunk cabbage have escaped the confines of the nursery and are considered invasive species by conservationists overseas.

everywhere the plant can find ground to grow, a blanket of skunk cabbage. Indian Springs is one place where you can see a lot of skunk cabbage. This unique plant blossoms in early, early spring, when there is still snow on the ground. It generates enough heat to melt the snow around it, pushing up the dark cocoon of red petals that protect the flower head. The plant gives off an odor of rotting flesh that attracts flies and other pollinators. After pollination, the leafy greens appear, storing up energy all summer for next year's cycle. The plant's unique scent can be experienced any time by breaking a leaf, although yanking vegetation is not proper etiquette for a nature hike.

At the far northwest corner of the hike, a side trail leads back to Timberland Lake and offers a look at the adjoining fen. The return path to the trailhead is more of the same. There are several rain shelters spread along the hike, and before you get back to the start, the trail leaves the woods for a quick look at a pond.

From the pond you can walk the paved paths over to the Lupine Loop that connects to the Environmental Discovery Center. At some point everyone should visit the center. In addition to the usual nature center exhibits, the center has a glass

These wetlands at Indian Springs are the source of the Huron River.

Indian Springs Metropark

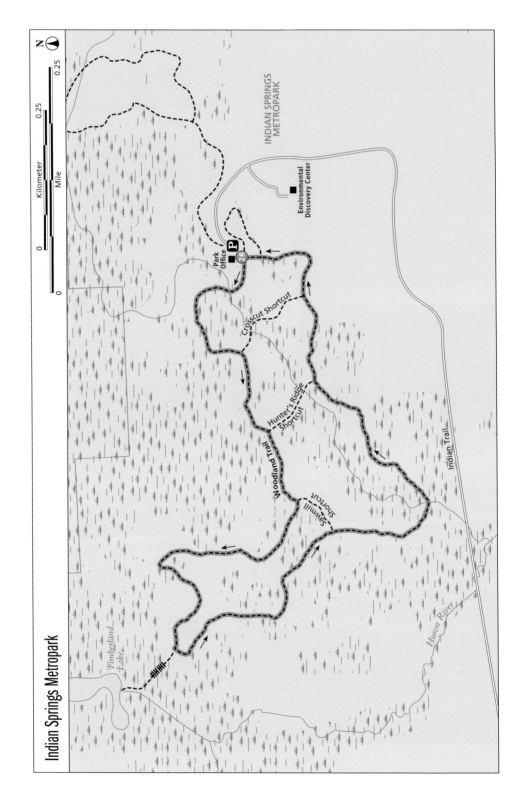

INDIAN SPRINGS
METROPARK

Environmental
Discovery Center

Park
Office

Crosscut Shortcut

Hunter's Ridge
Shortcut

Woodland Trail

Sawmill
Shortcut

Timberland
Lake

Indian Trail

Huron River

N

Kilometer

Mile

0.25

0.25

0

THE MICHIGAN RATTLER

The only venomous snake in Michigan is the Massasauga. Officially named the eastern Massasauga rattlesnake (*Sistrurus catenatus*), locals often call it the Michigan rattler. In Chippewa, massasauga means "great river mouth," and that hints at where hikers might stumble upon this intriguing reptile. Its natural habitat is near grassy wetlands and neighboring woody uplands.

The Massasauga is sometimes confused with the eastern hognose snake or the eastern milk snake. But should you stumble upon any of these snakes while hiking, the same rules apply: Keep your distance, and restrain pets. If someone in the hiking party gets bitten, call 911.

Thankfully the Michigan rattler is not an aggressive snake, just a dangerous one to mess with.

observation tunnel that leads out from the lower level of the building and under the adjacent pond. Though the water is often cloudy, it's an interesting look at pond life. And once you peel yourself away from the educational side of Indian Springs, there's the Spray 'n' Play Park. And while that is certainly a great addition to a hike if you've brought kids along, there's no rule that says adults can't hit the splash pads too.

Miles and Directions

0.0 Start at the trailhead behind the park office, and head out on the Woodland Trail.

0.4 The Crosscut Shortcut comes in from the left. Keep straight.

0.6 The next path on your left is the Hunter's Ridge Shortcut. The best is yet to come, however, so keep going. (*Option:* Turn left here to shorten the hike to 1.25 miles.)

0.8 A 2.0-mile loop can be made by turning left onto the Sawmill Shortcut. Bear right instead.

1.5 The trail to your right leads back almost 0.2 mile to Timberland Lake. The overlook trail also includes a peek at the nearby fen. This path is all on boardwalk. Keep left to stay on the Woodland Trail.

2.0 The trail on your left is the back end of the Sawmill Shortcut.

2.2 An unofficial path here leads off to the right, connecting the nature trail to the 8.0-mile paved bike-and-hike path that runs through the park. Taking this right and then a left on the paved path leads out to the main road right near the golf course.

2.7 The trail on your left is the back end of the Hunter's Ridge Shortcut.

2.9 The trail on your left is the back end of the Crosscut Shortcut.

3.1 The trail ends back at the park office.

Hike Information

Local Events/Attractions: Diehl's Orchard & Cider Mill, 1479 Ranch Rd., Holly; (248) 634-8981; diehlsorchard.com. All Michiganders know of the grand tradition of visiting apple orchards in the fall. Diehl's is a drive no matter where you're coming from, but from Indian Springs it's an easy 7 miles. This is a classic no-frills orchard. That means they have great cider; hot, greasy doughnuts dredged in cinnamon and sugar; and apples, apples, apples.

GREEN TIP:
When hiking in a group, walk single file on established trails to avoid widening them. If you come upon a sensitive area, spread out so that you don't cut one path through the landscape. Don't create new trails where there were none before.

29 Pontiac Lake State Recreation Area

Pontiac Lake State Recreation Area is not known for its hiking trails. There's just the one—an out-and-back connecting the campground with the beach on Pontiac Lake. But this 3.6-mile route takes you through some of the most beautiful forest in the area. With several steep hills, the rugged trail makes you work a little, which is great during the hottest days of summer, when you can cool off with a mid-hike swim in Pontiac Lake.

Start: Southeast corner of the campground between Sites 113 and 114
Distance: 3.6-mile out-and-back
Hiking time: About 1.5 hours
Difficulty: Moderate to difficult due to steep climbs
Trail surface: Packed dirt
Best season: Summer
Other trail users: None
Canine compatibility: Leashed dogs permitted

Fees and permits: Recreation Passport required
Schedule: Open 8 a.m.–dusk
Maps: TOPO! CD: Michigan, Ohio, Indiana, disc 4; maps available at park office and on website
Trail contacts: Pontiac Lake State Recreation Area, 7800 Gale Rd., Waterford, MI 48327; (248) 666-1020; michigan.gov/pontiaclake
Special considerations: Portions of the trail are on land open to hunting.

Finding the trailhead: The recreation area is in White Lake, approximately 40 miles northwest of Detroit. From M-59 (Highland Road) west of Pontiac, turn right onto North Williams Lake Road. After 1 mile turn left onto Gale Road. Drive 2.7 miles to Teggerdine Road. Turn right and drive a little less than 1 mile to the park entrance (Maceday Road). Continue to the eastern section of the campground, and park near the restrooms. The trailhead is at the southeast corner of the campground between sites 113 and 114. GPS: N42 41.085' / W83 27.901'

The Hike

Pontiac Lake State Recreation Area—best known for its shooting range and a sandy beach on Pontiac Lake—is an area park you may not have heard of. The park has 3,745 acres of rolling forest and wetland and several miles of frontage on the lake. The shooting range and the beach are at the east end of the park and take up very few acres. Aside from the campgrounds (a modern campground with 176 sites and an equestrian campground with 24), the rest of the park is dedicated to bridle paths and mountain bike trails.

In fact, there is only one dedicated hiking trail here—the 1.8-mile track between the campground and the beach. There are two ways to approach this classic out-and-back hike. You can park at the beach on Gale Road, hike to the campground, hike back, and then go swimming. Or you can park at the campground, hike to the beach, go swimming, and then hike back. It all depends on whether you like to swim at the

end of a hike or in the middle. Both tacks have their pros and cons, but this chapter will presume the latter option, giving you a mid-hike break.

Beginning from the campground, the best place to park is near the restrooms. It's a short walk around the campground loop to the trailhead, which is near Site 113. Once in the woods, you quickly cross the first of several bridle paths that get tangled up with the hiking trail. The woods here are full of oak, maple, and pine. Less than 0.2 mile in you will see a wall of earth through the trees. Approaching this steep hill, it almost appears to be a dead end, but the path cuts to the right at the last moment and climbs a steep 50 feet to the highest point on the hike.

> A century ago there was no Pontiac Lake in the Huron River watershed. There was Lime Lake, a much smaller body of water. Lime Lake was dammed in 1926, creating the 585-acre Pontiac Lake.

From here the trail descends—not as steeply, but you are going downhill for nearly 0.25 mile. The forest is stunning here. The trail passes around a wooded bowl and, but for a few hills, continues the descent to the lake. After the next few intersections, and a portion of trail where you share the route with horseback riders, the woods recede a bit and you come out into open meadow.

The lack of shade here can be a real concern on a hot summer afternoon. There is essentially no sustained tree cover from here to the beach. The trail straightens out and crosses a mountain bike path on its way to Gale Road. Once you cross the road, the trail parallels the shore to the beach day-use area. To your left is a fine tree with shade, under which you can take a break from the sun. Restrooms with flush toilets and water are just a short walk away. Between the parking lot and the water, there are two beach houses, perfect for changing into a suit and taking a quick dip. Once you are refreshed, it's time to return to the trail.

The walk back is a lot different from the first leg of the hike. The return to the high point on the route has you climbing an accumulated 280 feet in 1.5 miles. The gentle descents that eased the walk down seemed like they would be easy enough on the return, but be ready to climb. For the first 1.0 mile there are no real descents at all, only climbing. Passing through the same beautiful woods from the other direction, the perspective is a little different and offers a different look at the forest and rugged terrain.

The trail comes to an end in the park's wooded campground. Though busy in the summer months, camping here can be low key in spring and fall, and the hiking trail is only one of several great trails in the area. See the hikes for Indian Springs Metropark and Highland State Recreation Area for more options nearby.

◁ *There are few straight paths at Pontiac Lake.*

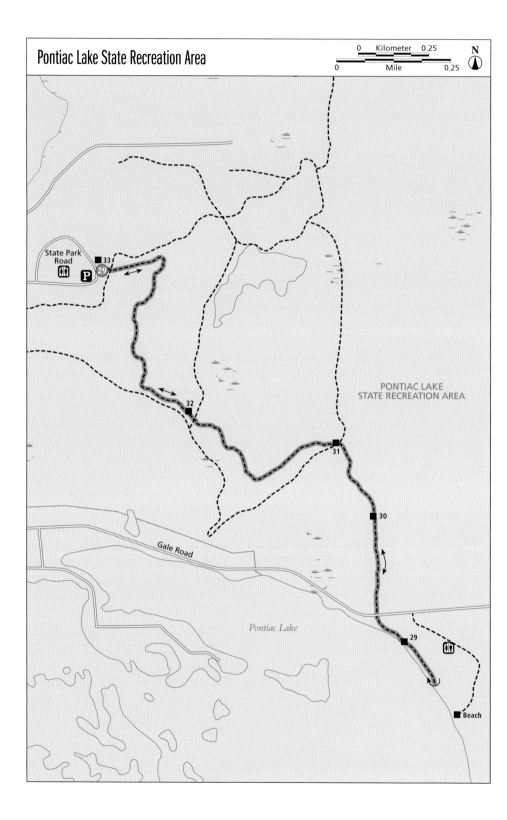

Pontiac Lake State Recreation Area

0   Kilometer   0.25

0   Mile   0.25

N

State Park Road

33

29

32

31

30

PONTIAC LAKE
STATE RECREATION AREA

Gale Road

Pontiac Lake

29

Beach

Miles and Directions

0.0 Start from trail marker 33, near Campsite 113. An equestrian trail crosses your path right at the start. Continue across the trail and into the woods.

0.3 Soon after the start of the hike, you come to the highest point on the trail. As you walk through the woods, the trail seems to be heading for a wall. While it's not all downhill after this, you are descending more than you are climbing.

0.5 Come to a T in the path; turn left. For the next 0.2 mile, you are on the equestrian trail.

0.7 At trail marker 32, the equestrian trail splits to the right and left. The hiking path continues straight ahead, which involves your taking a right and then a quick left.

1.2 Here at trail marker 31, an equestrian trail enters from the right and then in 30 yards splits off to the left.

1.4 After a stretch of open meadow, at trail marker 30 the path crosses a mountain bike trail.

1.7 The hike across the field is a straight shot to Gale Road. You cross the road here.

1.8 The trail ends at trail marker 29, on the edge of the Pontiac Lake beach area. Ahead you can see a wide lawn, picnic areas, restrooms, beach houses, and sandy beach. This is your turnaround point.

3.2 As you might expect from the long descent to the lake, the return trip is mostly uphill. There are a few doozies at the start, but the biggest climb begins less than 0.5 mile from the end of the line.

3.6 Like every out-and-back, this trail ends where it began, at trail marker 33.

Hike Information

Restaurants: Anthony's Pizza, 6301 Williams Lake Rd., Waterford; (248) 666-2399. To the uninitiated, Anthony's Pizza looks like every other party store in southeast Michigan—a place for beer, liquor, and snacks—but this joint serves up the best breadsticks and cheese dip around. They also serve pizza by the slice (they call them "squares"). Be sure to order your squares with sausage.

30 West Bloomfield Woods Nature Preserve

West Bloomfield Woods is 162 acres of prime real estate in the heart of the 'burbs set aside for the preservation of nature. From upland forest to wetlands, from the chirp of spring peepers to nesting great blue herons, the preserve offers an amazing escape from the suburban environment that surrounds it on all sides.

Start: Small parking lot off Arrowhead Road
Distance: 2.2-mile double loop
Hiking time: About 1 hour
Difficulty: Easy to moderate; some climbing, not much
Trail surface: Gravel
Best season: Summer
Other trail users: None
Canine compatibility: Leashed dogs permitted

Fees and permits: None
Schedule: Open 8 a.m.–dusk
Maps: Maps available on website; TOPO! CD: Michigan, Ohio, Indiana, disc 4
Trail contacts: West Bloomfield Parks and Recreation Commission, 4640 Walnut Lake Rd., West Bloomfield, MI 48323; (248) 738-2500; http://westbloomfieldparks.org/parks/2011TrailBrochure.pdf

Finding the trailhead: The preserve is in West Bloomfield Township, 25 miles northwest of Detroit. From the north and south you want to get on Orchard Lake Road. (That's exit 5 off I-696; Orchard Lake crosses Telegraph just south of Pontiac.) At the intersection of Orchard Lake Road and Pontiac Trail, drive west. At 1.6 miles turn left onto Arrowhead Road. The parking area for the woods is on your left, 0.3 mile from Pontiac Trail. The trailhead is just south of the parking area. GPS: N42 34.068' / W83 23.590'

The Hike

West Bloomfield Woods Nature Preserve is something special. The land was purchased by early settlers, who never ended up building on it. Later, around the turn of the last century, the land was purchased by the Ward family, who maintained its pristine nature as a sales tool. Preserving the woods, they added bridle paths, accessorized the forest with evergreens, and called it a community park—an attractive feature for those buying up waterfront property nearby. Then in the 1980s, when it seemed the value of the land couldn't be ignored by developers any longer, the city stepped in and arranged to purchase the property to create a preserve.

For a piece of land in a place like West Bloomfield to remain nearly in its natural state into the twenty-first century is truly amazing.

The preserve is only 167 acres, but the varied terrain gives it the feel of a much larger park. From swamps and streams to upland forest, there's a real sense of nature here. Tucked in as it is between a host of subdivisions, the trail skirts a few backyards as it goes. There are the usual distant sounds of traffic, but in a way these only heighten the sense of seclusion, of being somewhere not in the city.

A wide platform overlooks an algae-covered pond, which is full of wetland birds, amphibians, and other wildlife.

A hike at West Bloomfield Woods Nature Preserve is pretty straightforward. If you take a wrong turn, you will simply make a loop and arrive back where you began. The one exception is where the path crosses the West Bloomfield Trail. If you make a wrong turn onto this rail-to-trail project, you end up over by Haggerty Road.

The trail begins at the preserve entrance. A large sheltered information station across from the parking lot is your starting point; the path leads off to the right. After a short walk through the woods, you come to a wetland overlook. Spring peepers and wood frogs can fill the woods here with a chorus of croaks and chirrups. If you are patient you will see frogs, snakes, turtles, and any number of birds.

The side trail near the deck turnoff is the return path to the parking lot. Continue straight ahead for upland forest. After a nice climb and descent, the path passes a cedar swamp and then climbs again. To your left the land falls away. The stream you crossed earlier lies at the bottom of this narrow valley. The path curves around to the north, and you come to a second observation deck. The view of the forest here in the fall is impressive.

GREEN TIP:
Never let your dog chase wildlife.

MICHIGAN WADING BIRDS

The bird family with the scientific name Ardeidae includes bitterns, herons, and egrets. There are twelve species common to Michigan, but the most frequently sighted and talked about are the American and least bittern, the great blue heron, and the snowy egret.

AMERICAN AND LEAST BITTERN

The bitterns are the smallest and most elusive of the wading birds. The American bittern can get as long as 33 inches, but the least bittern averages 12 inches. Unlike the blue heron and the snowy egret, the bittern's color helps it blend into the marsh grasses. Its reaction to a threat is to try and make itself invisible.

GREAT BLUE HERON

The great blue heron can have a wingspan of more than 6 feet. You will often see these large birds standing near the shore in open water. If you chance to see one walking in the water, look to its feet, which can be 8 inches from tip to heel. Herons nest in trees, often dead trees found in wetlands. Their nests are about 3 feet across and are quite easy to spot if you're in the right place.

SNOWY EGRET

The snowy egret gets its name from its pure white plumage, easy to spot across a marsh or swamp. Smaller than great blue herons, and casting a narrower silhouette than swans, they're easy to identify from a distance. Snowy egrets nest in colonies, so you will often see them together in groups.

Crossing a bridge over the stream again, you soon come to a T in the path. To the right the path leads in the direction of Mirror Lake Drive. Turn to the left. Through the trees to the right (north of the trail) lies a small lake. The woods between you and the lake are prime nesting grounds for several species of wading bird, including the great blue heron. Hikers are especially prohibited from straying from the path at this point.

The rest of the trail is more of the same. You will come to the end of the south loop, turn right, and take the right at the observation deck. This leads across the West Bloomfield Trail, through a short patch of woods, and back to the parking lot.

To make the hike an educational experience, go to the preserve's website and download the self-guided tour map. This short brochure expounds on many of the park's natural features.

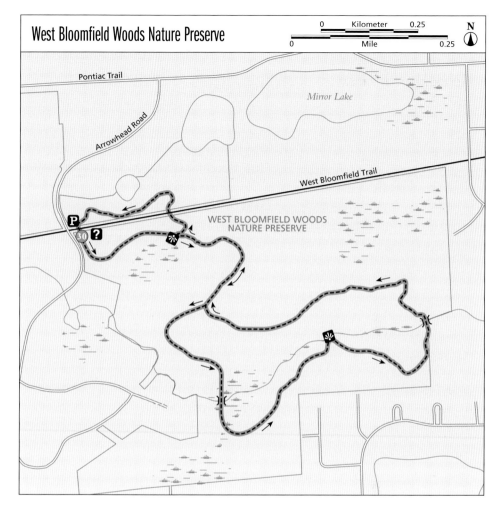

West Bloomfield Woods Nature Preserve

Miles and Directions

0.0 Start at the trailhead, just south of a small parking lot off Arrowhead Road. A large interpretive shelter offers information about the preserve.

0.2 A deck stretches out into an adjacent marsh. You can continue straight ahead or walk out to see what kind of wildlife you can spot. Look carefully; the most interesting things are often hidden in plain sight.

0.4 You will come back to this intersection at the end of the loop. For now, continue straight ahead.

1.0 The terrain in the preserve is surprisingly varied. The stream that passes through the woods has cut a deep valley, and from the observation deck here, you can get a better idea of what that looks like.

1.2 Continue across the bridge.

1.3 Come to a T in the path; turn left.

1.4 Signs on your right indicate that you are near a wading bird nesting area. Stay on the trail!

1.7 You've come full circle on the second loop. Turn right at the intersection.

2.0 Arrive back at the observation deck; turn right again and then cross the West Bloomfield Trail. You are now on the final short loop.

2.2 The hike ends at the southeast corner of the parking lot.

Hike Information

Local Events/Attractions: West Bloomfield Trail, West Bloomfield Parks and Recreation Commission, 4640 Walnut Lake Rd., West Bloomfield, MI 48323; (248) 738-2500; westbloomfieldparks.org. The West Bloomfield Trail is a rail-to-trail project that connects the West Bloomfield Woods Nature Preserve with Haggerty Road to the west and Inkster to the east.

31 Orchard Lake Nature Sanctuary

Surrounded by the palatial homes of Orchard Lake Village, Orchard Lake Nature Sanctuary preserves 50 acres of natural woodland on Orchard Lake. Though small—the sanctuary only has 1.5 miles of trails—the park offers a variety of natural settings, from views of the lake to a walk through tall trees to a prairie overflowing with flowers.

Start: North end of the sanctuary parking lot
Distance: 1.0-mile loop
Hiking time: About 30 minutes
Difficulty: Easy; very gentle loops with some stairs
Trail surface: Packed dirt
Best season: Summer
Other trail users: None
Canine compatibility: Dogs not permitted

Fees and permits: None
Schedule: Open dawn to dusk
Maps: Map posted at the trailhead; TOPO! CD: Michigan, Ohio, Indiana, disc 4
Trail contacts: City of Orchard Lake, 3955 Orchard Lake Rd., Orchard Lake, MI 48323; (248) 682-2400; cityoforchardlake.com/departments/nature_sanctuary.php

Finding the trailhead: The sanctuary is in Orchard Lake, approximately 25 miles northwest of Detroit. From the north and south you want to get on Orchard Lake Road. (That's exit 5 off I-696; Orchard Lake crosses Telegraph just south of Pontiac.) At the intersection of Orchard Lake Road and Pontiac Trail, drive west. The nature sanctuary is on your right, less than 1 mile from Orchard Lake Road. The trailhead is at the end of the parking lot. GPS: N42 34.406' / W83 22.591'

The Hike

Orchard Lake Village is named for the large lake that takes up 1.2 of the town's 4.1 square miles. In a county with a lot of lakes, Orchard Lake is a big one. Its 795 acres are second only to nearby Cass Lake, which tops 1,200. In the middle of the lake is Apple Island. When settlers came to this part of Michigan, they planted apple trees on the island and thus settled a score of place names in one swipe.

Since those early years of frontier living, the area has changed dramatically. Today Orchard Lake is surrounded by homes. In contrast to the sounds of wind in the trees and the occasional woodpecker, the summer air is now filled with the distant hum of traffic and the chainsaw buzz of motorboats and personal watercraft. There remains, however, a sanctuary from all this progress. Orchard Lake Nature Sanctuary straddles 50 acres between Orchard Lake and Upper Straits Lake. By way of the park's 1.5 miles of trails, you are quickly subsumed into the forest, leaving the traffic on Pontiac Trail behind.

Throughout the sanctuary there are reminders of where you are. On the far shore of Upper Straits Lakes, large houses sit all in a row, and the shoreline is dotted with

The small clearing at the center of the sanctuary is overflowing with summer flowers.

moored pontoon boats, motorboats, and personal watercraft. At several points the trail passes close behind a house, where landscaped backyards blend seamlessly into the sanctuary grounds. The property, however, remains secluded and makes for a perfect midsummer hike.

The hike begins in the gravel parking lot and heads north. Vines have been enjoying a carbon dioxide feast for quite a few years now, and the result is the Virginia creeper and poison ivy you see wrapped around the trees. In fact, there's a bit of poison ivy here, so be sure you know what it looks like. Or stay on the safe side—if it has "leaves of three, let it be." Take the first right, and the path heads east, just north of a small pond that stays out of view.

This is a good time to point out that the map at the trailhead seems to be in error on several points. Deeper in the park near the fishing dock, there's a map carved in marble and set in fieldstone. This is a much more accurate representation of the trails as they are in the sanctuary; unfortunately it's not terribly portable.

The path takes you through a forest of tall oaks. As it turns north and passes Orchard Lake, the tree fall has allowed for a great view of the water. There's a bench here if you want to stay and think on that for a bit. Turning back into the park, the trail eventually comes to the chalet. This open-air shelter is a great spot for getting out of the rain. The chalet marks a great meeting of trails. To the left, the path leads back to the parking lot. To the north is a walk through a mix of hardwoods and evergreens. Straight ahead the path passes through woodland prairie before descending toward Upper Straits Lake.

▶ **The SS. Cyril and Methodius Seminary on the northeast shore of Orchard Lake was once the Michigan Military Academy. In 1879 William Tecumseh Sherman (remember Sherman's march to Atlanta?) spoke to the graduating class. More than 10,000 people came to hear him give a version of his "War Is Hell" speech.**

The prairie is often full of blooming flowers, and it's not uncommon to see deer grazing near the edge of the woods. It's a short walk through the open field. Once back in the woods you come to the stone map mentioned earlier. From here the route takes us to the left (south), but not before you walk out to the fishing dock for a view of the lake. On weekday mornings water-skiers and motorboaters are rare, and the scene is peaceful.

The return path takes you through some wetlands. Though the trail is not always wet, a few boardwalks help during the soggy seasons. The trail then climbs a set of

Stone steps make the one climb on this loop a breeze.

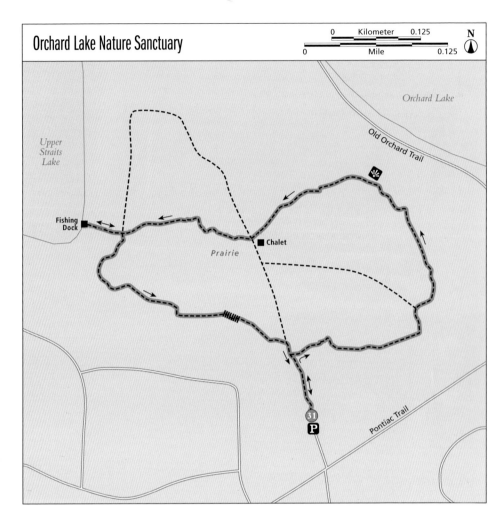

stone stairs set in the side of the hill and comes to an intersection with the sanctuary's central path. After turning right, you are back at the start.

During the humid evenings of summer, mosquitoes are plentiful at Orchard Lake Nature Sanctuary. In fact, they seem to live on the few hikers who wander into the park. Bug repellent is a big help—so is waiting until the nights are bit cooler.

Miles and Directions

0.0 Start from the trailhead at the north end of the parking lot. After about 100 yards, take the first trail on your right.

0.3 As the path heads east and then north, the side of the hill is cleared enough of trees to offer a stunning look at Orchard Lake and a bench to rest your weary feet.

0.4 Many paths meet here at the "chalet."

0.6 A stone marker here shows a map of the park. The trail straight ahead leads to a fishing dock on Upper Straits Lake. To the right is another loop through the north section of the nature area.

0.8 Stone stairs set in the hill help with the steep climb.

0.9 Turn right to head back to the parking lot.

1.0 The trail ends where it began.

Hike Information

Historical Tours: Greater West Bloomfield Historical Society, 3951 Orchard Lake Rd., West Bloomfield; (248) 757-2451; gwbhs.com. In addition to a museum (open the second Sunday of the month, 1–4 p.m.), the historical society leads tours to Apple Island. A pontoon boat takes you across, and the tour includes a look at the island's natural features and historic sites.

GREEN TIP:
If you see others littering, muster up the courage to ask them not to. (Or at least pick up after them.)

32 Lloyd A. Stage Nature Center

Rarely will you find a nature preserve surrounded by so much suburbia. Though hemmed in by subdivisions, the Lloyd A. Stage Nature Center makes a lot out of its nearly 100 acres. Two miles of trails wander through wetlands and wooded uplands along the Rouge River. The property is a gathering place for deer, which seem very comfortable with people passing through, and nearly 200 different bird species have been spotted here.

Start: Behind the nature center building
Distance: 1.5-mile double loop
Hiking time: About 40 minutes
Difficulty: Easy; well traveled and designed for accessibility
Trail surface: Wood chips and boardwalk
Best season: Summer
Other trail users: None
Canine compatibility: Dogs not permitted

Fees and permits: No fees or permits required
Schedule: Trails open dawn until dusk. (Trails are open even when the nature center is closed.)
Maps: TOPO! CD: Michigan, Ohio, Indiana, disc 4; maps available at the nature center
Trail contacts: Managed by the Troy Nature Society, 6685 Coolidge Hwy., Troy, MI 48098; (248) 688-9703; troynaturesociety.org

Finding the trailhead: The nature center is located in Troy, about 30 miles north of Detroit. Take the exit for Big Beaver Road, exit 69, off I-75 and head west 1.3 miles to Coolidge Highway. Turn right and drive 3.8 miles. The Nature Center will be on your left. The trails begin behind the center. When the center is open, you must go through the building. Otherwise, walk around back. GPS: N42 36.983' / W83 11.522'

The Hike

The Lloyd A. Stage Nature Center comprises 100 acres of natural space in the far northwest corner of Troy, one of the busiest suburbs in Metro Detroit. Of all the great things Troy is known for, natural space is not on the top of people's lists. After all, there are only 900 acres of it, accounting for 4 percent of the city. Therefore the nature center is even more special because of its uniqueness.

The Rouge River, more like a stream here, cuts through the nature center, flowing west to east. Given its size, the property has a surprising diversity of habitat. Just south of the nature center building is a large sugar bush—that is, a grove of sugar maples. Following the river upstream, the property flows through a rich marsh. To the south of that are forested uplands surrounding sedge meadows. And throughout the park you will find wildlife. The nature center maintains a host of nesting boxes that have attracted dozens of birds through the property.

The nature trails here are open every day from dawn until dusk. When the nature center is open, the gate to the trails is closed, meaning you have to pass through

A white-tailed deer peers through the trees at a passing hiker.

the nature center building to access the trails. The staff there is very well informed. Though the center is owned by the City of Troy, the day-to-day operations and natural education programming are in the hands of the Troy Nature Society. These are the people who clean out the nesting boxes, clear the trails, and take groups of children into the woods. They often have an interesting story to tell about wildlife at the center.

The nature center has four trails, none of them adding up to more than a mile. (In fact, only one is longer than 0.5 mile.) Together, however, they make for a great 1.5-mile hike. As you walk out the back door of the nature center building, a paved path leads back to a bridge. This is the start of the Sugar Maple Loop. The wide path is groomed with wood chips and bordered by branches. Following the loop you quickly come to the tail of the Blackbird Loop. Taking a right here, and another right soon after, you walk through a forest mixed hardwoods.

The understory here is mainly clear of vegetation. The forest floor is covered with dead leaves and broken twigs. Nesting boxes in the trees attract different songbirds. When you get to the boardwalk, you know the marsh is near. Turning right on the next trail puts you on the Fox Trail, which circles around to the north and takes you to a raised platform, the Marsh Tower, with its view of the cattails.

After the marsh tour the trail comes to a T on the Blackbird Loop. Turn right; the trail climbs into more woods above a long meadow to the east. These woods and the adjacent meadow are often teeming with white-tailed deer. The deer seem to have little aversion to people, and their comfort level with your presence might make you a bit uncomfortable, especially if you've ever seen a "when deer attack" video on YouTube. So far the deer have proved harmless, but don't get too friendly. They are still wild animals.

At the end of the Blackbird Loop, you cross over and complete the Sugar Maple Loop. The trail crosses over the Rouge River and then backtracks to the nature center building. Along the way you will pass the Sugar Shed, where staff members demonstrate how to make maple syrup in spring.

There's no charge to walk the nature center's trails. However, the Troy Nature Society is a not-for-profit organization. If you live nearby and appreciate the small bit of natural space they've been able to secure, stop by the nature center building and inquire about volunteering your time or making a donation.

Miles and Directions

0.0 Start from behind the nature center. A paved path leads back to the trails. Once across the bridge, take the path to the right.

0.1 For the first leg of the hike you are on the Sugar Maple Loop. At the first intersection, take a right for the Blackbird Loop.

0.2 Take another right to follow Blackbird in a counterclockwise fashion.

0.3 Turn right yet again. Crossing the bridge over the Rouge River puts you on the Fox Trail.

0.4 The nature center's outdoor classroom is on your left. The boardwalks along this stretch of trail tell you a little about how wet the ground is. To your south is a marsh on the Rouge River.

0.5 Bear left here for the short jaunt out to the Marsh Tower, an overlook that offers some height for your viewing. On the return, turn left.

0.7 You are now back on the Blackbird Loop. Turn right into the woods. For the next 0.25 mile the trail climbs very gently. The field and woods here are often packed with deer that seem to have little fear of humans.

1.0 Coming out of the woods, you are at the other end of the clearing. The trail descends a bit. On your left is the Bluebird Trail. This trail is named for the bluebirds that have taken up residence in the nature area's nesting boxes, many of which are in the clearing you just passed. Continue straight on the Blackbird Loop.

1.1 Take a right at the T to return to the Sugar Maple Loop.

1.2 You are back on the Sugar Maple Loop. Take the path to the right. This part of the trail, as the name suggests, passes through a grove of maple trees.

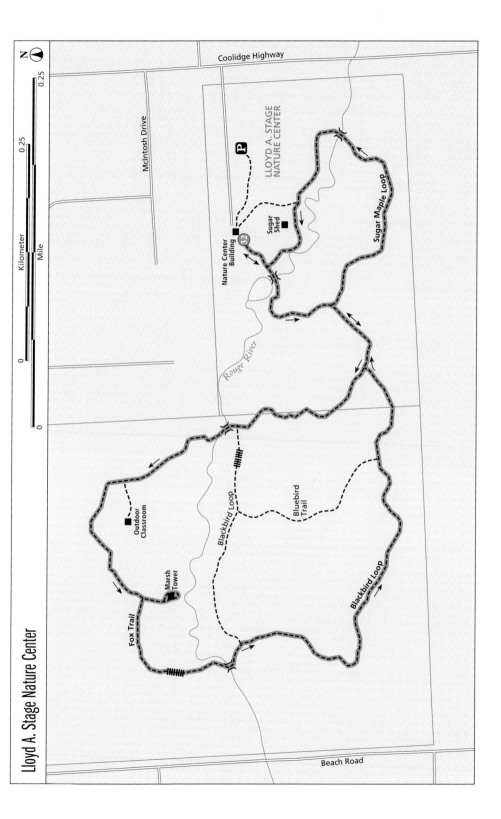

Lloyd A. Stage Nature Center

1.4 When the nature center building is closed, the path on the right here is your way back to the parking lot. When it's open, the path is blocked with a gate, and you must head back into the building to get back to your car.

1.5 The trail passes the Sugar Shed, where maple syrup is made in spring, and then ends behind the nature center building.

Hike Information

Restaurants: Hippo's Hot Dogs, 1648 Rochester Rd., Troy; (248) 524-9778; hippos hotdogs.com. So what that they serve their Coney dog on a poppy-seed bun? This is a Chicago-style hot dog joint, so you make allowances. Great dogs; great price. Just north of Maple on Rochester Road.

Kalamata Greek Grill, 3149 Crooks Rd., Troy; (248) 643-2600; kalamatagreek .com. You can't live in Detroit long before you dine at a Greek restaurant, which we call Coneys. In fact, most of the Coneys around were begun by Greek families. That's why the Coney on the corner serves gyros and baklava. And if it's gyros you crave, you have to get to Kalamata.

33 Stony Creek Metropark

Few parks can compare to Stony Creek Metropark when it comes to nature trails. Nearly half the park, from 28 Mile Road to 31 Mile, is laced with trails. The Habitat Trail near the nature center begins near Stony Creek but then widens out to include oak savanna and mixed hardwood forest. Using a short connector, you can also add a 3.5-mile loop north of Inwood Road.

Start: To the left (south) of the nature center
Distance: 2.7-mile loop
Hiking time: About 1 hour
Difficulty: Easy to moderate
Trail surface: Crushed rock, packed dirt
Best season: Summer
Other trail users: None
Canine compatibility: Leashed dogs permitted
Fees and permits: Metropark Motor Vehicle Permit required

Schedule: Apr–Oct 6 a.m.–10 p.m.; Nov–Mar 7 a.m.–8 p.m.
Maps: Maps available at park office and on website; TOPO! CD: Michigan, Ohio, Indiana, disc 4
Trail contacts: Stony Creek Metropark, 4300 Main Park Rd., Shelby Township, MI 48316; (586) 781-4242; metroparks.com

Finding the trailhead: The metropark is just north of Rochester, about 30 miles north of Detroit. From M-59 take exit 46 for Rochester Road north. Drive 2.5 miles to Avon Road. After 2.2 miles the road makes a 90-degree left and becomes Dequindre Road. Drive another 2.4 miles to Mount Vernon Road and turn right. From there signs lead you into Stony Creek Metropark. Once in the park, follow the signs for the nature center. The trailhead is to the left of the nature center when you're facing the entrance. GPS: N42 45.572' / W83 04.569'

The Hike

The two best-known Detroit-area metroparks are Kensington, near Milford, and Stony Creek, near Rochester. In some ways they are both very similar. Both are huge parks with a large central lake. Both also have a lot of developed recreation area. Stony Creek has two beaches, boat rentals, a golf course and a disc golf course, a paved bike path, mountain bike trails, cross-country skiing trails, and a nature center with interpretive nature trails. In fact, Stony Creek has the most expansive system of nature trails of all the Huron-Clinton Metroparks. In addition to several loops that begin near the nature center, the park offers the East Lake Trails and Osprey Trail along the road leading up to the nature center and more than 4 miles of trails to the north of Inwood Road.

The Habitat Trail is a 2.7-mile loop through the north part of the park near the park's nature center. To get an idea of how big Stony Creek actually is, note that the drive from the park entrance to the nature center is 4.5 miles. If you are looking for a parking area that doesn't commit you to nearly 10 miles of in-park driving, there is

▶ Follow Stony Creek south of the park. Where the creek crosses Tienken Road, you have the site of historic Stoney Creek Village, originally settled in 1823.

a lot outside the park on Inwood Road. It's intended for those hiking the Inwood Trails, but a connector path to the south links to the Habitat Trail. You'll still need a metropark sticker to park in the Inwood lot.

The trailhead for the Habitat Trail is to the south of the nature center—that's on your left as you approach from the parking lot. The path passes under a power line pylon and descends to a bridge that crosses Stony Creek. On the other side is a sign marking the start of the hike, pointing you to the right. The trail begins next to Stony Creek, but the two quickly part ways. After turning right at the first intersection (left is for the Landscape Trail) you will find yourself traversing a broad oak savanna (that is, a prairie with occasional oak trees).

The prairie is full of wildflowers in summer, including coneflower, milkweed, and black-eyed Susan. The prairie is also the kind of habitat that the Massasauga

Summer flowers bloom alongside the trail, especially at the north end of the loop.

From north to south, the metropark follows the curve of Stony Creek.

rattlesnake loves. Some interpretive signage along the way explains the snake. The takeaway is: Enjoy the flowers, keep on the path, and if you see a snake, don't mess with it.

The first bench you come to is under a large oak and offers a great view. The next bench, farther along, marks the trail that connects north with the Inwood Trails. Pretty soon you are in the woods, passing yet another bench. This loop appears to have a bench about every 0.2 mile, often placed in the most scenic spots.

The Habitat Trail is relatively level. There are some small gentle hills here and there, but you will do the most climbing at the beginning and end—marking the divide between uplands and the river lowlands. After crossing the path of the power lines, you enter woods with a high maple canopy. When you exit the woods, the meadow to your right is dotted with nesting boxes. To your left is a trail that offers a shortcut back to the start by way of the Landscape Trail. At some point you should plan on walking the Landscape Trail. The loop has a wooded kettle (always great for scenery) and goes around a vernal pond.

Continuing on the Habitat Trail, the path continues through wood and meadow, steadily climbing. At the next set of benches, you've reached the highest point of the hike. The route quickly descends to the level of the river, which it follows back to the north. Continuing on this trail would take you back to the trailhead near that

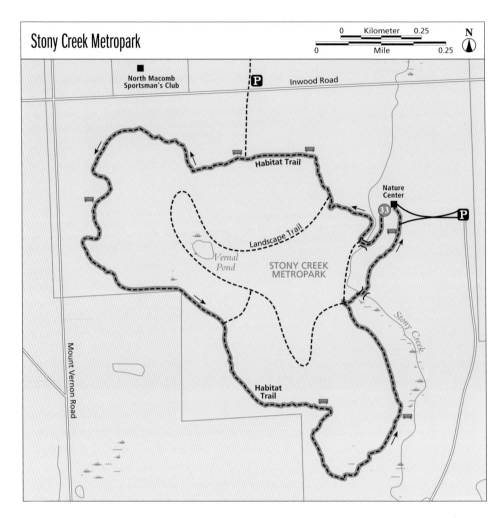

first bridge. About 250 yards before that point, however, a trail leads off to the right over another bridge. This is the continuation of the loop. The path cuts through the woods, passes one last bench, and deposits you back out in front of the nature center.

Miles and Directions

0.0 Start from the trailhead south of the nature center. Facing the entrance, follow the path to the left that passes underneath the power line pylon. The trailhead is down the hill and over the bridge. Turn right at the trailhead sign. To the left is the 0.5-mile Reflection Trail.

0.3 The trail follows along next to Stony Creek for a little bit and then heads into the woods. Turn right at the intersection. To the left is the 1.0-mile Landscape Trail.

0.4 Once into the wide-open oak savanna, pass a bench under an old oak as the trail turns westward. There are numerous benches along this loop—some in the trees, some overlooking prairie, and some on the water. All are situated for maximum scenic effect.

0.6 The bench here marks the connector trail that heads due north to the trails off Inwood Road.

1.1 The trail passes beneath the power lines and enters a forest of tall maple trees.

1.5 The connector trail on the left links up with the shorter Landscape Trail. Continue straight ahead for the planned loop.

1.8 Come to a bench at the bend in the trail. Just beyond this turn the trail descends 65 feet.

2.0 Stay to the left.

2.2 There are some benches here by the creek.

2.5 The loop continues with your turning right at this intersection and crossing the bridge over Stony Creek. (**Option:** Continuing straight puts you on the tail end of the Reflection Trail, heading back to the trailhead.)

2.6 The loop cannot end without one more bench. This one is in the woods just yards from the end of the hike.

2.7 The loop ends at the paved paths in front of the nature center.

Hike Information

Local Events/Attractions: Farmers' market, corner of East Third and Water Streets, Rochester; (248) 656-0060; downtownrochestermi.com/farmers-market. Held every Saturday morning from May through October.

Rochester Hills Museum, 1005 Van Hoosen Rd., Rochester Hills; (248) 656-4663; rochesterhills.org/index.aspx?NID=88. The museum is open to the public Friday and Saturday 1–4 p.m.

Restaurants: Rochester Mills Beer Co., 400 Water St., Rochester; (248) 650-5080; beercos.com. For great beer and an upscale pub menu, check out the Beer Company.

Sukho Thai, 54 West Auburn Rd., Rochester Hills; (248) 844-4800; sukhothai-thaicuisine.com. There are a lot of Thai places in Rochester. This one is a bit classier than the usual grab-and-go Thai carryout. Nice atmosphere, creative menu.

34 Wolcott Mill Metropark

In the dead center of Macomb County, Wolcott Mill Metropark has a 2.0-mile hiking trail that explores the North Branch of the Clinton River and nearby wetlands. The trail is located at the park's historic mill site. After the hike, take some time to visit the old mill and perhaps take part in one of the programs run on the weekends.

Start: Far north end of the Wolcott Mill Historic Center parking lot
Distance: 2.0-mile loop
Hiking time: About 1 hour
Difficulty: Easy; some elevation changes, but none too challenging
Trail surface: Grass and packed dirt
Best season: Summer and fall
Other trail users: None
Canine compatibility: Leashed dogs permitted

Fees and permits: Metropark Motor Vehicle Permit required
Schedule: Open dawn to dusk
Maps: TOPO! CD: Michigan, Ohio, Indiana, disc 4; maps available at park office and on website
Trail contacts: Administered by Stony Creek Metropark, 4300 Main Park Road, Shelby Township, MI 48316; (586) 781-4242; metroparks .com

Finding the Trailhead: The park is located northwest of Lake St. Claire, about 45 miles north of Detroit. From M-59 in Utica/Sterling Heights, take M-53 north 7.5 miles. Take the exit to continue north on Van Dyke. Cross 28 Mile Road; after 1 mile turn right onto 29 Mile Road. In just under 4 miles, turn left onto Kunstman Road. The entrance to the Wolcott Mill Historic Center is 0.5 mile up on your right. Follow the park road to where it ends at a parking lot. The trailhead is at the far end of the parking lot on the left. GPS: N42 45.938' / W82 55.738'

The Hike

Wolcott Mill Metropark comprises 2,625 acres on the North Branch of the Clinton River. The park has a working public farm, a historic mill site, a model plane airfield, equestrian trails, and a golf course. Each of these areas is its own site and has its own park entrance. The hiking trails are at the Wolcott Mill Historic Site.

Wolcott Mill is a gristmill built in 1847. The mill was in operation for 120 years. Not too many years after the mill was shut down in 1967, the dam that directed water toward the wheel was damaged. In other words, you don't come to Wolcott Mill to see grain turned to flour. But much of the equipment has been restored to give you a picture of the working mill during different periods. Other buildings on the site have different exhibits. These include a restored 1927 Model T dump truck, a barn museum, a garage, and a workshop.

The 2.0-mile Settlers Trail is the longest of the three loops at Wolcott Mill. The Mill Race and Mother Earth Trails both come in under a mile and are nice short hikes if you have young kids in tow. The Settlers Trail loop begins at the north end of

The historical attractions at Wolcott Mill mean there's plenty to do after your hike.

the parking lot for the Wolcott Mill Historic Center. As you face the brick walk to the historic mill site, the trailhead is on your left.

The trail begins as a level, wide path mown into the grass. The first 1.0 mile of the Settlers Trail runs parallel to the North Branch of the Clinton River. When the nearby river overflows its banks, this lowland area near the trailhead is inundated with water; even during a dry summer, the ground is damp. Walking through the grassy meadow, which becomes increasingly more wooded as you go, you can hear the rush of the river just through the trees. Two hundred yards from the trailhead, there's a bench near the water. Perhaps a little early in the trek for resting your feet, it would be a nice place for some peaceful contemplation.

The path overlaps the Mother Earth Trail—a 0.75-mile loop that explores the area's pre-European human history. A brochure at the mill tells the story of how Native Americans, the Potawatomi especially, lived on the land. Their moving from summer villages to winter lodges, girdling trees to create clearings for basic farming, and the traditions of hunting and gathering all tell a great story.

At 0.3 mile the Mother Earth Trail turns to the left and continues a separate loop. The Settlers Trail begins to climb, eventually reaching the top of a bluff 20 to 30

GREEN TIP:
When choosing trail snacks, go with unpackaged homemade goodies.

feet above the river. Here the trail goes from grassy to packed dirt to sand. For a time the trail and river separate, and the trees open up onto meadow. Eventually the river is on your right again.

Just shy of 1.0 mile into the hike, you come to a four-way intersection. The trail to your right descends steeply to the water. With a little peering, you can see that the way is blocked. Straight ahead is a field, which is often used by model airplane enthusiasts. Your path lies to the left (south). As you walk through a scrubby field, the trail passes a cement pad in the woods that marks the halfway point, but it's not until you cross the park road that you come to the "second half" of the hike.

Once you head back into the woods, firmly leaving the river behind, the wetlands begin. Several boardwalks make parts of this trek passable. Shortly the trail comes out of the woods at the south end of the parking lot and your hike is done.

In addition to the historic mill, the metropark's Farm Center is worth a visit. This is the only public farm in the state with all six of the heritage breeds of dairy cows, which are milked every day at 10 a.m.

Miles and Directions

0.0 Start from the trailhead at the north end of the parking lot (on your left facing the path to the historic center).

0.2 Come to a bench by the water, and enjoy the sounds of the South Branch of the Clinton River passing by.

0.3 To the left is the shorter Mother Earth Trail. Continue to the right for the Settlers Trail. After this point the trail is gravel and sand; you're now passing through woods.

0.7 Steady on: Trails seem to pass willy-nilly through this section of the path. Continue straight.

0.8 Come to a T; turn left. You soon come to a split. The right path cuts along the top of the ridge; the left—the more official of the two—takes a conservative route farther from the edge. They both meet back together after about 20 yards.

0.9 This intersection marks the farthest west the Settlers Trail will take you. The path down the hill to the right is a dead end. Straight ahead is the field used by model airplane aficionados. Your path lies to the left.

1.0 The halfway point is marked with a cement pad in the woods. Not an intentional trail marker, it's helpful nonetheless.

1.2 The path takes you across the main service road.

1.3 Reach the first of two lengthy boardwalks. This one is nearly 0.1 mile long.

1.5 Cross the power line path.

1.6 Come to the second boardwalk, this one slightly longer than 0.1 mile.

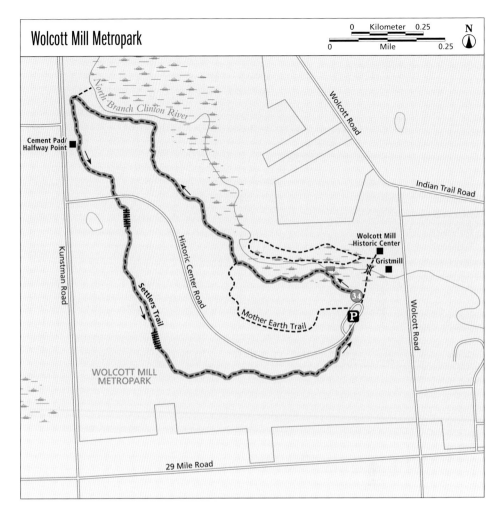

0 Kilometer 0.25

0 Mile 0.25

N

Wolcott Road

North Branch Clinton River

Cement Pad/
Halfway Point

Indian Trail Road

Wolcott Mill
Historic Center

Gristmill

Kunstman Road

Historic Center Road

Settlers Trail

Mother Earth Trail

WOLCOTT MILL
METROPARK

34

P

Wolcott Road

29 Mile Road

2.0 A three-way intersection indicates you're nearing the end. Turn left for the parking lot and the hike is done.

Hike Information

Local Events/Attractions: Westview Orchards, 65075 Van Dyke Rd., Washington Township; (586) 752-3123; westvieworchards.com. One of the nicer orchards in the area; in fall there's a ton of activities for the kids, not to mention great cider and doughnuts.

Wolcott Mill Civil War Skirmish, 64100 Kunstman Road, Ray; facebook.com/pages/Wolcott-Mill-Civil-War-Skirmish/242067112485822. Every year in October dozens of reenactors play out a Civil War skirmish at the Wolcott Mill Historic Center.

Wolcott Mill Metropark Farm Center, 65775 Wolcott Rd., Ray; (586) 752-5932; metroparks.com. The farm center puts on a country fair one weekend in June. Check the website for details.

35 Cranberry Lake Park

This little township park north of Rochester is easily overshadowed by nearby Addison Oaks. The two are so different; it's like comparing apples and orchards. As a result, you can expect to have this short nature hike all to yourself. The simple 1.0-mile-long loop can be expanded to 3.0 miles by parking in the Romeo Road lot and making it a lollipop route.

Start: Parking lot just west of historic farm site
Distance: 1.0-mile loop
Hiking time: About 30 minutes
Difficulty: Easy
Trail surface: Mowed grass, gravel two-track, wood chips
Best season: Best in the height of summer; nice in fall too
Other trail users: Cyclists and equestrians
Canine compatibility: Leashed dogs permitted

Fees and permits: No fees or permits required
Schedule: Open 30 minutes before sunrise to 30 minutes after sunset
Maps: Map available on website; TOPO! CD: Michigan, Ohio, Indiana, disc 4
Trail contacts: Charter Township of Oakland, Parks and Recreation Office, 4480 Orion Rd., Second Floor, Rochester, MI 48306; (248) 651-7810; oaklandtownship.org

Finding the trailhead: The park is about 7 miles north of Rochester. From M-59 take the Rochester Road exit, heading north. Drive 11 miles to Predmore Road and turn left (west). The park is 0.5 mile down the road, on the right (north) side. Parking is just west of the farm site; the trailhead is at the north end of the lot. GPS: N42 47.114' / W83 08.823'

The Hike

The village of Rochester enjoys a great balance. To the south is the best Metro Detroit has to offer—shopping, culture, etc. To the north you have the best of country living—a number of apple orchards, Addison Oaks county park, a couple state recreation areas, numerous nature areas, the Paint Creek Trail (which begins right in town), and the Stony Creek Metropark. Adding depth to this mix is the area's rich history and a group of people who are excited about preserving that history.

The historical and natural come together in a little township park just south of Addison Oaks. Cranberry Lake Park comprises 203 acres stretched between Predmore and Romeo Roads. Adjacent to the park is a 16-acre historic farmstead, Cranberry Lake Farm. Behind the farm a 1.0-mile-long trail loops through prairie, wetlands, and forest.

The loop begins in the parking lot and ends just to the east behind Cranberry Lake Farm. The trails at Cranberry Lake are a combination of mown paths, old gravel doubletrack, and trails groomed with wood chips. The main loop is about 1.0 mile

New England aster is just one of the flowers blooming in the park's many fields.

long, but by parking on Romeo Road and adding a long out-and-back, you can make this a 3.0-mile lollipop trek.

The first part of the trail passes through open field. Summer flowers like the ubiquitous goldenrod and Queen Anne's lace are often in bloom. The path quickly turns into the woods and, following an old shady drive, heads north. The path here is a worn gravel doubletrack, and one can almost imagine a farmer driving his Model A Ford pickup or perhaps a Ford 8N tractor following the ruts to the back end of a long-ago farm field.

The meadow at Cranberry Lake surrounds (and is in places surrounded by) wetlands. So when the path leaves the trees heading east, you are walking a relatively narrow strip of dry land. After you turn again and head south, the path will cross a few wetlands. Trees along the trail are few here, and much of the trail at Cranberry Lake is out in the open. Sunny days require sunscreen, but even overcast days in summer can result in a burn if you're not prepared.

▶ **In the early part of the twentieth century, Detroit businessmen bought farms north of the city and used them as country retreats.**

Addison Oaks, the 1,140-acre county park to the north on Romeo Road, recently built a connector path that links its trail system with the trails at Cranberry Lake. The

The paths at Cranberry Lake are not the typical well-trod dirt trails.

trails here are open to mountain biking, but level paths mean they're seldom used for this purpose. Perhaps the connector will bring more bike traffic through; perhaps not.

As you walk through the meadow, the loop ends behind the historic Cranberry Lake Farm. Also known as the Axford-Coffin Farm, the main building was built in the 1840s by John Axford. It is a classic example of a nineteenth-century Greek Revival farmhouse. The farm was then sold to Jacob Kline, whose family held onto the property for more than seventy-five years but then lost it to foreclosure during the Great Depression. In the 1930s Detroit businessman Howard Coffin bought the farm as a family retreat. He added a bulky stone fireplace sometime before he sold the property in the 1950s. Oakland Township acquired the property in 1996 and has been busy making it into a historic community center. The Flumerfelt Barn, a recent addition to the property, was built in the late 1800s and moved here by the Oakland Township Historical Society in 2004.

Miles and Directions

0.0 Start from the parking lot, just west of historic Cranberry Lake Farm. The trailhead is at the north end of the lot, impossible to miss.

0.1 After walking through a prairie, turn left when you come to the first trail. Then take a right on the doubletrack drive that heads due north.

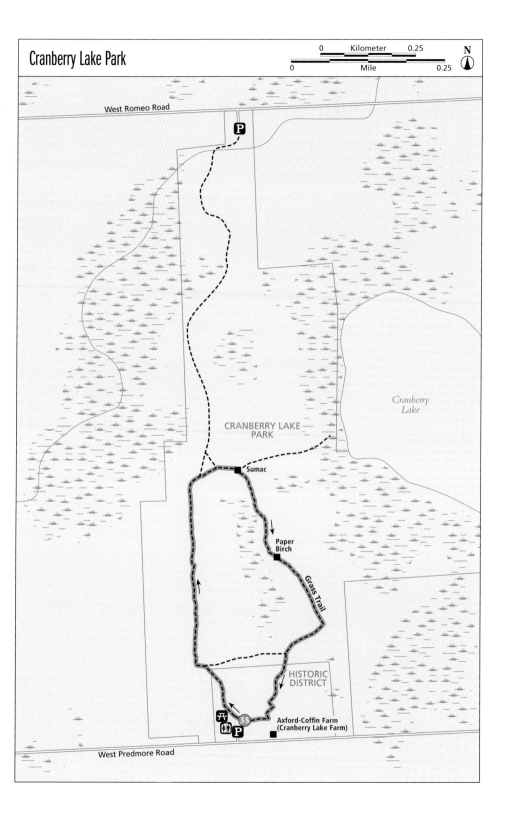

0.4 Before you reach the end of the drive, a path branches off to the right. Follow this into the clearing. Halfway across the clearing, a path enters from the left. This leads to the parking area on Romeo Road. Continue straight ahead.

0.5 Ahead, the trail continues in the direction of Cranberry Lake, though it stops short of a lake view. Instead turn right. Now heading south, the path passes through a small grove of sumac.

0.7 Cross a boardwalk; there's an impressive stand of paper birch to the left.

0.8 A trail comes in on your right; take it.

0.9 After just a short ways you come to a small outbuilding, which means it's time to turn left.

1.0 After you pass a few more outbuildings, the trail ends behind the historic farm.

Hike Information

Local Events/Attractions: Rochester Cider Mill, 5125 North Rochester Rd., Rochester; (248) 651-4224; rochestercidermill.com. The Rochester Cider Mill has been around since the early 1980s, but the family has been pressing apples for generations. This is a great source for unpasteurized cider (and, of course, there's no excuse for passing on their excellent cider doughnuts).

36 Addison Oaks County Park

Addison Oaks has trails for everyone—equestrians, mountain bikers, hikers, and in-line skaters. (Skaters, in particular, will appreciate the 2.5-mile paved loop around Buhl Lake.) Some trails are designated for horses and hikers, others for hikers and bikers, and a handful for all three. That means you have to take note of trail signage and stay alert at bends in the path. You never know what might be coming around the corner.

Start: Parking lot just north of the summer checkpoint
Distance: 3.6-mile loop
Hiking time: About 1 hour, 15 minutes
Difficulty: Easy to moderate
Trail surface: Some pavement, gravel two-track, packed dirt
Best season: Best in the height of summer; nice in fall too
Other trail users: Cyclists and equestrians
Canine compatibility: Dogs permitted on leashes no longer than 6 feet

Fees and permits: Daily vehicle permit (reduced price for Oakland County residents)
Schedule: Open daily 7 a.m.–9 p.m. during camping season; otherwise 8 a.m.–30 minutes past sunset
Maps: Map available on website; TOPO! CD: Michigan, Ohio, Indiana, disc 4
Trail contacts: Addison Oaks, 1480 West Romeo Rd., Leonard; (248) 693-2432; oakgov .com/parks/parksandtrails/Addison-Oaks/ Pages/default.aspx

Finding the trailhead: The park is about 7 miles north of Rochester. From M-59 take the Rochester Road exit, heading north. Drive 11.5 miles to West Romeo Road and turn left (west). The park is 1.7 miles down the road, on the right (north) side. Parking is just past the contact station (open in the summer), and you follow the paved path west to the trailhead. GPS: N42 48.149' / W83 10.115'

The Hike

Addison Oaks has something of a split personality. Outdoor enthusiasts know the park for its campground, lakes, picnic areas, and extensive network of trails. (The swimming beach has been closed until further notice.) Other visitors are more familiar with the park because they've attended one of the countless weddings held at the historic Buhl Estate.

The estate itself goes back to 1927, when much of the property that is now Addison Oaks was bought by Lawrence and Cora Buhl. Lawrence was the founder of the Buhl Aircraft Company (1925–1933). Robert O. Derrick designed the home to look like an English Tudor cottage. Wood from area barns was used give the home authenticity. In 1965, the property was purchased by Dr. D. J. Boucher. He eventually established the Tudor Hills Gun Club and Game Preserve. By 1969, however, there wasn't enough money to keep the venture going, and the property was acquired

The trails at Addison Oaks are prone to flooding in the spring.

by the Oakland Parks and Recreation Commission.

Today, the estate is managed by Oak Management and is used to host events. Occasionally, Oakland County Parks will offer guided tours of the estate, and visitors have a chance to learn the building's history and how it has changed over the years.

For outdoor recreation, Addison Oaks is one of the finest parks in the county. There are trails here for mountain biking, horseback riding, and hiking or trail running. Some of the trails are designate for one use. Other trails are open to two different groups of users. And others are open to all users. On the map it can look confusing, but once your feet are traipsing the trails, the signage is pretty clear. Just be aware: Sometimes trails overlap for a bit. You want to keep an eye (and an ear) out for folks on bikes. They can approach quickly from behind or ahead just beyond that next blind curve.

While all the trails at Addison Oaks are worth a hike, the one outlined here has a nice mix of terrain and offers over 4 miles of walking that never gets boring. There are hills and dips, piney woods and maple forest, and open prairie. In the spring, trails might be blocked by expanding vernal ponds. In the fall, the leaves that shaded hikers all summer turn to pleasing shades of burnt orange. In the winter, you can always snowshoe.

This route starts near the park entrance and winds through the west side of the property. To the west, the trails are bound by Lake George Road. To the south, our route stops where Romeo Road used to continue west to Lake George. (A portion of that road was decommissioned when the park acquired land south along Kline Road.) If you like history, the decommissioned section of Romeo Road is still visible if you know what to look for. Today it looks like another trail—maybe a little wider and straighter than the others in the park. This trail, however, is lined by old trees and as you walk along, a careful eye will see evidence of roadbuilding.

▶ **Much of Addison Oaks was once part of the Buhl Estate. In the late 1920s, a number of local barns were deconstructed so that the architect would have aged hand-hewn beams to give the English Tudor–style home an authentic look.**

There are hiking trails south of here—in particular, the E loop—but we're sticking with the D loop for this trip. Once into the woods, the trail rises dramatically for southeast Michigan. The first section you

When the leaves are down, you can see the Buhl Estate from the trails.

hike is a wide two-track road, mostly gravel, used by park maintenance. As you leave the main path at marker 17, the trail descends into woods before you come out into a large open field. This section is followed by a long winding path through the woods. On the map it looks like you're pacing through the forest, but it doesn't feel that way on the ground. The rolling terrain keeps the route interesting, and though there are no huge hills, your legs will get a bit of a workout.

Eventually the route spits you back out on that maintenance road, which you follow to the trailhead.

Miles and Directions

0.0 Start from the parking lot near the contact station, next to Adams Lake.

0.0 The trail officially begins west of the park entrance, a two-track gravel road, winding up into the woods.

0.3 Continue straight ahead through this intersection of trails.

0.4 At trail marker 17 turn left and follow the path south into the woods.

0.6 At trail marker 16 the trail forks. Take the left path.

0.6 Trail marker 18 sits at the northwest corner of a large field. Continue south, staying at the edge of the clearing.

Addison Oaks County Park

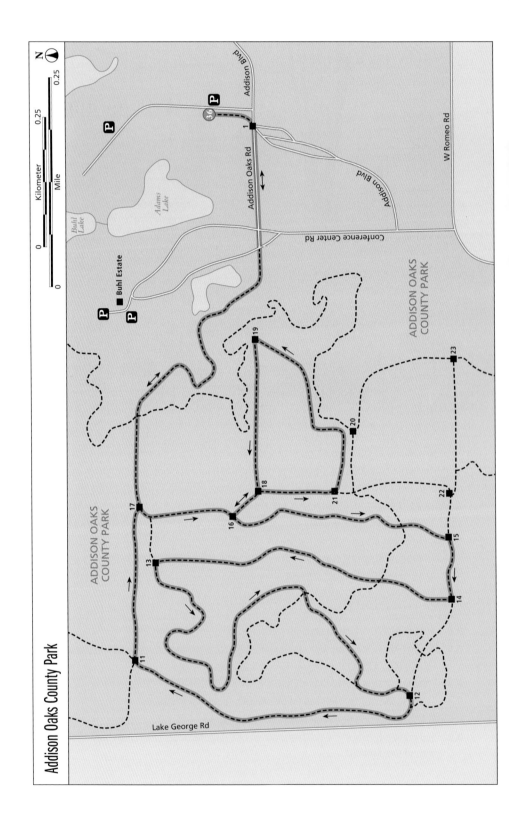

In the winter, this route is used by fat-tire cyclists.

0.7 Continue past trail marker 21, banking east.

1.0 The trail continues east and north to trail marker 19 at the northeast edge of the field. Turn west back to markers 18 and 16.

1.2 At marker 16, take the path not taken earlier and turn south.

1.5 Turn right at marker 15, follow the road a short way to marker 14.

1.6 Turn back into the woods at trail marker 14.

1.9 At trail marker 13 you can take a short connector to the right and shorten the loop significantly. But there are more hills and trees ahead.

2.6 Turn right at trail marker 12; the path here runs parallel to Lake George Road for a good stretch.

2.9 At trail marker 11 turn right, to the east, and follow that path back to the start.

3.6 Return to the trailhead.

Hike Information

Local Events/Attractions: Upland Hills Farm, 481 Lake George Rd., Oxford; (248) 628-1611; uplandhillsfarm.com. Upland Hills Farm offers a host of programs that expose school kids to nature. They are open to the public designated Sundays in the summer, and they put on a great fall festival for the whole family.

37 Bald Mountain State Recreation Area

For a long hike with lots of trees and hills, there are few spots in southeast Michigan that can beat the North Unit trails at Bald Mountain in Lake Orion. The two loops, split by Harmon Road, take in a half dozen lakes and ponds and skirt some wetlands (but not too close). For an easier hike, just tackle one of the loops—both start from the same parking area.

Start: South end of the parking lot on Harmon Road, where it meets Predmore

Distance: 6.7-mile double loop

Hiking time: About 2.5 hours

Difficulty: Difficult; lots of hills

Trail surface: Packed dirt

Best season: Fall

Other trail users: Mountain bikers

Canine compatibility: Leashed dogs permitted

Fees and permits: Recreation Passport required

Schedule: Open 8 a.m.–dusk

Maps: TOPO! CD: Michigan, Ohio, Indiana, disc 4; maps available at park office and on website

Trail contacts: Bald Mountain State Recreation Area, 1330 East Greenshield Rd., Lake Orion, MI 48360; (248) 693-6767; michigan.gov/baldmountain

Special considerations: This trail passes through state land open to hunting. Wear bright orange clothing during hunting season.

Finding the trailhead: The hike starts in Lake Orion, approximately 35 miles north of Detroit. From M-24 in Lake Orion, take Clarkston Road 2.2 miles east to Adams Road. Turn left (north) and drive 0.5 mile to Stoney Creek Road. Turn right and then make a quick left onto Harmon Road. The trailhead is 0.5 mile north on the left. The trailhead is at the south end of the parking lot. GPS: N42 46.951' / W83 11.819'

The Hike

To the east and south, the village of Lake Orion is surrounded by the Bald Mountain State Recreation Area. The 4,637-acre park is divvied up into three units. The heart of the park is the South Unit. The park office is there, and around Upper and Lower Trout Lakes you will find a beach, a boat launch, and picnic areas. Trails here connect to the Paint Creek Trail, a rail-to-trail path that begins all the way down in Rochester and connects with the Polly Ann Trail to the north. The little-visited West Unit, on the other end of the spectrum, is primarily farmland.

The North Unit is where you find the park's best trails, and not just for hiking. Twenty years ago it was hard to find decent mountain bike trails in southeast Michigan. Since then land managers have worked with the mountain bike community and developed some excellent trail systems. These include the trails at Pinckney Recreation Area near Ann Arbor and the outstanding Holly-Holdridge Mountain Bike Trail, which is part of Holly State Recreation Area. Here in Lake Orion there are the

A family makes for the hills, surrounded by the sounds of frogs in the nearby wetlands.

three lovely loops in the North Unit at Bald Mountain, and they are not solely for cycling.

Two of the North Unit loops, the White and Blue Trails, lie west of Harmon Road. The third, the Orange Trail, is to the east. From a parking area on Harmon Road where it meets Predmore Road, you can access them all. Bikers here share the path with hikers. Mountain bikers seem to prefer the Orange Loop, and most ride on weekends. During the week, and earlier in the season when the trails can get damp, you tend to see fewer cyclists on the trail. Even when you do, the interaction is usually positive.

Bald Mountain Recreation Area has over 4,637 acres of rolling hills. The terrain here can be described as nothing less than rugged, and the backcountry portions of the North Unit are the most rugged of all. Your hike begins at the parking area on Harmon. You will head south and work your way clockwise around Heart and Carpenter Lakes. This loop is actually two trails. Beginning on the White Trail at trail marker 3, you will jump on the Blue Trail, which meets back up with the original loop a bit later on.

This section of the hike offers the steepest climbs. In fact, even though it's a little shorter than the Orange Trail, the White-Blue Loop has more accumulated elevation gain, climbing 360 feet (and descending 350 feet) in 3.1 miles. The back side of

ALLEGHENY MOUND ANT

How many people live in your house? Two? Four? Eight? The mounds you see alongside the trail are home to the Allegheny mound ant, and a mound 19 inches tall may house 250,000 of the little buggers. The ants build their mounds in fields and clearings, and as big as they look from the outside, they are downright huge on the inside. Some nests have galleries that go down 6 feet below the surface.

The mound ant is a field ant and is common across most of the United States. The ants like their nests out in the open. They're taking care of eggs in there, so they need the sun to heat the mound. That means shade is the enemy. In order to clear out vegetation, the ants have evolved this neat little trick: They bite neighboring trees and shrubs and inject a little formic acid into the wound. The formic acid goes to work and the plant dies. A few bites are usually enough, though larger trees might require many treatments.

Of course this clearing of vegetation makes the ant a nuisance to a lot of people. Orchards and Christmas tree nurseries, for example, have room between the rows for mounds, and the ants aren't particular about what kind of tree they're trying to take down. As a native species, the Allegheny mound ant has struck a deal with the local ecology. It knows the boundaries; people just sometimes change the rules.

You can recognize the mound ant by its unique coloring. It looks like a reddish ant wearing black pants. And did you know that an Allegheny mound ant colony can have more than one queen? This is pretty unusual among ants. The aforementioned 19-inch mound might have a thousand queens cranking out brand-new Allegheny mound ants.

As you're walking through the woods, the ants pose no danger. Take note, however: It's best not to disturb their mounds. These ants are known to "aggressively defend" a disturbed mound, and while the formic acid in their bite won't kill you, it certainly gives their bite a little something extra.

Carpenter Lake is wetlands, and where the trail approaches the north end of the lake, you get a scenic look at cattails and the marsh. Still in the woods, you connect back up with the White Trail. After a short stretch to the north, the trail heads almost due east back to Harmon Road.

Once across the road, the Orange Trail loops around West and East Graham Lakes, ducking under Prince Lake and Duck Pond. After a long stretch of rolling forested hills, the trail hits a low spot running along the eastern edge of East Graham Lake. In spring, and after a rain, the mud here becomes nearly impassable.

The combination of trails, connectors, and spurs means you can turn this one hike into three. There's parking at the northwest corner of Predmore and Lake George Roads. A short spur here makes the Orange Trail a nice lollipop loop. The same can be done from the parking area on Miller Road, where you have your choice of a white lollipop or a blue one.

> Mountain bikers should always give you a heads-up when they pass from behind. Typically they will indicate the side on which they plan to pass by saying, for example, "On your left!"

Miles and Directions

0.0 Start from the trailhead at the parking lot on Harmon Road, where it meets Predmore. The trailhead (trail marker 1) is to the south down a grassy slope.

0.1 Trail marker 2 is for the side trail on the left, which cuts east and north and connects with the Orange Trail. Continue straight.

0.2 The mixed hardwood forest is beautiful along this stretch. From the trail you can see one of the park's rental cabins.

0.5 The White Trail continues straight ahead. Instead turn left to follow the Blue Trail.

0.8 The steepest climb of the hike begins with the steepest drop. The path can be tricky—loose stones, etc.

1.2 Pass trail marker 4. Continue straight ahead.

1.5 Bear to the left.

1.6 Bear to the right.

1.7 To your right there's a scenic look at the marsh that connects Chamberlain Lake to the north with Carpenter Lake to the south.

2.1 The Blue Trail ends at trail marker 5. There's a bench where the path meets up with the White Trail. Turn left.

2.3 An unofficial trail to the left leads to a parking area on Miller Road, just east of downtown Lake Orion. Turn right.

3.1 At trail marker 6 continue straight to cross the road. When you come to marker 7, turn left. You're now on the Orange Trail.

3.7 Trail marker 8 marks a trailhead on Miller Road.

4.1 Stop at marker 9 for a view of Prince Lake.

4.4 At marker 10 a really short side trail moves off to the left.

4.5 At marker 11 the short side trail returns to the path.

5.1 At marker 12 you will find the parking lot on Lake George Road.

5.5 A connector trail on the left at trail marker 13 leads down to the parking lot on Predmore, at the east end of the park. Continue straight.

6.0 Around the 6.0-mile mark, the trail reaches a low point. Wet weather means a muddy hike.

6.2 At marker 14 the trail crosses the drive for parking on East Graham Lake.

6.3 There's another side trail at marker 15. Just keep going.

6.6 You are back at marker 7. Turn left, cross the road, and at marker 6 turn left again.

6.7 The trail ends at the north end of the parking lot.

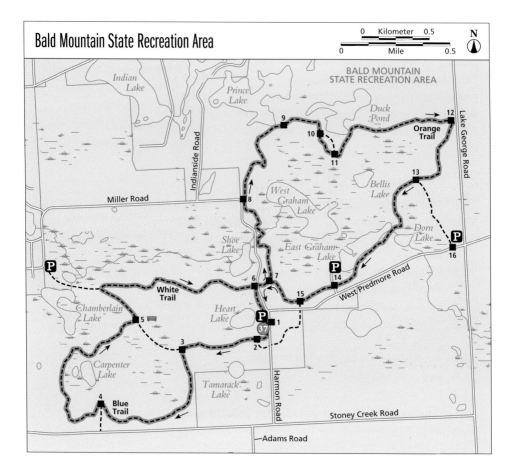

Hike Information

Restaurants: Sagebrush, 28 South Broad St., Lake Orion; (248) 693-0100; mysage brushcantina.com. The original Sagebrush burned down several years ago, but Lake Orionites would not be denied their favorite restaurant. This is perhaps the most popular dining in town, serving Mexican with a touch of Tex-Mex.

Palazzo di Bocce, 4291 South Lapeer Rd., Lake Orion; (248) 371-9987; palazzo dibocce.com. The tagline at Palazzo di Bocce is "Eat Italian . . . Play Bocce!" That about sums it up. This fine Italian eatery has regulation bocce courts spread throughout.

38 Independence Oaks County Park

Just a few miles north of the quaint village of Clarkston, Oakland County maintains more than 1,200 acres of park around Crooked and Upper Bushman Lakes. The park is defined by its glacial features—rolling moraines and low outwash plains—and the wetlands here are the headwaters of the Clinton River. Begin the hike near the nature center, and follow the trail through the woods to some of the highest points in the area.

Start: Northwest corner of the nature center parking lot

Distance: 1.8-mile loop

Hiking time: About 45 minutes

Difficulty: Easy to moderate hike; an easy trail with several steep climbs

Trail surface: Packed dirt, gravel

Best season: Spring through fall; trails groomed for cross-country skiing in winter

Other trail users: None on unpaved trails

Canine compatibility: Dogs permitted on leashes no longer than 6 feet

Fees and permits: Daily vehicle permit (reduced price for Oakland County residents)

Schedule: Open daily, dawn to dusk

Maps: Map available at the contact station when you first drive into the park; TOPO! CD: Michigan, Ohio, Indiana, disc 4

Trail contacts: Independence Oaks, 9501 Sashabaw Rd., Clarkston, MI 48348; (248) 625-0877; oakgov.com/parks/parksandtrails/Independence-Oaks/Pages/default.aspx

Finding the trailhead: The park is in Clarkston, about 40 miles northwest of Detroit. From I-75 take exit 89 at Sashabaw Road and drive north. Independence Oaks is less than 2.4 miles north of the interstate and 1.4 miles past the light at Clarkston Road, on the west side of the road. Once in the park, follow the signs for the nature center. The trailhead is at the northwest corner of the nature center parking lot. GPS: N42 46.87' / W83 23.747'

The Hike

Like many of the hikes in this book, the rugged and varied terrain of Independence Oaks is a bit unexpected. Morning commuters wending their way down Sashabaw Road on a weekday morning may little realize how big the park really is, and its varied terrain may be a total unknown. Even many of the folks who pack the park beach in summer, holding family reunions and graduation parties on the tended grounds, little suspect that just across Crooked Lake wait rolling moraines, tall shady woodlands, and forested wetlands full of peepers.

Other Oakland County parks feature more organized recreation—golf courses, water parks, BMX racing—but Independence Oaks is more about nature. An education in the ecological qualities of the park begins at the Wint Nature Center. Hands-on exhibits are a great way for kids (and adults) to learn about the park's more interesting inhabitants, such as the Michigan (Massasauga) rattler and the newly returned bluebird.

For a while bluebirds were pretty rare at Independence Oaks (as they were across the Midwest). An aggressive nesting box strategy has reversed the negative trend here somewhat, and the River Loop hike offers opportunities for birders to catch a glimpse of this treasured songbird. Located on the east side of Crooked Lake, the River Loop passes over the Clinton River twice, crossing through the grassy outwash plain.

West of Crooked Lake, the park's terrain changes dramatically. Thousands of years ago a retreating glacier left behind hills of stones and dirt. When pieces of the glacier broke off, they hit the ground (with a thud, presumably), creating a hole that was eventually filled by the melting ice. This is how we explain the glacial moraines and kettle ponds you find at Independence Oaks today.

Three trails wind through this section of the park. The Rockridge Loop is mapped out here, but two others are popular with hikers as well. At more than 3.0 miles, the Springlake Loop is the longest of the bunch. Hikers can add the Ted Gray Loop (the

Independence Oaks is graced with prairies and woodland.

Turkeys are a common sight at the park.

shortest of the three) to the Springlake Loop for a combined 4.1 miles. This would be the most challenging walk in these woods. Not only is the route longer but the climbs are steeper and the trails more uneven than the Rockridge trail.

The Rockridge Loop features some steep climbs, but while half the loop climbs forested hills, the other half follows the lakeshore. All told, it comes in under 2.0 miles. The paths are wide and relatively smooth. A highlight of this route is the wildlife-viewing platform near the halfway point. The view from the top is impressive and in the fall offers a sweep of autumn color. In fact, fall is one of the best times to visit Independence Oaks. The falling leaves create a carpet of yellows and reds that mirror the colors above.

One of the reasons Independence Oaks offers such wide and smooth trails is that the trail system is groomed in winter for cross-country skiing. Hikers will see signage along the trail that indicates direction, such as "One Way" and "Hill Bypass." These are intended to facilitate orderly skiing. Though a "hill bypass" might be quite comfort-ing for a weary visitor, there's no need for hikers to pay attention to these directions.

The hike begins near the nature center and quickly dives into the woods. After 1.0 mile or so of hilly terrain and the climb to the observation tower, tired legs can take comfort in the relatively level path along Crooked Lake back to the parking lot. Take a moment to walk out onto the fishing pier. Across the water you just might

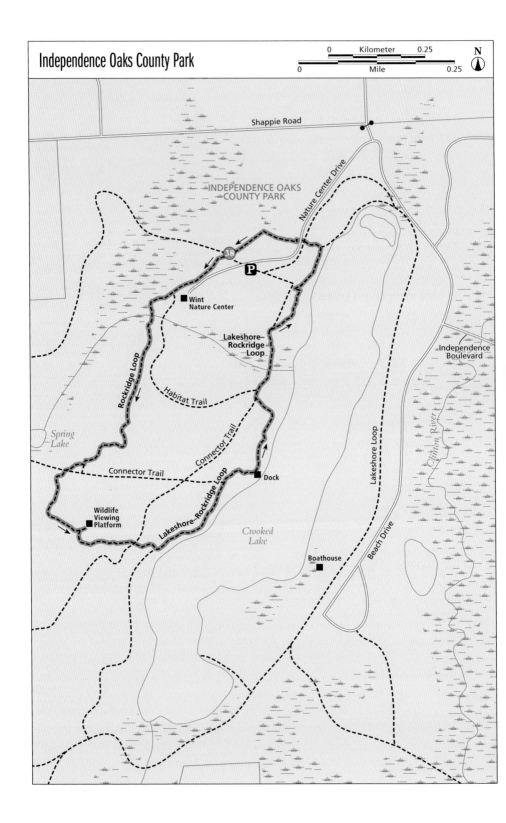

Independence Oaks County Park

| 0 | Kilometer | 0.25 |
| 0 | Mile | 0.25 |

N

Shappie Road

INDEPENDENCE OAKS COUNTY PARK

Nature Center Drive

38

P

Wint Nature Center

Lakeshore–Rockridge Loop

Rockridge Loop

Habitat Trail

Independence Boulevard

Spring Lake

Connector Trail

Connector Trail

Lakeshore Loop

Clinton River

Wildlife Viewing Platform

Lakeshore–Rockridge Loop

Dock

Crooked Lake

Boathouse

Beach Drive

see a sunbather looking back, wondering what all the fuss is about over there "in the woods."

Miles and Directions

0.0 Start from the west end of the parking lot for the Wint Nature Center.

0.15 Arrive at intersection with the nature center's Habitat Trail (to the left).

0.45 A connector trail here bypasses the hill ahead.

0.5 The connector trail returns to main path.

0.7 The wildlife viewing platform is on your left.

0.8 Pass the Connector Trail, then turn left onto the Lakeshore/Rockridge Loop.

1.0 Another connector trail enters on the left.

1.1 The dock on the lake to your right is for fishing.

1.3 This crazy intersection has paths leading off in all directions. Left heads back to the nature center. Straight ahead is the parking lot. The Lakeshore/Rockridge Loop follows the shoreline northward and around to the right.

1.5 Say goodbye to the Lakeshore Loop; turn left.

1.6 The trail crosses a bike path and the road you drove in on. Most folks give up here when they see their car in the nearby parking lot. Obsessive types continue following the path as it cuts behind the other side of the parking lot.

1.8 The trail ends back at the nature center parking lot.

Hike Information

Local Events/Attractions: Cook's Farm Dairy, 2950 East Seymour Lake Rd., Ortonville; (248) 627-3329. Bring a fascination for cows, a tolerance for the unique smells of a dairy farm, and an appetite for the best ice cream you'll have this summer. Just also be sure to bring cash, because they don't take credit cards.

DTE Music Theatre, 7774 Sashabaw Rd., Clarkston; (248) 377-0100; dteenergy musictheatre.org. For locals the DTE Music Theatre will always be called Pine Knob—its name for thirty years, but whatever the name, it is one of the best places in the Midwest to enjoy a summer concert.

Restaurants: Union Woodshop, 18 South Main St., Clarkston; (248) 625-5660; unionwoodshop.com. Building on the success of the Clarkston Union—an upscale neighborhood restaurant located in a former church building in the middle of town—the Woodshop specializes in barbecue and boasts a decent beer list. Kid Rock is a local, and his beer, American Badass Beer, is a hometown favorite.

GREEN TIP:
Hiking and snowshoeing are great carbon-free winter activities!

39 Ortonville State Recreation Area

One of Oakland County's best fall hikes, Ortonville Recreation Area offers two official loops for hikers or, more accurately, one large loop with a shortcut in the middle. Take the longer loop for an extended hike through rolling forested hills—great in spring and summer, but even better with autumn color.

Start: East side of the recreation area parking lot
Distance: 2.6-mile loop
Hiking time: About 90 minutes
Difficulty: Moderate to difficult; plenty of climbing
Trail surface: Packed dirt to sandy to grassy
Best season: Fall
Other trail users: Mountain bikers
Canine compatibility: Leashed dogs permitted
Fees and permits: Recreation Passport required

Schedule: Summer 8 a.m.–10 p.m.; closes at dusk in winter
Maps: Maps available at park office and on website; TOPO! CD: Michigan, Ohio, Indiana, disc 4
Trail contacts: Ortonville State Recreation Area, 5779 Hadley Rd., Ortonville, MI 48462; (810) 797-4439; michigan.gov/ortonville
Special considerations: This trail passes through state land open to hunting. Wear bright orange clothing during hunting season.

Finding the trailhead: Ortonville Recreation Area is 53 miles north of Detroit. From I-75 take exit 91 for MI 15. Drive north through Ortonville. About 9.5 miles north of the interstate, turn right onto Oakwood Road. Drive 0.5 mile to Sands Road and turn left. Drive another 0.5 mile to State Park Road and turn right. The entrance to the park is 0.3 mile on your left. The trailhead is on the east side of the parking lot. GPS: N42 52.138' / W83 26.288'

The Hike

Crisp autumn days, burnt orange and red in the trees, and blankets of leaves on the ground. Autumn is one of the best times to enjoy a hike at the Ortonville State Recreation Area. And you won't be the only one. On weekend mornings couples walk by with their dogs, looking not unlike a page from an L.L.Bean catalog. Spring and summer are also acceptable times to hike Ortonville Rec—the ground isn't particularly wet (except in one spot), and the trails don't become overgrown as summer wears on—but there's something special about hiking here in the fall.

The 2.6-mile loop in the Bloomer 3 section of the Ortonville State Recreation Area begins at the northeast corner of a dirt parking lot a little ways off State Park Road, which is north of the village of Ortonville. The loop is popular with hikers and mountain bikers—the latter riding the route clockwise, while the former typically

From the trailhead, the gravel path leads up and into the woods. ▶

walk the trail counterclockwise. A middle trail that offers an alternate path back to the parking area shortens the hike for those on foot but is closed to bikes.

These rules, like the one about dogs being on leashes, are often overlooked. Your best bet is to be aware that there are mountain bikes out there from time to time and that they may be approaching you from behind. And if you're walking your dog and using a leash to keep it from tangling with other dogs, other owners may not be so considerate.

The trail begins with a long slow climb, so gentle in the beginning you might not even notice it. Before you have reached the 0.5-mile mark, however, the climb has grown steeper and the trail breaks into the wooded rolling moraines that dominate this section of the park. This makes for some great hiking—the trail sometimes descending and turning and then climbing again, at other times delicately balancing on the top of a ridge.

As the trail skirts the park's eastern boundary, a farm is visible through the trees for a short stretch. The path then turns back west, the hills seem to flatten, and the trees thin. At trail marker 5 you've reached the halfway point. Less than 0.5 mile after that, you come to trail marker 6, which marks the intersection for taking the shorter alternate loop.

The alternate return is steep and winding, passing close to the park's rental cabin. Though the cabin is accessed by side trails, it's visible through the trees and brush. Ignore the shorter route if you can. Continuing on the described route will take you back to more rolling hills and high-roofed forest. Here you will find the steepest climb of the loop.

The loop might be best hiked in the fall, although large portions of the trail run through land open to hunting. Fall hikers are advised to wear a bright orange safety vest and hat to distinguish themselves from deer. (When the deer start wearing orange, we're all in trouble.) Afterward, if you're here in the fall and the mood is right, head over to Ashton Orchards on Seymour Lake Road for cider and a doughnut.

Miles and Directions

0.0 Start from the east side of the parking lot. As you drive in, east is to your right.

0.1 Trail marker 2. Turning left here would allow you to divvy up the main loop and hike only the western portion. Go straight instead.

0.4 Trail marker 3. This is the beginning of the moraine terrain, with quick ups and downs. Great for mountain biking.

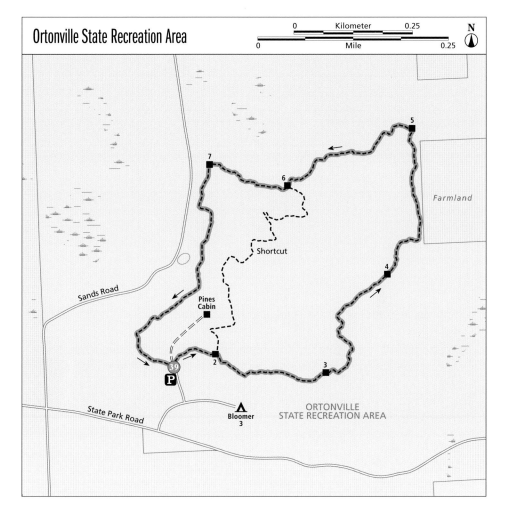

Ortonville State Recreation Area

0 Kilometer 0.25
0 Mile 0.25

N

Farmland

7

6

5

Shortcut

4

Sands Road

Pines
Cabin

3

2

39

P

State Park Road

Bloomer
3

ORTONVILLE
STATE RECREATION AREA

0.8 The trail becomes grassy near trail marker 4, going from woods to open field (trees, bushes, etc.) and from hard-packed dirt to a narrow path with a mowed grass shoulder. If you hear shooting, it's likely the nearby shooting range.

1.1 There's a field on your right. When the trees are less leafy, you can see right across to the barn.

1.3 At trail marker 5 turn left and follow the path to trail marker 6. The path is wide and there are some woods, but the trees aren't very tall.

1.7 Trail marker 6. Continue straight for the full loop. (***Option:*** Follow the trail left, which is a shorter path back to the parking lot, limiting your hike to the eastern portion of the loop.)

1.9 Trail marker 7; turn left.

2.6 The trail returns to the parking area.

Hike Information

Restaurants: A&W Drive-In, 470 South St., Ortonville; (248) 627-2670; facebook
.com/AWOrtonville. Coney connoisseurs take note: This A&W is better than the rest,
serving an authentic Detroit Coney where others fail by serving the so-so franchise
chili. Generations of folks from Ortonville have made this a summer tradition (closed
in winter).

40 Metamora-Hadley State Recreation Area

The Metamora-Hadley State Recreation Area in south Lapeer County offers that feeling of heading "up north" without having to fight the I-75 up-north traffic. Centered on an attractive 80-acre lake, the park has 5 miles of trails that wind through open meadow, hardwood forest, and assorted wetlands. You might want to bring a tent, swimming suit, or fishing pole to take full advantage of the place.

Start: Parking lot next to the camp store
Distance: 3.4-mile loop
Hiking time: About 1–1.5 hours
Difficulty: Moderate
Trail surface: Packed dirt
Best season: Summer
Other trail users: None
Canine compatibility: Leashed dogs permitted
Fees and permits: Recreation Passport required

Schedule: Summer 8 a.m.–10 p.m.; closes at dusk in winter
Maps: TOPO! CD: Michigan, Ohio, Indiana, disc 4; maps available at park office and on website
Trail contacts: Metamora-Hadley State Recreation Area, 3871 Herd Rd., Metamora, MI 48455; (810) 797-4439; michigan.gov/metamorahadley

Finding the trailhead: The recreation area is in Metamora, 50 miles north of Detroit. From I-75 take exit 81 for M-24 north. After passing through Lake Orion and Oxford, about 19 miles from the interstate, turn left onto Pratt Road. Drive 2.3 miles and turn left onto Hurd Road. The park entrance is 0.7 mile south, on the left side of the road. Once in the park, take a right just past the welcome station. Parking and the trailhead are on your left—next to the camp store. GPS: N42 56.639' / W83 21.274'

The Hike

The South Branch of Farmers Creek flows north through the Metamora-Hadley State Recreation Area. A tributary of the Middle South Branch of the Flint River, the creek continues north and then west through Flint and then heads north again, eventually emptying into Lake Huron by way of the Saginaw River. There's not much to the creek here in Metamora, but damming the flow has created 80-acre Lake Minnewanna.

The recreation area comprises 723 acres of woods, meadows, and wetlands surrounding this man-made lake. The north shore of the lake has been cleared for

▶ **The Metamora Hunt was established in 1928 and continues the British tradition of fox hunting—on horseback with hounds.**

a beach and picnic grounds—complete with restrooms and concessions. The park's North Campground sits on the south shore of the lake. Of the two campgrounds

A short wooden bridge cuts across an offshoot of Lake Minnewanna and completes the loop by way of the beach.

(214 campsites in all), the North Campground is more accessible to RVs and trailers. The South Campground is a bit more tent friendly, but you can expect to find larger campers as well.

There are about 5 miles of nature trails around the property, accessing all but the southwestern corner of the park. Several spurs connect a larger loop to the South Campground and the beach, allowing you to choose from a mix of entry and exit points and create your own path.

Our loop begins at the main trailhead (trail marker 1). The camp store is at the far southeast end of a parking lot. Park at the other end of the lot; the trailhead is a short walk up the road. From the start, the trail heads into a mixed hardwood forest. The path climbs gently, and in about 0.75 mile the woods fall back and you are hiking through a meadow. You go up a grassy swell and then down, and then enjoy a nice walk back into the trees.

The soil is sandy here, and you will see a trail to your left that leads back to the South Campground. The trail ahead continues to climb, and before you reach the next connector trail back to the campground, the loop peaks at 1,033 feet and then begins its descent. Once past Farmers Creek there are some hills, but nothing too challenging. The trail traces the eastern shore of Lake Minnewanna.

An arm of the lake juts out to the east, connected by a narrow channel. The bridge here creates an opportunity. By continuing around to the east and bypassing the bridge, you leave the lake behind, enjoy some more hills, and add 0.4 mile to the loop. Instead cross the bridge here and take the trail to the left that follows the wet edge of the lake. The path is sometimes wet, and tree roots can be tricky to navigate, but being this close to the water makes it worth it. The trail is used mainly by anglers, and short paths cut off to the right (in the direction of the parking lot) and left (down to the water).

After a stretch you come out on the beach parking lot. On hot days it makes sense to include a swimming suit in your pack. There are places to change, and a quick dip makes a nice detour. Crossing the picnic grounds, the route takes the road across the earthen dam and cuts through to the trailhead.

In winter the trails are open for cross-country skiing. In summer consider making your hike part of a camping weekend. The South Campground at Metamora-Hadley is one of the nicest this close to the city. It can get crowded on the weekend, but it's usually a quiet campground full of families having fun.

Miles and Directions

0.0 Start from trailhead, just west of the main drive and north of the parking area next to the camp store.

0.8 After you travel for some time under a tall canopy of trees, the forest opens up to a wide meadow.

1.2 At trail marker 3 continue straight. The path to the left leads to the campground.

2.0 At trail marker 4 continue straight and cross the stream. The path to the left also connects to the campground.

2.3 On this side of the bridge is trail marker 7. Cross the bridge to trail marker 6 and turn left, following the shoreline.

2.8 At trail marker 10 a connector trail enters on your right. This leads back to a parking area used by anglers. Continue straight.

2.9 At trail marker 11 the dense forest relents. Here the clearing is the park's popular day-use area. There's a sandy beach on Lake Minnewanna, restrooms, and frequently concessions. Cross the clearing to the road on the other side.

3.0 Follow the road across the earthen dam.

3.2 Just past the parking area for the fishing pier, the trail picks up on the left.

3.4 The trail ends across the street from the trailhead; the parking area is left down the road.

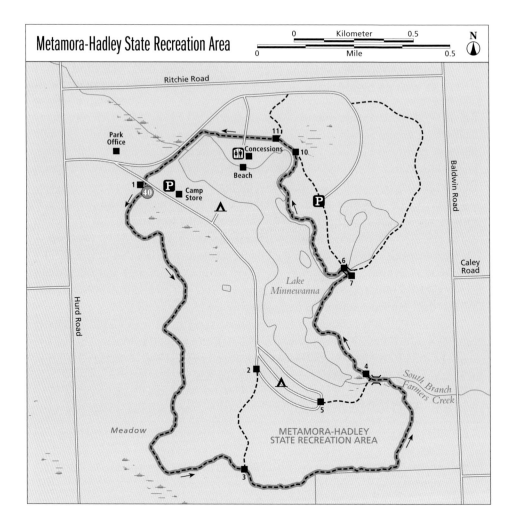

Metamora-Hadley State Recreation Area

Hike Information

Local Events/Attractions: Metamora Country Days and Balloon Festival, downtown Metamora; metamorachamber.org. Metamora holds this annual festival in late August. There's an art and craft show, petting zoo, bouncy castles for the kids, and helicopter rides—as well as a stunning hot air balloon launch.

Restaurants: Sundance Grille, 3817 South Lapeer Rd., Metamora; (810) 678-8998; facebook.com/SundanceGrille. Plan to hit the trail a little later in the morning and stop for breakfast at the Sundance Grille. It may seem dodgy from the road, but this place is a favorite with the locals and serves up great bacon, French toast, etc., and is easy on the pocketbook.

41 Seven Ponds Nature Center

When looking for a place to hike with younger kids, you want an easygoing trail, access to unique natural environments, opportunities to learn something, and flush toilets. Seven Ponds Nature Center has it all. Before hitting the trails, take some time to explore the exhibits at the interpretive center. The stuffed beaver is pretty cool, and chatting with staff members provides insight that makes for a more enjoyable visit.

Start: Sidewalk in front of the nature center
Distance: 1.2-mile double loop
Hiking time: About 40 minutes
Difficulty: Easy; wide, groomed trails with no significant elevation changes
Trail surface: Wood chip and boardwalk
Best season: Summer
Other trail users: None

Canine compatibility: Dogs not permitted
Fees and permits: Small fee charged
Schedule: Open 9 a.m.–5 p.m. Tues–Sun
Maps: Maps available in the interpretive center; TOPO! CD: Michigan, Ohio, Indiana, disc 4
Trail contacts: Seven Ponds Nature Center, 3854 Crawford Road, Dryden, MI 48428; (810) 796-3200; sevenponds.org

Finding the trailhead: The nature center is in Dryden, 40 miles north of Detroit. From I-75 take exit 81 for M-24 north. After passing through Lake Orion and Oxford, about 18 miles, turn right onto Dryden Road. Drive 4.5 miles to Calkins Road and turn right. (The road name changes to Crawford Road.) About 1 mile from Dryden Road, the nature center is on your right. The trailhead is in front of the interpretive center. GPS: N42 55.661' / W83 11.364'

The Hike

Metamora is Michigan's horse country, and the village has become synonymous with the horsey set. The boundaries of this informal community extend beyond Metamora itself. Oxford, Hadley, and Dryden all play a part, with stables, horse-riding schools, and the associated trappings that make up the equestrian lifestyle.

Take a Sunday drive down country roads here and you will pass palatial estates, acres and acres of white-fenced pasture, and a goodly number of horses. Of course this all doesn't come cheap, and some of Detroit's wealthiest families have maintained country retreats in Metamora for generations.

This is beautiful country, to be sure. It's so beautiful and "natural" that it's easy to forget that much of what you see on these back roads is artificial. Someone had to clear the land of trees and rocks, and for decades people have worked to maintain those verdant meadows. Just east of Metamora and south of Dryden, the Seven Ponds Nature Center offers another perspective on the natural history of this corner of Lapeer County.

The nature center comprises 486 acres of ponds, marshes, woods, and prairie. The property is maintained with an eye to protecting and cultivating a natural space. Eight

A robin guards its young against passing hikers at Seven Ponds Nature Center.

After the petals have faded on the wild rose, birds will feast on the remaining rose hips.

miles of trails offer access to nearly every corner of this nature sanctuary. The nonprofit that owns and operates the nature center uses the property to educate the public (children especially) on the importance of nature, developing in them an "environmental ethic." But first and foremost it is intended to be a nature sanctuary in the fullest sense of that word—both a safe place where nature can thrive and a safe haven to which visitors can escape.

When you arrive and park, the first thing you see is the interpretive center. Inside you can observe an active beehive, inspect native plant species in the Lischer Herbarium, learn about more than 150 native birds, or get the dirt on the area's fossils, rocks, and minerals. There are activities and exhibits especially for kids, and the Bird Feeding Area allows visitors to view birds up close.

The interpretive center is also where you pay the small admission fee, pick up a nature center map, and ask the staff about goings-on in the sanctuary. And it's a good place to browse and buy books on Michigan's natural history: The Rookery is one of the best-stocked nature center bookstores around.

The trail that wanders the southern part of the nature center begins in front of the interpretive center. As you face the front doors, a path leads off to the left and down the rise to the level of the ponds. Don't be surprised to meet groups of children getting a tour and learning about the sanctuary's flora and fauna.

The first pond you encounter is one of the nature center's smallest, Tree Top Pond. The trail follows its eastern shore for a short ways and then heads west, crossing the channel that connects Tree Top to the even smaller Little Pond. The bridge here is unique. The A-frame design doesn't support a flat platform. Rather, steps lead up to the top of the bridge and then back down. From the apex you can see both ponds. Keep your eyes open as you walk. You will sometimes see deer drinking from the pond; they're never far off.

Beyond the bridge the trail eases to the right and enters a wood. A side trail on the right leads to an observation deck for a look at Big Pond, but otherwise it's all trees (a

An overgrown boardwalk carries visitors across the park's cedar swamp.

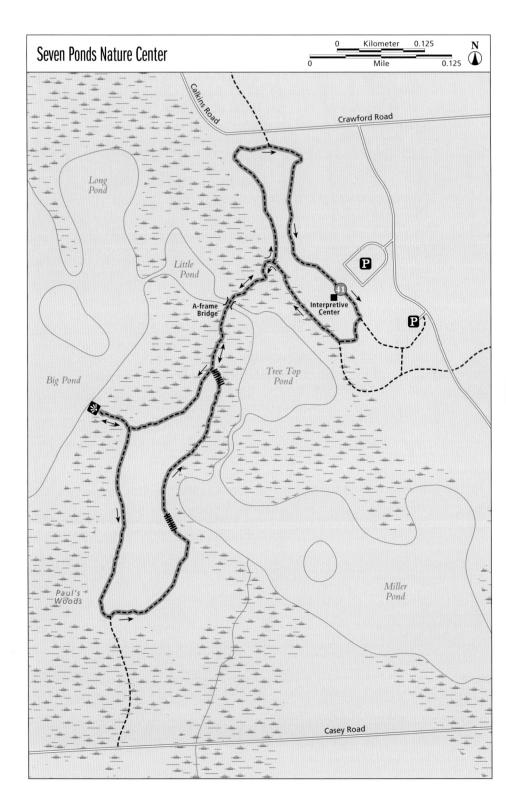

Seven Ponds Nature Center

Calkins Road

Crawford Road

Long Pond

Little Pond

A-frame Bridge

Big Pond

Tree Top Pond

Interpretive Center

41

P

P

Paul's Woods

Miller Pond

Casey Road

0   Kilometer   0.125

0   Mile   0.125

N

lot of maple). At the end of this leg, the trail turns sharply left and returns via a raised walkway through a cedar swamp.

Your path brings you back over the bridge and to the left, skirting Little Pond before climbing for an upland stroll back to the interpretive center. After the hike, embrace the local culture and plan lunch at the Historic White Horse Inn in Metamora—or the slightly more blue-collar Lenny Miller's in Dryden.

Miles and Directions

0.0 Start from the sidewalk in front of the interpretive center. The trail leads off to the left of the building and down some stairs. At the bottom, turn right.

0.1 Come to an intersection. Turn left.

0.2 A unique A-frame bridge offers a great view of Tree Top and Little Ponds.

0.3 Stay to the right at the intersection.

0.4 A short path on the right leads out to the observation tower with views of Big Pond. Return to the main loop and turn right.

0.5 Turn left for the cedar swamp boardwalk. (Continuing straight here leads to a dead end at Casey Road.)

0.8 The trail comes to a T; turn left. Then turn right to head back to the bridge.

0.9 Turn left at the T instead of returning the way you came.

1.0 Take the path on the right. (The trail on the left crosses the road and accesses the loops north of Crawford Road.)

1.2 The trail ends at the interpretive center.

Hike Information

Local Events/Attractions: Polly Ann Trail, PO Box 112, Leonard, MI 48367; (248) 969-8660; pollyanntrailway.org. The Polly Ann Trail is an ongoing rail-to-trail project that currently extends from south of Lake Orion to north of Imlay City. The trail passes right through Dryden. Visit the website for maps and parking information.

Restaurants: Lenny Miller's, 5800 Dryden Rd., Dryden; (810) 796-2470. Restaurants are often hard to judge out in the country. The best places often look the same as the worst. Lenny Miller's does an outstanding job. The salad bar alone is worth the trip, and people rave over the chicken noodle soup.

Historic White Horse Inn, 1 East High St., Metamora; (810) 678-2150; thewhite horseinn.com. Since 1850 travelers have been made welcome at the White Horse. This makes it the oldest restaurant in the state. The inn continues to have a reputation for serving great food in a historic atmosphere.

GREEN TIP:
Pass it down: The best way to instill green habits
in your children is to set a good example.

The Art of Hiking

When standing nose to nose with a cougar in the Upper Peninsula, you're probably not too concerned with the issue of ethical behavior in the wild. No doubt you're just terrified. But let's be honest. How often are you nose to nose with a cougar? (In fact, how many cougars are there really in the UP?) For hiking here in southeast Michigan, heading into the "wild" means driving to a trailhead parking lot. Sure you can mourn over how civilized we've become—how GPS units have replaced natural instinct and Gore-Tex stands in for true grit—but the silly gadgets of civilization aside, we have plenty of reason to take pride in how we've matured. With our local wild places conquered, we have come to understand that we have a responsibility to protect them: It is our wild places, not we, that are at risk. So please do what you can. The following section will help you understand better what it means to "do what you can" while still making the most of your hiking experience. Anyone can take a hike, but hiking safely and well is an art requiring preparation and proper equipment.

Trail Etiquette

Leave no trace. Always leave an area just like you found it—if not better than you found it. Pack out all of your trash and extra food.

Stay on the trail. It's true that a path anywhere leads nowhere new, but purists will just have to get over it. Trails serve an important purpose: They limit impact on natural areas. Straying from a designated trail may seem innocent, but it can cause damage to sensitive areas—damage that may take years to recover, if it can recover at all. Even simple shortcuts can be destructive. So, please, stay on the trail.

Leave no weeds. Invasive species are one of the biggest threats to the ecological health of our parks and recreation areas. Noxious weeds tend to overtake other plants, which in turn affects animals and birds that depend on them for food. To minimize the spread of noxious weeds, hikers should regularly clean their boots and hiking poles of mud and seeds. Also brush your dog to remove any weed seeds before heading off into a new area.

Keep your dog under control. You can buy a flexi-lead that allows your dog to go exploring along the trail while allowing you the ability to reel him in should another hiker approach or should he decide to chase a rabbit. Always obey leash laws, and be sure to pick up your dog's waste.

Respect other trail users. Often you're not the only one on the trail. Here in Metro Detroit, trails may be shared with bikes and horses. These are noted in this guide's trail descriptions. If you hear activity ahead, step off the trail just to be safe. Note that you won't always be able to hear a mountain biker coming, so be prepared and know ahead of time whether you share the trail with the two-wheel set. Cyclists should always yield to hikers, but that's little comfort to the hiker. Be aware. When you approach horses or pack animals on the trail, always step quietly off the trail, preferably on the downhill side, and let them pass. If you're wearing a large backpack, it's often a good idea to sit down. To some animals, a hiker wearing a large backpack might appear threatening. Make sure your dog doesn't harass these animals.

Getting into Shape

Hiking is a great way of getting in shape, but sometimes you need to get in shape before you go hiking. If you're terribly out of shape, start with a 15-minute walk during your lunch hour or after work, and gradually increase your walking time to an hour. You should also increase your elevation gain. Walking briskly up hills really strengthens your leg muscles and gets your heart rate up. If you work in a storied office building, take the stairs instead of the elevator. If you prefer going to a gym, walk the treadmill or use a stair machine. You can further increase your strength and endurance by walking with a loaded backpack. Stationary exercises you might consider are squats, leg lifts, sit-ups, and push-ups. Other good ways to get in shape include biking, running, aerobics, and of course short hikes. Stretching before and after a hike keeps muscles flexible and helps avoid injuries.

Preparedness

It's been said that failing to plan means planning to fail. So do take the necessary time to plan your trip. Whether going on a short day hike or an extended backpack trip, you should always prepare for the worst. In order to survive—and to stay reasonably comfortable—you need to concern yourself with the basics: water, food, and shelter. For the majority of the hikes in this book, you won't need a meal on the trail, and shelter means having appropriate clothing and a car. But don't go on a hike without having these bases covered.

Water. Even in frigid conditions, you need at least two quarts of water a day to function efficiently. Add heat and taxing terrain, and you can bump that figure up to one gallon. That's simply a base to work from—your metabolism and your level of conditioning can raise or lower that amount. For most of these hikes, a thirty-two-ounce water bottle should be enough, but a hot day on a long trail will require more.

Unless you're packing in water treatment, avoid filling your bottle from natural water sources. These sources can be loaded with intestinal disturbers, such as bacteria, viruses, and fertilizers. *Giardia lamblia*, the most common of these disturbers, is a protozoan parasite that lives part of its life cycle as a cyst in water sources. The parasite spreads when mammals defecate in water sources. Once ingested, Giardia can induce cramping, diarrhea, vomiting, and fatigue within two days to two weeks after ingestion. Giardiasis is treatable with prescription drugs. If you believe you've contracted giardiasis, see a doctor immediately.

Food. In most cases you can grab a bite before or after your hike, but snacks are nice, and if you're hiking with kids (more on that below), snacks are a necessity. Skip the candy bars and chips and other high-sugar, high-fat food. Instead bring along foods that are easy to pack, nutritious, and high in energy (e.g., bagels, nutrition bars, dehydrated fruit, gorp, and jerky).

First Aid

You may find that carrying a first-aid kit on a 2-mile hike is more of a hassle than it's worth. Unless you're prone to blisters, it may suffice just to have one in the car (a good idea, even if you're not a regular hiker). Many companies produce lightweight, compact first-aid kits. Just make sure yours contains at least the following:

- adhesive bandages
- moleskin or duct tape
- various sterile gauze pads and dressings
- white surgical tape
- Ace bandage
- antihistamine
- aspirin
- Betadine solution
- first-aid book
- antacid tablets
- tweezers
- scissors
- antibacterial wipes
- triple-antibiotic ointment
- plastic gloves
- sterile cotton-tip applicators
- syrup of ipecac (to induce vomiting)
- thermometer
- wire splint

Here are a few tips for dealing with, and hopefully preventing, certain ailments.

Sunburn. Take along sunscreen or sunblock, protective clothing, and a wide-brimmed hat. If you do get a sunburn, treat it with aloe vera gel, and protect the area from further sun exposure. At higher elevations, the sun's radiation can be particularly damaging to skin. Remember that your eyes are vulnerable to this radiation as well. Sunglasses can be a good way to prevent headaches and permanent eye damage from the sun, especially in places where light-colored rock or patches of snow reflect light up in your face.

Blisters. Be prepared to take care of these hike-spoilers by carrying moleskin (a lightly padded adhesive), gauze and tape, or adhesive bandages. An effective way to apply moleskin is to cut out a circle of moleskin and remove the center—like a doughnut—and place it over the blistered area. Cutting the center out will reduce the pressure applied to the sensitive skin. Other products can help you combat blisters. Some are applied to suspicious hot spots before a blister forms to help decrease friction to that area; others are applied to the blister after it has popped to help prevent further irritation.

Insect bites and stings. You can treat most insect bites and stings by applying hydrocortisone 1% cream topically and taking a pain medication such as ibuprofen or acetaminophen. If you forgot to pack these items, a cold compress or a paste of mud and ashes can sometimes assuage the itching and discomfort. Remove any stingers by using tweezers or scraping the area with your fingernail or a knife blade. Don't pinch the area—you'll only spread the venom.

Some hikers are highly sensitive to bites and stings and may have a serious allergic reaction that can be life-threatening. Symptoms of a serious allergic reaction can include wheezing, an asthma attack, and shock. The treatment for this severe type of reaction is epinephrine. If you know that you are sensitive to bites and stings, carry a prepackaged kit of epinephrine, which can be obtained only by doctor's prescription.

Ticks. Ticks can carry Lyme disease. The best defense is of course prevention. If you know you're going to be hiking through an area littered with ticks, wear long pants and a long-sleeved shirt. You can apply a permethrin repellent to your clothing and a DEET repellent to exposed skin. At the end of your hike, do a spot check for ticks (and insects in general). If you do find a tick, grab the head of the tick firmly— with a pair of tweezers if you have them—and gently pull it away from the skin with a twisting motion. (Companies like REI carry a very useful tick-removal tool called the Tick Key.) Sometimes the mouth parts linger, embedded in your skin. If this happens, try to remove them with a disinfected needle. Clean the affected area with an antibacterial cleanser, and then apply triple antibiotic ointment. Monitor the area for a few days. If irritation persists or a white spot develops, see a doctor for possible infection.

Poison ivy and sumac. These skin irritants can be found most anywhere in North America and come in the form of a bush or a vine and having leaflets in groups of three, five, seven, or nine. Learn how to spot the plants. The oil they secrete can cause an allergic reaction in the form of blisters, usually about twelve hours after exposure. The itchy rash can last from ten days to several weeks. The best defense against these irritants is to wear clothing that covers the arms, legs, and torso. For summer, zip-off cargo pants come in handy. There are also nonprescription lotions you can apply to exposed skin that guard against the effects of poison ivy/sumac and can be washed off with soap and water. If you think you were in contact with the plants, wash with soap and water after hiking (or even on the trail during longer hikes). Taking a hot shower with soap after you return home from your hike will also help to remove any lingering oil from your skin. Should you contract a rash from any of these plants, use an antihistamine to reduce the itching. If the rash is localized, create a light bleach/water wash to dry up the area. If the rash has spread, either tough it out or see your doctor about getting a dose of cortisone (available both orally and by injection).

Snakebites. Snakebites are rare in North America, even rarer in Michigan. Unless startled or provoked, the majority of snakes will not bite. If you are wise to their habitats and keep a careful eye on the trail, you should be just fine. When stepping over logs, first step on the log, making sure you can see what's on the other side before stepping down. Though your chances of being struck are slim, it's wise to know what to do in the event you are.

If a nonvenomous snake bites you, allow the wound to bleed a small amount and then cleanse the wounded area with a Betadine solution (10% povidone iodine). Rinse the wound with clean water (preferably) or fresh urine (it might sound ugly, but it's sterile). Once the area is clean, cover it with triple antibiotic ointment and a clean bandage. Infection can be a dangerous outcome of snakebite. Keep the area as clean as possible, and get medical attention immediately.

If somebody in your party is bitten by a venomous snake, follow these steps:

1. Calm the patient.
2. Remove jewelry, watches, and restrictive clothing, and immobilize the affected limb. Do not elevate the injury. Medical opinions vary on whether the area should be lower or level with the heart, but the consensus is that it should not be above it.
3. Make a note of the circumference of the limb at the bite site and at various points above the site as well. This will help you monitor swelling.
4. Evacuate your victim. Ideally he should be carried out to minimize movement. If the victim appears to be doing okay, he can walk. Stop and rest frequently, and if the swelling appears to be spreading or the patient's symptoms increase, find a way to get your patient transported.
5. If you are waiting for rescue, make sure to keep your patient comfortable and hydrated (unless he begins vomiting).

Snakebite treatment is rife with old-fashioned remedies: You used to be told to cut and suck the venom out of the bite site or to use a suction cup extractor for the same purpose; applying an electric shock to the area was even in vogue for a while. Do not do any of these things. Do not apply ice, do not give your patient painkillers, and do not apply a tourniquet. All you really want to do is keep your patient calm and get help. If you're alone and have to hike out, don't run—you'll only increase the flow of venom throughout your system. Instead, walk calmly.

Dehydration. Have you ever hiked in hot weather and had a roaring headache and felt fatigued after only a few miles? More than likely you were dehydrated. Symptoms of dehydration include fatigue, headache, and decreased coordination and judgment. When you are hiking, your body's rate of fluid loss depends on the outside temperature, humidity, altitude, and your activity level. On average, a hiker walking in warm weather will lose four liters of fluid a day. That fluid loss is easily replaced by normal consumption of liquids and food. However, if a hiker is walking briskly in hot, dry weather and hauling a heavy pack, he or she can lose one to three liters of water an hour. It's important to always carry plenty of water and to stop often and drink fluids regularly, even if you aren't thirsty.

Heat exhaustion is the result of a loss of large amounts of electrolytes and often occurs if a hiker is dehydrated and has been under heavy exertion. Common symptoms of heat exhaustion include cramping, exhaustion, fatigue, lightheadedness, and nausea. You can treat heat exhaustion by getting out of the sun and drinking an electrolyte solution made of one teaspoon of salt and one tablespoon of sugar dissolved in a liter of water. Drink this solution slowly over a period of one hour. Drinking plenty of fluids (preferably an electrolyte solution/sports drink) can prevent heat exhaustion. Avoid hiking during the hottest parts of the day, and wear breathable clothing, a wide-brimmed hat, and sunglasses.

Hypothermia is one of the biggest dangers, especially for day hikers in the summertime. That may sound strange, but imagine starting out on a hike in midsummer when it's sunny and 80 degrees out. You're clad in nylon shorts and a cotton T-shirt. About halfway through your hike, the sky begins to cloud up, and in the next hour a light drizzle begins to fall and the wind starts to pick up. Before you know it, you are soaking wet and shivering—the perfect recipe for hypothermia. More advanced signs include decreased coordination, slurred speech, and blurred vision. When a victim's temperature falls below 92 degrees, the blood pressure and pulse plummet, possibly leading to coma and death.

To avoid hypothermia, always bring a windproof/rainproof shell; a fleece jacket; long underwear made of a breathable, synthetic fiber; gloves; and hat when you are hiking in the mountains. Learn to adjust your clothing layers based on the temperature. If you are climbing uphill at a moderate pace, you will stay warm; but when you stop for a break, you'll become cold quickly unless you add more layers of clothing.

If a hiker is showing advanced signs of hypothermia, dress her in dry clothes and make sure she is wearing a hat and gloves. Place the victim in a sleeping bag in a tent or shelter that will protect her from the wind and other elements. Give warm fluids to drink, and keep her awake.

Frostbite. When the mercury dips below 32 degrees, your extremities begin to chill. If a persistent chill attacks a localized area, say, your hands or your toes, the circulatory system reacts by cutting off blood flow to the affected area—the idea being to protect and preserve the body's overall temperature. And so it's death by attrition for the affected area. Ice crystals start to form from the water in the cells of the neglected tissue. Deprived of heat, nourishment, and now water, the tissue literally starves. This is frostbite.

Prevention is your best defense against this situation. Most prone to frostbite are your face, hands, and feet, so protect these areas well. Wool is the traditional material of choice because it provides ample air space for insulation and draws moisture away from the skin. Synthetic fabrics, however, have made great strides in the cold-weather-clothing market. Do your research. A pair of light silk liners under your regular gloves is a good trick for keeping warm. They afford some additional warmth, but more important they'll allow you to remove your mitts for intricate work without exposing the skin.

If your feet or hands start to feel cold or numb due to the elements, warm them as quickly as possible. Place cold hands under your armpits or bury them in your crotch. If your feet are cold, change your socks. If there's plenty of room in your boots, add another pair of socks. Do remember, though, that constricting your feet in tight boots can restrict blood flow and actually make your feet colder more quickly. Your socks need to have breathing room if they're going to be effective. Dead air provides insulation. If your face is cold, place your warm hands over your face, or simply wear a head stocking.

Should your skin go numb and start to appear white and waxy, chances are you've got or are developing frostbite. Don't try to thaw the area unless you can maintain the warmth. In other words, don't stop to warm up your frostbitten feet only to head back on the trail. You'll do more damage than good. Tests have shown that hikers who walked on thawed feet did more harm, and endured more pain, than hikers who left the affected areas alone. Do your best to get out of the cold entirely and seek medical attention, which usually consists of performing a rapid rewarming in water for 20 to 30 minutes.

The overall objective in preventing both hypothermia and frostbite is to keep the body's core warm. Protect key areas where heat escapes, like the top of the head, and maintain the proper nutrition level. Foods that are high in calories aid the body in producing heat. Never smoke or drink when you're in situations where the cold is threatening. By affecting blood flow, these activities ultimately cool the body's core temperature.

Natural Hazards

Besides tripping over a rock or tree root on the trail, there are some real hazards to be aware of while hiking. Even if where you're hiking doesn't have a plethora of venomous snakes, poisonous plants, insects, and dangerous animals, there are a few weather and other conditions you may need to take into account.

Lightning. Thunderstorms regularly roll across the Midwest in summer, bringing with them high winds and lightning. Thankfully we often can tell these storms are coming way ahead of time. Check the weather before you set out on the trail. If you are caught in a thunderstorm, avoid standing in high or exposed areas.

Flash floods. Flash floods are not common in our area, though they do occur after periods of excessive rain. If you plan on hiking near a river after a storm, check the National Weather Service for flash flood warnings.

Other considerations. Hunting is a popular sport in the United States, especially during rifle season in October and November. Hiking is still enjoyable in those months in many areas, so just take a few precautions. First, learn when the different hunting seasons start and end in the area in which you'll be hiking. During this time frame, be sure to wear at least a blaze orange hat, and possibly put an orange vest over your pack. Don't be surprised to see hunters in camo outfits carrying bows or rifles around during their season. If you would feel more comfortable without hunters around, find a park where hunting is not allowed.

Navigation

Even if you are going on a short hike in a familiar area, you should always be equipped with the proper navigational equipment—at the very least a detailed map and a sturdy compass.

Maps. The hike descriptions in this book come with decent maps. For more detail you can track down the park's official trail map. For those of you interested in hiking some of Michigan's more ambitious trails, here's some advice on finding a map:

There are many different types of maps available to help you find your way on the trail. Easiest to find are USDA Forest Service and Bureau of Land Management (BLM) maps. These maps tend to cover large areas, so be sure they are detailed enough for your particular trip. You can also obtain national park maps as well as high-quality maps from private companies and trail groups. These maps can be obtained from either outdoor stores or ranger stations.

US Geological Survey topographic maps are particularly popular with hikers—especially serious backcountry hikers. These maps contain the standard map symbols such as roads, lakes, and rivers, as well as contour lines that show the details of the trail terrain like ridges, valleys, passes, and mountain peaks. The 7.5-minute series (1 inch on the map equals approximately ⅔ mile on the ground) provides the closest inspection available. USGS maps are available by mail (US Geological Survey, Map Distribution Branch, PO Box 25286, Denver, CO 80225), or online at usgs.gov/pubprod/.

If you want to check out the high-tech world of maps, you can purchase topographic maps on CD-ROM. These software-mapping programs let you select a route on your computer, print it out, then take it with you on the trail. Some software mapping programs let you insert symbols and labels, download waypoints from a GPS unit, and export the maps to other software programs.

The art of map reading is a skill that you can develop by first practicing in an area you are familiar with. To begin, orient the map so that it is lined up in the correct direction (i.e., north on the map is lined up with true north). Next, familiarize yourself with the map symbols and try to match them up with terrain features around you, such as a high ridge, mountain peak, river, or lake. If you are practicing with a USGS map, notice the contour lines. On gentler terrain these contour lines are spaced farther apart; on steeper terrain they are closer together. Pick a short loop trail, and stop frequently to check your position on the map. As you practice map reading, you'll learn how to anticipate a steep section on the trail or a good place to take a rest break.

Compasses. First off, the sun is not a substitute for a compass. So, what kind of compass should you carry? Here are some characteristics you should look for: a rectangular base with detailed scales, a liquid-filled housing, a protective housing, a sighting line on the mirror, luminous alignment and back-bearing arrows, a luminous north-seeking arrow, and a well-defined bezel ring.

You can learn compass basics by reading the detailed instructions included with your compass. If you want to fine-tune your compass skills, sign up for an orienteering class or purchase a book on compass reading. Once you've learned the basic skills of using a compass, remember to practice these skills before you head into the backcountry.

If you are a klutz at using a compass, you may be interested in checking out the technical wizardry of the GPS (Global Positioning System) device. The GPS was developed by the Pentagon and works off twenty-four NAVSTAR satellites, which were designed to guide missiles to their targets. A GPS device is a handheld unit that calculates your latitude and longitude with the easy press of a button. The Department of Defense used to scramble the satellite signals a bit to prevent civilians (and spies!) from getting extremely accurate readings, but that practice was discontinued in May 2000, and GPS units now provide nearly pinpoint accuracy (within 30 to 60 feet).

There are many different types of GPS units available, and they range in price from $100 to $400. In general, all GPS units have a display screen and keypad where you input information. In addition to acting as a compass, the unit allows you to plot your route, easily retrace your path, track your traveling speed, find the mileage between waypoints, and calculate the total mileage of your route.

Before you purchase a GPS unit, keep in mind that these devices don't pick up signals indoors, in heavily wooded areas, on mountain peaks, or in deep valleys. Also, batteries can wear out or other technical problems can develop. A GPS unit should be used in conjunction with a map and compass, not in place of those items.

Pedometers. A pedometer is a small, clip-on unit with a digital display that calculates your hiking distance in miles or kilometers based on your walking stride. Some units also calculate the calories you burn and your total hiking time. Pedometers are available at most large outdoor stores and range in price from $20 to $40.

Trip Planning

Planning your hiking adventure begins with letting a friend or relative know your trip itinerary so they can call for help if you don't return at your scheduled time. Your next task is to make sure you are outfitted to experience the risks and rewards of the trail. This section highlights gear and clothing you may want to take with you to get the most out of your hike.

- ❑ camera
- ❑ compass/GPS unit
- ❑ daypack

- ❑ first-aid kit
- ❑ fleece jacket
- ❑ food

- ❏ guidebook
- ❏ hat
- ❏ headlamp/flashlight with extra batteries and bulbs
- ❏ insect repellent
- ❏ knife/multipurpose tool
- ❏ map
- ❏ pedometer
- ❏ rain gear
- ❏ sunglasses
- ❏ sunscreen
- ❏ swimsuit and/or fishing gear (if hiking to a lake)
- ❏ watch
- ❏ water
- ❏ water bottles/water hydration system

Equipment

With the outdoor market currently flooded with products, many of which are pure gimmickry, it can be difficult to differentiate and choose among them. Do I really need a tropical-fish-lined collapsible shower? (No, you don't.) The only defense against the maddening quantity of items thrust in your face is to think practically—and to do so before you go shopping. The worst buys are impulsive buys. Since most name brands will differ only slightly in quality, it's best to know what you're looking for in terms of function. Buy only what you need. You will, don't forget, be carrying what you've bought on your back. Here are some things to keep in mind.

Clothes. Clothing is your armor against Mother Nature's little surprises. Hikers should be prepared for any possibility, especially when hiking in mountainous areas. Adequate rain protection and extra layers of clothing are a good idea. In summer a wide-brimmed hat can help keep the sun at bay. In the winter months the first layer you'll want to wear is a "wicking" layer of long underwear that keeps perspiration away from your skin. Wear long underwear made from synthetic fibers that wick moisture away from the skin and draw it toward the next layer of clothing, where it then evaporates. Avoid wearing long underwear made of cotton, which is slow to dry and keeps moisture next to your skin.

The second layer you'll wear is the "insulating" layer. Aside from keeping you warm, this layer needs to "breathe" so that you stay dry while hiking. A fabric that provides insulation and dries quickly is fleece. One type of fleece is made out of recycled plastic. Purchasing a zip-up jacket made of this material is highly recommended.

The last line of layering defense is the "shell" layer. You'll need some type of waterproof, windproof, breathable jacket that will fit over all your other layers. It should have a large hood that fits over a hat. You'll also need a good pair of rain pants made from a similar waterproof, breathable fabric. Some Gore-Tex jackets cost as much as $500, but there are more affordable fabrics out there that work just as well.

Now that you've learned the basics of layering, don't forget to protect your hands and face. In cold, windy, or rainy weather you'll need a hat made of wool or fleece and insulated, waterproof gloves that will keep your hands warm and toasty. As mentioned earlier, buying an additional pair of light silk liners to wear under your regular gloves is a good idea.

Footwear. If you have any extra money to spend on hiking, put that money into boots or trail shoes. Poor shoes will bring a hike to a halt faster than anything else. To avoid this, buy shoes that provide support and are lightweight and flexible. A lightweight hiking boot is better than a heavy, leather mountaineering boot for most day hikes and backpacking. Trail-running shoes provide a little extra cushion and are made in a high-top style that many people wear for hiking. These running shoes are lighter, more flexible, and more breathable than hiking boots. If you know you'll be hiking in wet weather often, purchase boots or shoes with a Gore-Tex liner, which will help keep your feet dry.

When buying your boots, be sure to wear the same type of socks you'll be wearing on the trail. If the boots you're buying are for cold-weather hiking, try the boots on while wearing two pairs of socks. Speaking of socks, a good cold-weather sock combination is to wear a thinner sock made of wool or polypropylene covered by a heavier outer sock made of wool or a synthetic/wool mix. The inner sock protects the foot from the rubbing effects of the outer sock and prevents blisters. Many outdoor stores have some type of ramp to simulate hiking uphill and downhill. Be sure to take advantage of this test, as toe-jamming boot fronts can be very painful and debilitating on the downhill trek.

Once you've purchased your footwear, be sure to break them in before you hit the trail. New footwear is often stiff and needs to be stretched and molded to your foot.

Hiking poles. Hiking poles help with balance and, more importantly, take pressure off your knees. The ones with shock absorbers are easier on your elbows and knees. Some poles even come with a camera attachment to be used as a monopod. And should, heaven forbid, you meet a mountain lion, bear, or unfriendly dog, the poles can make you look a lot bigger.

Backpacks. No matter what type of hiking you do, you'll need a pack of some sort to carry the basic trail essentials. A daypack should have some of the following characteristics: a padded hip belt that's at least 2 inches in diameter (avoid packs with only a small nylon piece of webbing for a hip belt); a chest strap (the chest strap helps stabilize the pack against your body); external pockets to carry water and other items that you want easy access to; an internal pocket to hold keys, a knife, a wallet, and other miscellaneous items; an external lashing system to hold a jacket; and, if you so desire, a hydration pocket for carrying a hydration system (which consists of a water bladder with an attachable drinking hose).

For short hikes, some hikers like to use a fanny pack to store just a camera, food, a compass, a map, and other trail essentials. Some fanny packs have pockets for two water bottles and a padded hip belt.

Cell phones. Most hikers carry their cell phones on day hikes in case of emergency. That's fine, but please remember that cell phone coverage is not always consistent and is no substitute for being prepared. Use your brain to avoid problems, and if you do encounter a problem, first use your brain to try to correct the situation. Only use your cell phone, if it works, in true emergencies.

Hiking with Children

Hiking with children isn't a matter of how many miles you can cover; it's about seeing and experiencing nature through their eyes.

Kids like to explore and have fun. They like to stop and point out bugs and plants, look under rocks, jump in puddles, and throw sticks. If you're taking a toddler or young child on a hike, start with a trail that you're familiar with. Trails that have interesting things for kids, like piles of leaves to play in or a small stream to wade through in summer, will make the hike much more enjoyable for them and will keep them from getting bored.

You can keep your child's attention if you have a strategy before starting on the trail. Using games is not only an effective way to keep a child's attention; it's also a great way to teach him or her about nature. Quiz children on the names of plants and animals. Pick up a family-friendly outdoor hobby like Geocaching (geocaching .com) or Letterboxing (atlasquest.com), both of which combine the outdoors, clue solving, and treasure hunting. If your children are old enough, let them carry their own daypack filled with snacks and water. So that you are sure to go at their pace and not yours, let them lead the way. Playing follow the leader works particularly well when you have a group of children. Have each child take a turn at being the leader.

With children, a lot of clothing is key. The only thing predictable about weather is that it will change. Especially in mountainous areas, weather can change dramatically in a very short time. Always bring extra clothing for children, regardless of the season. In winter have your children wear wool socks and warm layers such as long underwear, a fleece jacket and hat, wool mittens, and good rain gear. It's not a bad idea to have these along in late fall and early spring as well. Good footwear is also important. A sturdy pair of high-top tennis shoes or lightweight hiking boots is the best bet for little ones. If you're hiking in summer near a lake or stream, bring along a pair of old sneakers that your child can put on when he or she wants to go exploring in the water. Remember when you're near any type of water, watch your child at all times. Also keep a close eye on teething toddlers, who may decide a rock or leaf of poison ivy is an interesting item to put in their mouth.

From spring through fall you'll want your kids to wear a wide-brimmed hat to keep their face, head, and ears protected from the hot sun. Also, make sure your children wear sunscreen at all times. Choose a brand without PABA—children have sensitive skin and may have an allergic reaction to sunscreen that contains PABA. If you are hiking with a child younger than six months, don't use sunscreen or insect repellent. Instead be sure that their head, face, neck, and ears are protected from the sun with a wide-brimmed hat, and that all other skin exposed to the sun is protected with the appropriate clothing.

Remember that food is fun. Kids like snacks, so it's important to bring a lot of munchies for the trail. Stopping often for snack breaks is a fun way to keep the trail interesting. Raisins, apples, granola bars, crackers and cheese, cereal, and trail mix all make great snacks. Also, a few of their favorite candy treats can go a long way toward heading off a fit of fussing. If your child is old enough to carry her own backpack, let her fill it with some lightweight "comfort" items such as a doll, a small stuffed animal, or a little toy (you'll have to draw the line at bringing the ten-pound Tonka truck). If your kids don't like drinking water, you can bring some powdered drink mix or a juice box.

Avoid poorly designed child-carrying packs—you don't want to break your back carrying your child. Most child-carrying backpacks designed to hold a forty-pound child will contain a large carrying pocket to hold diapers and other items. Some have an optional rain/sun hood.

Hiking with Your Dog

Bringing your furry friend with you is always more fun than leaving him behind. Our canine pals make great trail buddies because they never complain and always make good company. Hiking with your dog can be a rewarding experience, especially if you plan ahead.

Getting your dog in shape. Before you plan outdoor adventures with your dog, make sure he's in shape for the trail. Getting your dog into shape takes the same discipline as getting yourself into shape, but luckily, your dog can get in shape with you. Take your dog with you on your daily runs or walks. If there is a park near your house, hit a tennis ball or play Frisbee with your dog.

Swimming is also an excellent way to get your dog into shape. If there is a lake or river near where you live and your dog likes the water, have him retrieve a tennis ball or stick. Gradually build your dog's stamina over a two- to three-month period. A good rule of thumb is to assume that your dog will travel twice as far as you will on the trail. If you plan on doing a 5-mile hike, be sure your dog is in shape for a 10-mile hike.

Training your dog for the trail. Before you go on your first hiking adventure with your dog, be sure he has a firm grasp on the basics of canine etiquette and behavior. Make sure he can sit, lie down, stay, and come. One of the most important commands you can teach your canine pal is to "come" under any situation. It's easy for your friend's nose to lead him astray or possibly get lost. Another helpful command is the "get behind" command. When you're on a hiking trail that's narrow, you can have your dog follow behind you when other trail users approach. Nothing is more bothersome than an enthusiastic dog that runs back and forth on the trail and disrupts the peace of the trail for others—or, worse, jumps up on other hikers and gets them muddy. When you see other trail users approaching you on the trail, give them the right of way by quietly stepping off the trail and making your dog lie down and stay until they pass.

Equipment. The most critical pieces of equipment you can invest in for your dog are proper identification and a sturdy leash. Flexi-leads work well for hiking because they give your dog more freedom to explore but still leave you in control. Make sure your dog has identification that includes your name and address and a number for your veterinarian. Other forms of identification for your dog include a tattoo or a microchip. You should consult your veterinarian for more information on these last two options.

You can purchase collapsible water and food bowls for your dog. These lightweight bowls can easily be stashed in your pack. If you are hiking on rocky terrain or in the snow, you can purchase footwear for your dog that will protect his feet from cuts and bruises.

Always carry plastic bags to remove feces from the trail. It is a courtesy to other trail users and helps protect local wildlife.

The following is a list of items to bring when you take your dog hiking: collapsible water bowls, a collar and a leash, plastic bags for feces, flea/tick powder, paw protection, and water.

First aid for your dog. Your dog is just as prone—if not more prone—to getting in trouble on the trail as you are, so be prepared. Here's a rundown of the more likely misfortunes that might befall your pet.

Bees and wasps. If a bee or wasp stings your dog, remove the stinger with a pair of tweezers and place a mudpack or a cloth dipped in cold water over the affected area.

Porcupines. One good reason to keep your dog on a leash is to prevent it from getting a nose full of porcupine quills. You may be able to remove the quills with pliers, but a veterinarian is the best person to do this nasty job because most dogs need to be sedated.

Skunks. Here's another good reason to keep your dog on a leash. When dogs tangle with skunks, it's the owners who lose. Your local pet supply store will have specialty shampoo to help eliminate the odor.

Heat stroke. Avoid hiking with your dog in really hot weather. Dogs with heat stroke will pant excessively, lie down and refuse to get up, and become lethargic and disoriented. If your dog shows any of these signs on the trail, have him lie down in the shade. If you are near a stream, pour cool water over your dog's entire body to help bring his body temperature back to normal.

Heartworm. Dogs get heartworms from mosquitoes that carry the disease in the prime mosquito months of July and August. Giving your dog a monthly pill prescribed by your veterinarian easily prevents this condition.

Plant pitfalls. One of the biggest plant hazards for dogs on the trail is foxtails. Foxtails are pointed grass seed heads that bury themselves in your friend's fur, between his toes, and can even get in his ear canal. If left unattended, these nasty seeds can work their way under the skin and cause abscesses and other problems. If you have a long-haired dog, consider trimming the hair between his toes and giving him a summer haircut to help prevent foxtails from attaching to his fur. After every hike, always look over your dog for these seeds—especially between his toes and in his ears.

Other plant hazards include burrs, thorns, and thistles. Remove any burrs or thistles you find on your dog as soon as possible, before they become an unmanageable mat. Thorns can pierce a dog's foot and cause a great deal of pain. If your dog is limping, stop and check his feet for thorns. Also note that dogs are not only susceptible to poison ivy but also can pick up the plant's oil and transfer it to you.

Protect those paws. Be sure to keep your dog's nails trimmed to avoid soft-tissue or joint injuries. If your dog slows and refuses to go on, check to see that his paws aren't torn or worn. You can protect your dog's paws from trail hazards such as sharp gravel, foxtails, and thorns by purchasing dog boots.

Sunburn. Dogs with light skin are susceptible to sunburn on the nose and other exposed skin areas. Applying a nontoxic sunscreen to exposed skin areas will help protect your dog from overexposure to the sun.

Ticks and fleas. Ticks can easily give your dog Lyme disease as well as other diseases. Before you hit the trail, treat your dog with a flea and tick spray or powder. You can also ask your veterinarian about a once-a-month application that repels fleas and ticks.

Mosquitoes and deerflies. These little flying machines can do a job on your dog's snout and ears. Spraying your dog with fly repellent for horses helps discourage both pests.

Mushrooms. Make sure your dog doesn't sample mushrooms along the trail. They could be poisonous.

When you are finally ready to hit the trail with your dog, keep in mind that many parks do not allow dogs on trails. Always call ahead to see what the restrictions are.

Further Reading

Bragg, Amy Elliott. *Hidden History of Detroit*. Charleston, SC: The History Press, 2011.

Fletcher, Colin, and Chip Rawlins. *The Complete Walker IV*. New York: Knopf, 2002.

Kershaw, Linda. *Trees of Michigan*. Auburn, WA: Lone Pine Publishing International, 2006.

Reznicek, Anton A., and Edward G. Voss. *Field Manual of Michigan Flora*. Ann Arbor, MI: University of Michigan Press, 2012.

Tekiela, Stan. *Birds of Michigan Field Guide*. Cambridge, MN: Adventure Publications, 2004.

Tekiela, Stan. *Wildflowers of Michigan Field Guide*. Cambridge, MN: Adventure Publications, 2000.

Clubs and Trail Groups

Hiking Michigan: hikingmichigan.com. Check out the website and send an e-mail to sign up for the southeast Michigan hiking newsletter. Each month there are several hikes scheduled, which often follow paths not on the "official" maps. There is no fee to participate.

School for Outdoor Leadership, Adventure and Recreation (aka SOLAR), PO Box 220, Farmington Hills, MI 48334; solaroutdoors.com. SOLAR meets the first Tuesday of every month in Southfield. There's an annual membership fee to join in the activities, and the meeting is the best way to find out what the club has to offer. Club members lead outings and teach classes on all sorts of outdoor activities—hiking, biking, paddling, etc.

The Sierra Club: Southeast Michigan Group; michigan.sierraclub.org/semg. The Sierra Club leads quite a number of group hikes throughout the year. A paltry $1 donation is requested for participating in day hikes.

Hike Index

About the Author

Matt Forster began walking in earnest as a boy who regularly missed the school bus. He grew into a young man to whom hiking seemed more a trudge to be endured than an activity to be enjoyed. Thankfully the wisdom of age conquered this adolescent ignorance, and today he hikes as a respite from deskwork. Michigan's outdoors offer endless appeal, and Matt has spent years hiking, biking, and paddling throughout these pleasant peninsulas.

Matt's other books on Michigan include *Backroads & Byways of Michigan*, *Michigan's Best Nature Centers and Wilderness Preserves*, and *Best Tent Camping Michigan*. When not exploring the Mitten, Matt travels with his wife, Kim, and their two children. Their family adventures in Colorado (Kim's home state) resulted in a travel guide for the Rocky Mountain State, *Colorado: An Explorer's Guide*.